Backing

into the

Future

By Bernard Knox

Oedipus at Thebes: Sophocles' Tragic Hero and His Time

Oedipus the King

The Heroic Temper

Word and Action: Essays on the Ancient Theater

Essays Ancient and Modern

The Oldest Dead White European Males

The Cambridge History of Classical Literature, volume I, Greece *(coeditor and contributor)*

The Norton Book of Classical Literature *(editor)*

The Norton Anthology of World Masterpieces *(coeditor)*

Backing into the Future

The Classical Tradition and Its Renewal

Bernard Knox

W. W. Norton & Company

New York   London

First Edition

The text of this book is composed in 12/14.5 Centaur
with the display set in Poster Bodoni Compressed.
Composition and manufacturing by the Haddon Craftsmen, Inc.
Book design by Margaret M. Wagner

Library of Congress Cataloging-in-Publication Data

Knox, Bernard MacGregor Walker.
Backing into the future : the Classical tradition and its renewal /
Bernard Knox.
p. cm.
Includes index.
I. Classical literature—History and criticism. 2. Civilization, West-
ern—Classical influences. 3. Literature, Modern—Classical influ-
ences. 4. Influence (Literary, artistic, etc.) 5. Classical literature—Ap-
preciation. 6. Homer—Influence. 7. Classicism. I. Title.
PA3009.K59 1994
880.'09—dc20   93-22732
ISBN 0-393-33117-2

W.W. Norton & Company, Inc.
500 Fifth Avenue, New York, N.Y. 10110
W.W. Norton & Company Ltd.
10 Coptic Street, London WCIA IPU

1 2 3 4 5 6 7 8 9 0

For Bianca, once more

Contents

Contents

Foreword

Prospective readers puzzled by the somewhat enigmatic title *Backing into the Future* may well come to the conclusion that it is a reference to the amusing film produced in 1985 called *Back to the Future*. But in fact the source of the title is much older. The phrase is based on a number of expressions found in ancient Greek literary texts: the chorus's description of its bewilderment in Sophocles' *Oedipus the King*, for example—"not seeing what is here nor what is behind"—or the characterization of an older men in Homer's *Odyssey* as "the only one who sees what is in front and what is behind." The natural reaction of the modern reader is to understand the first of these expressions as "not seeing the present nor the past," and the second as "who sees the future and the past." But the Greek word *opiso*, which means literally "behind" or "back," refers not to the past but to the future. The early Greek imagination envisaged the past and the present as in front of us—we can see them. The future, invisible, is behind us. Only a few very wise men can see what is behind them;

some of these men, like the blind prophet Tiresias, have been given this privilege by the gods. The rest of us, though we have our eyes, are walking blind, backward into the future.

Paradoxical though it may sound to the modern ear, this image of our journey through time may be truer to reality than the medieval and modern feeling that we face the future as we make our way forward into it. The Christian Church from its beginnings and all through the Middle Ages waited with unshaken faith for the Second Coming of Christ; as the year 999 drew to its close, Western Europeans, some in panic fear and others in joyful anticipation, looked forward to the beginning of the thousandth year since the birth of Christ, the year that would see the end of this world and the establishment of the kingdom of God. In later centuries, ushered in by the Enlightenment and the Industrial Revolution, the idea of human progress generated a host of new visions of the future. The human race would still look forward, but its eyes would be set not on the Last Judgment but on Utopian dreams of a perfect society on this earth—the stateless, creative liberty of the Anarchists, the universal prosperity that would be created by the uninhibited free play of the market, the classless society that would succeed the dictatorship of the proletariat as the state withered away, and many another dream that turned out to be a delusion and in some cases a disaster.

These modern futuramas have their irreconcilable differences, but they have one thing in common: they all resolutely reject the past. "History," said one of the great builders of modern industrial progress, "is more or less bunk. It's tradition. We don't want tradition." Today our literary curriculum is under attack by educational reformers who, though expressing themselves in language more arcane than the plain speech of Henry Ford, are planning to abolish the cultural tradition on which the West's sense of its unity and identity is founded. They propose, in the name of multiculturalism, feminism, and political correctness, to replace such patriarchal and racist texts as Homer, the Bible, Plato, Dante, Shakespeare, Goethe, and Flaubert with works that will presumably direct the eyes of the young forward to the new world of universal sister- and brotherhood.

Such a total and sudden abolition of cultural traditions that link the present to the past is not without historical precedent. Violent cultural and social change, inspired by new ideologies, has more than once been imposed on a people by revolutionary government. The results have not been impressive. Most of the cultural innovations are eventually, sometimes quickly, discarded, and sometimes the experiment ends in a collapse into chaos. The visionaries of the French Revolution, for example, abolished the Catholic religion, replacing it with the worship of the Supreme Being. They changed the names of the months; in 1793 the winter season consisted of Nivose, Pluviose, and Ventose—Snowy, Rainy, and Windy. They abolished all aristocratic titles—Duc, Comte, Vicomte, Marquis—and even changed the form of salutation between equals—Monsieur and Madame were replaced by Citoyen and Citoyenne. And they replaced ancestral weights and measures with the metric system. Of all these radical innovations, the metric system was the only one that lasted more than a few years. For it, and for whatever benefits the Revolution may have brought the French people, they had to pay a disproportionately high price in the blood of their sons as a Corsican military dictator plunged Europe into more than a decade of war.

Many years later, the Russian Bolsheviks, at enormous cost in human life and suffering, imposed on the inhabitants of one-sixth of the earth's surface a system designed to substitute for what Marx called "the cash nexus between man and man" the bond of comradeship in the struggle to create the classless society. Their Brave New World has collapsed in what threatens to become chaos as the state system of production and distribution withers away, as the Orthodox Church begins to reclaim its hold on the Russian soul, St. Petersburg reassumes its traditional name, and the separate nations the czars had welded into an empire reclaim their independence.

The ambitions of our academic radicals are of course not comparable in scale with those of the revolutionaries who created modern France and have come close to destroying modern Russia. They envisage not a social revolution (though their phraseology abounds with nostalgic echoes of Karl Marx and Friedrich Engels) but a cultural revolution— or rather, since from their academic positions of vantage they aim to impose change from above, a cultural *coup d' état*. But if they should succeed, they may do just as much damage in the cultural sphere as the Jacobins and the Bolsheviks did in the political.

A society that turns its back on its past, abolishes its traditions and tries to replace them overnight with newfangled substitutes geared to a new ideology, is headed, history seems to suggest, for catastrophe. On the other hand, societies and cultures so bound by tradition that they resist gradual adjustment to new circumstances and ideas, that look resolutely backward to the past as an inviolable, even sacred, pattern, are bound for either stagnation or revolution, or both in turn. A cultural tradition must not be allowed to ossify, to become an oppressive orthodoxy. It must be continually renewed and expanded, to include new masterpieces, embrace new aspirations, new visions of the human condition. But renewal, in the words of one of the great innovators of modern music, Igor Stravinsky, "is only fruitful when it goes hand in hand with tradition."

One of the essays in this book deals with just such a renewal of tradition—Derek Walcott's magnificent poem *Omeros*. In this masterpiece, the only epic poem in English that will stand comparison with Milton's *Paradise Lost*, Walcott has done for the inhabitants of his birthplace, the small island of St. Lucia in the Antilles, what Joyce did for his fellow Dubliners in *Ulysses*. Walcott's characters, black fishermen in the village of Gros Islet, reenact the duel of Hector and Achilles, while his black Helen casts her spell not only on these two but also on the British ex-officer Major Plunkett, whose namesake, Midshipman Plunkett, was killed in 1782 in the naval battle off St. Lucia that assured England's possession of the island for the next 150 years. Achille (the native language is a French patois) is blown in a dream Odyssey clear across the Atlantic to meet his ancestor in West Africa. Walcott himself, who first heard the modern Greek name of Homer—Omeros—from "a voice/ that hummed in the vase of a girl's throat," appears in the poem and eventually meets Homer, in the form of a blind man from the village known as Seven Seas.

Walcott has appropriated the Homeric tradition to assert

the dignity of his black villagers and to give depth and reso-
nance to his modern themes—the "afterglow of empire," the
replacement of colonial exploitation by a native version ("Ireland shall have her freedom," Yeats wrote, "and you still
break stone"), the displacement of peoples—the Aruac Indians dispossessed by French colonists and their African slaves,
his own displacement as a black poet living in Boston. Like
Joyce (who also appears in the poem), Walcott has expanded
and renewed the tradition; he looks back at the past to illuminate the present and give form to his brooding on the future.

I

Poets and Heroes

Godlike Achilles

There are in the *Iliad* two human beings who are god-like, Achilles and Helen. One of them has already come to a bitter recognition of human stature and moral responsibility when the poem begins. Helen, the cause of the war, is so preeminent in her sphere, so far beyond competition in her beauty, her power to enchant men, that she is a sort of human Aphrodite. In her own element, she is irresistible. Every king in Greece was ready to fight for her hand in marriage, but she chose Menelaus, king of Sparta. When Paris, the prince of Troy, came to visit, she ran off with him, leaving husband and daughter, without a thought of the consequences for others. Her willful action is the cause of all the deaths at Troy, those past and those to come. When she left with Paris she acted like a god, with no thought of

This essay originally appeared in *Grand Street*, vol. 9, no. 3 (Spring 1990), and as part of the Introduction to Homer's *Iliad*, translated by Robert Fagles. Copyright © 1990 by Bernard Knox. Translation copyright © 1990 by Robert Fagles. Reprinted by permission of Viking Penguin, a division of Penguin Books USA Inc.

anything but the fulfillment of her own desire, the exercise of her own power, the demands of her own nature.

But when the *Iliad* opens, she has already come to realize the meaning for others of her actions, to recognize that she is a human being. She criticizes herself harshly as she speaks to Priam:

> if only death had pleased me then, grim death,
> that day I followed your son to Troy, forsaking
> my marriage-bed, my kinsmen and my child . . .

She feels responsible for the human misery she sees all around her; something the gods never do. When Zeus and Hera, for example, settle their quarrel about the fate of Troy, Zeus gives way to Hera but claims her acquiescence whenever he in his turn wishes to destroy a city. Not only does she accept, she actually offers him three cities, those she loves best: Argos, Sparta, and Mycenae. That is how the fate of nations is decided. Human suffering counts for nothing in the settlement of divine differences. The gods feel no responsibility for the human victims of their private wars. But Helen has come at last to a full realization of the suffering she has caused; too late to undo it, but at least she can see herself in the context of humankind and shudder at her own responsibility. "My dear brother," she says to Hector,

> dear to me, bitch that I am—vicious, scheming
> a horror to freeze the heart! Oh how I wish
> that first day my mother brought me into the light
> some black whirlwind had rushed me out to the mountains
> or into the surf where the roaring breakers crash and drag,

> where the waves had swept me off before all this had
> happened!

This realization of her responsibility explains why she had resisted the goddess Aphrodite, who urged her to go to bed with Paris; in that scene she fell below the level of divine indifference—as from the human point of view she rose above it. She had ceased to be a mere existence, an unchanging blind self. She has become human and can feel the sorrow, the regret that no human being escapes.

At the beginning of the *Iliad*, Helen has already broken out of the prison of self-absorption, but this is the point at which Achilles enters it. The *Iliad* shows us the origin, course, and consequences of his wrath, his imprisonment in a godlike, lonely, heroic fury from which all the rest of the world is excluded, and also his return to human stature. The road to this final release is long and grim, strewn with the corpses of many a Greek and Trojan, and it leads finally to his own death.

There are, of course, objections that may be made to such a view of Achilles as a tragic hero, a fully created character whose motives and actions form an intelligible unity. Prominent among them are the contradictions and inconsistencies in Achilles' reactions to events that many critics claim to detect in the text of the poem. These are telltale signs, according to one school, of oral improvisation under the pressure of performance, the result, according to another, of later editorial activity. It may be, however, that the critics have underestimated the elegance and sophistication of Homer's narrative technique (a constant danger for those who persist in think-

ing of him purely in terms of oral composition). In his creation of character, Homer spares us the rich, sometimes su-
perfluous, detail we have come to associate with that word in
modern fiction; he gives us only what is necessary to his purpose. Similarly, in his presentation of motivation, he is eco-
nomical in the extreme. In those sections of the poem where
personal relationships and motives are important—the debate in Book 1, the embassy in Book 9, the meeting of Achilles
and Priam in Book 24—Homer's method is dramatic rather
than epic. The proportion of direct speech to narrative is
such that these scenes, the embassy in particular, could be
performed by actors, and, as is clear from Plato's dialogue *Ion*,
the later rhapsodes who gave Homeric recitations exploited
the dramatic potential of Homer's text to the full. Like a
dramatist, Homer shows us character and motivation not by
editorial explanation but through speech and action. And he
also invokes the response of an audience familiar with heroic
poetry and formulaic diction, counting on their capacity to
recognize significant omissions, contrasts, variations, and jux-
tapositions. We are not told what is going on in the mind of
his characters, we are shown. Homer, like the god Apollo at
Delphi in Heraclitus' famous phrase, does not say, nor does
he conceal—he indicates.

Achilles plays no part in the events described in Books
2–8; he sits by his ships on the shore, waiting for the fulfillment of his mother's promise. And by the end of Book 8, the
supplication of Thetis and the will of Zeus have begun to
produce results. The Greeks are in retreat, penned up in their
hastily fortified camp at nightfall, awaiting the Trojan assault
which will come with daybreak. And Agamemnon yields to
Nestor's advice to send an embassy to Achilles, urging him to

return to the battleline. Agamemnon admits that he was wrong and proposes to make amends:

> Mad, blind I was!
> Not even I would deny it . . .
> But since I was blinded, abandoned to such inhuman rage,
> now, at last, I am bent on setting things to rights:
> I'll give a priceless ransom paid for friendship.

In a bravura passage, he details the priceless ransom. Not only will he return Briseis and swear an oath that he has never touched her; he will give Achilles lavish gifts—gold, horses, and women among them. He will also offer him the hand of one of his three daughters, with seven cities as her dowry.

It is a magnificent offer, but there is one thing missing: Agamemnon offers no apology to Achilles, no admission that he was in the wrong. Quite the contrary. His confession that he was mad, at the beginning of his speech, is effectively canceled out by the way he ends it.

> Let him submit to me!
> Let him bow down to me! I am the greater king,
> I am the elderborn, I claim—the greater man.

This is a harsh summons to obedience. The word translated "bow down" is a passive form, *dmetheto*, of a verb *damno* which means "tame," "subdue." It is a word the Homeric poems use for the taming of wild asses, the taming of a bride by a man, the subjection of a people to a ruler, of a beaten warrior to the victor. Agamemnon will still not recognize Achilles' claim to honor as predominant in battle; in fact, these words reveal that the splendid gifts reflect honor on Agamemnon rather than on Achilles. They are the enormous bounty a ruler can, if he wishes, bestow on a subject, and will do so only if the subject recognizes his place.

Once the ambassadors arrive, Odysseus describes the plight of the Achaeans, begs Achilles to relent, and then launches into the recital of the magnificent gifts Agamemnon offers in recompense. The whole of the long recital, rich in detail and rising in intensity throughout, is repeated almost verbatim from Agamemnon's speech; the audience relished a repeat of such a virtuoso passage—this is one of the pleasures of oral poetry in performance. But this is no mere oral poet repeating mechanically, no mere servant of the tradition. We are suddenly reminded that Odysseus' speech is not just a welcome reprise of Agamemnon's brilliant catalogue of gifts—it is a speech of a wily ambassador in a delicate situation. Odysseus cuts short the repetition of Agamemnon's speech at "All this/I would extend to him if he will end his anger." And we remember what came next, what Odysseus has suppressed: "Let him submit to me!"

Achilles' reply is a long, passionate outburst; he pours out all the resentment stored up so long in his heart. He rejects out of hand this embassy and any other that may be sent; he wants to hear no more speeches. Not for Agamemnon, nor for the Achaeans either, will he fight again. He is going home, with all his men and ships. As for Agamemnon's gifts . . .

His gifts, I loathe his gifts . . .
I wouldn't give you a splinter for that man!
Not if he gave me ten times as much, twenty times over, all

he possesses now, and all that could pour in from the
    world's end—
not all the wealth that's freighted into Orchomenus, even
    into Thebes,
Egyptian Thebes where the houses overflow with the
    greatest troves of treasure . . .
no, not if his gifts outnumbered all the grains of sand
and dust in the earth—no, not even then could
    Agamemnon
bring my fighting spirit round until he pays me back,
pays full measure for all his heart-breaking outrage!

"Pays full measure / for all his heart-breaking outrage"—
this is the point. Achilles is a killer, the personification of
martial violence, but there is one area in which his sensibili-
ties are more finely attuned than the antennae of a radar scan-
ner—that of honor among men. And he senses the truth.
Odysseus did not report Agamemnon's insulting demand for
submission, but Achilles is not deceived. In all Odysseus did
say there was no hint that Agamemnon regretted his action,
no semblance of an apology, nothing that "pays full measure / for all his heart-breaking outrage." Seen in this context, the gifts are no gifts, they are an insult. Gold, horses,
women—he has no need of such bribes. And the offer of
Agamemnon's daughter is that of an overlord to a subject;
without an apology, an admission of equal status, it is one
more symbol of subordination. His father will find him a
bride at home; he will live there in peace, live out his life,
choose the other destiny his goddess mother told him he carried toward the day of his death:

if I make it back to the fatherland I love,
my pride, my glory dies . . .
true, but the life that's left me will be long . . .

This speech of Achilles is sometimes seen as a repudiation
of the heroic ideal, a realization that the life and death of
glory is a game not worth the candle.

Cattle and fat sheep can all be had for the raiding,
tripods all for the trading, and tawny heads of stallions.
Ah, but a man's life breath cannot come back again—
no raiders in force, no trading brings it back,
once it slips through a man's clenched teeth.

These are indeed strange words for Achilles, but in the context of the speech as a whole they are not inconsistent with
his devotion to honor. It is the loss of that honor, of that
recognition as the supreme arbiter of the war, which has
driven him to these formulations and reflections. He would
still be ready to choose the other destiny, a short life with
glory, if that glory had not been taken away from him by
Agamemnon, and were not even now, in the absence of an
apology, withheld.

In the face of this passionate rejection there is nothing
Odysseus can say. It is Phoenix, Achilles' tutor and guardian
from the days of his boyhood, who now takes up the burden.
In the name of that relationship he asks Achilles to relent.
Even the gods, he says, can be moved, by prayer and supplica-
tion. He goes on to describe the spirits of Prayer. *Litai* is the
Greek word and "prayer" is not an exact translation, for the
English word has lost some of its original sense of "supplica-

tion"—the root sense of the Greek. These "Prayers for forgiveness" are humble and embarrassed—"they limp and halt . . . can't look you in the eyes." Their attitude represents the embarrassment of the man who must apologize for his former insolence; it is hard for him to humble himself, it affects even his outward semblance. But he makes the effort, and the Prayers, the entreaties, come after the Spirit of Ruin to repair the damage done; they must not be refused.

But this appeal too will fall on deaf ears. And with some justice. Apollo relented in Book 1 but only after full restitution was made and a handsome apology, "Prayers for forgiveness." And where are the prayers, the embarrassed, lame pleas of Agamemnon? The Spirit of Ruin, Agamemnon's *Ate*, is all too plain, but Achilles has seen no prayers from him—only from Odysseus, and now from Phoenix. Who now tries again, with an example of another hero, Meleager, who relented, but too late—a prophetic paradigm in the framework of the poem. He too withdrew from the fighting in anger, endangered his city, refused entreaties of his fellow citizens and even of his father, refused the gifts they offered him, and finally when the enemy had set fire to the city, yielded to the entreaties of his wife and returned to the battle. But the gifts he had spurned were not offered again. You too, Phoenix is saying, will someday relent, if Hector drives the Achaeans back on their ships, but if so, you will fight without the gifts that are the visible symbols of honor, the concrete expression of the army's appreciation of valor. Phoenix is talking Achilles' language now, and it has its effect: Achilles admits that he finds Phoenix's appeal disturbing—"Stop confusing / my fixed resolve with this, this weeping and wailing." And he speaks now not of leaving the next day but of remaining by the ships and ends by announcing that the decision, to stay or to leave, will be taken on the morrow.

Ajax, the last to speak, does not mention Agamemnon, but dwells on the army's respect and affection for Achilles. It is the plea of a great, if simple, man, and again Achilles is moved. He still feels nothing but hate for Agamemnon, but he now decides that he will stay at Troy. But he will not fight until

> the son of wise King Priam, dazzling Hector
> batters all the way to the Myrmidon ships and shelters,
> slaughtering Argives, gutting the hulls with fire.

Since his ships, as we have been told, are drawn up on the far flank of the beachhead, this is small comfort for Agamemnon; the embassy is a failure.

The battle resumes and Zeus fulfills his promise to Thetis: Hector and the Trojans drive the Achaeans back on their ships. The main Achaean fighters, Agamemnon, Diomedes, and Odysseus, are wounded and retire from the melee. Achilles, watching all this from his tent, sends Patroclus off to inquire about another wounded man who has been brought back to the ships, Machaon, the physician of the Greek army. And he revels in the setbacks of the Achaeans. "Now," he says, "I think they will grovel at my knees, / our Achaean comrades begging for their lives." This passage is, of course, one of the mainstays of those who wish to attribute Book 9 to a later poet: it seems to them to show ignorance of the embassy to Achilles. But this is because they take it that Agamemnon's offer of gifts was a fully adequate satisfaction; Grote (the most eloquent champion of this view) even speaks of "the outpouring of profound humiliation" by the Greeks and from Agamemnon especially. But as we have seen, Odysseus' speech to Achilles contained not the slightest hint of apology on Agamemnon's part, and certainly nothing like what Achilles demands—that Agamemnon "pay full measure for his heart-breaking outrage." There was no supplication made on behalf of Agamemnon; Phoenix's mention of the *Litai* that come humbly and embarrassed to beg favor only underscored the point. Now, says Achilles, now they are beginning to feel the pinch, they will come to their knees, to the suppliant position of abject prostration, confession of utter weakness and dependence.

Patroclus comes back from the tents of the Achaeans with news of Machaon's wound and with a purpose: Nestor has primed him to ask Achilles, if he will not fight himself, to send Patroclus out in his armor. What Achilles now hears from Patroclus is the kind of balm for his wounded pride that he had hardly dared to hope for. Not only is Hector at the ships but

> there's powerful Diomedes brought down by an archer,
> Odysseus wounded, and Agamemnon too, the famous
>   spearman,
> and Eurypylus took an arrow-shot in the thigh . . .

This should be enough to satisfy even Achilles: no more dramatic proof of his superiority in battle could be imagined. And he begins to relent. He is still resentful of Agamemnon's treatment of him, but "Let bygones be bygones now. Done is done / How on earth can a man rage on forever?" He is willing to save the Achaens, now that they are suitably punished for the wrong they did him. Why, then, does he not go into battle himself? He tells us.

> Still by god, I said I would not relax my anger,
> not till the cries and carnage reached my own ships.
> So you, you strap my splendid armor on your back,
> you lead our battle-hungry Myrmidons into action!

But Patroclus is not to go too far. He is to drive the Trojans back from the ships, no more: above all, he is not to assault Troy. He is to win glory for Achilles by beating off the Trojan attack, and then—"they'll send her back, my lithe and lovely girl / and top it off with troves of glittering gifts." Unlike the Meleager of Phoenix's cautionary tale, he will receive the gifts once offered and refused, even though he does not join the fighting himself.

All through this speech, confused emotions are at war within him. What does he really want? He talks of the restitution of Briseis and gifts, the compensation offered and refused before. He talks of "the beloved day of our return." Perhaps he does not know himself at this moment. But at the end of the speech there comes out of him the true expression of the godlike self-absorption in which he is still imprisoned.

> Oh would to god—Father Zeus, Athena and Lord
>   Apollo—
> not one of all these Trojans could flee his death, not one,
> no Argive either, but we could stride from the slaughter,
> so we could bring Troy's hallowed crown of towers
> toppling down around us—you and I alone!

Clearly what he really wishes for is a world containing nothing but himself and his own glory, for Patroclus, whom he now sends out in his own armor, he regards as a part of himself. This solipsistic dream of glory—"every body dead but us two," as a scandalized ancient commentator summarized it—so offended the great Alexandrian scholar Zenodotus that he condemned the lines as the work of an interpolator who wished to inject into the *Iliad* the later Greek idea (for which the text gives no warrant) that Achilles and Patroclus were lovers.

All too soon the news comes from the battlefield: Patroclus is dead and the armies are fighting over his corpse. Achilles will return to the battle now, to avenge his friend; he sees the death of Patroclus as the fatal consequence of his quarrel with Agamemnon and wishes that "strife could die from the lives of gods and men." He will make peace with Agamemnon. "Enough. Let bygones be bygones. Done is done." But this is not regret or self-criticism: he is still angry. "Despite my anguish I will beat it down / the fury mounting inside me, down by force." But he is angrier still with Hector. "Now I will go and overtake that murderer, / that Hector who destroyed my dearest friend." His mother has just told him that his death is fated to come soon after Hector's, and though deeply disturbed by this news, he accepts his fate. Not to avenge Patroclus by killing Hector would be a renunciation of all that he stands for and has lived by, the attainment of glory, of the universal recognition that there is "no man my equal among the bronze-armed Achaeans."

He cannot go into battle at once, for he has no armor; his father's panoply has been stripped off the corpse of Patroclus.

Hector wears it now. Thetis goes off to have the god Hephaestus make new armor for her son, and when she brings it he summons an assembly of the Achaeans, as he had done at the very beginning of the poem. The wounded kings, Odysseus, Diomedes, Agamemnon, their wounds testimony to Achilles' supremacy in combat, come to hear him. His address is short. He regrets the quarrel with Agamemnon and its results. He is still angry—that emerges clearly from his words—but he will curb his anger: he has a greater cause for anger now. He calls for an immediate general attack on the Trojan ranks, which are still marshaled outside the city walls, on the level ground.

Agamemnon's reply to Achilles' short, impatient speech is long and elaborate. It is, in fact, an excuse. Achilles has come as close as he ever could to saying that he was wrong, but Agamemnon, even now, tries to justify himself as he addresses not only Achilles but also the army as a whole, which, as he is fully aware, blames him for the Achaean losses. In fact his opening lines are an extraordinary appeal to the assembly for an orderly reception of his speech. "When a man stands up to speak, it's well to listen. / Not to interrupt him, the only courteous thing." He disclaims responsibility for his action.

I am not to blame!
Zeus and Fate and the Fury stalking through the night.
They are the ones who drove that savage madness in my
heart . . .

He is the victim, he claims, of *Ate*, a word that means both the madness of self-delusion and the ruin it produces. "I *was*

blinded," he says, "and Zeus stole my wits." He is talking
now to a full assembly of the Achaeans, which includes

> Even those who'd kept to the beached ships till now,
> the helmsmen who handled the heavy steering-oars
> and stewards left on board to deal out rations—

At the council of the kings, when the embassy to Achilles was
decided on, he had spoken more frankly: "Mad, blind I
was! / Not even I would deny it." He does not make so hon-
est an admission here. And now he promises to deliver the
gifts that were offered and refused, to restore Briseis and to
swear a great oath that he has not touched her.

To all this, Achilles is utterly indifferent. He shows no interest in Agamemnon's excuses or in the gifts: clearly he feels
that this is all a waste of time. He has only one thing on his
mind: Hector. And he urges immediate resumption of the
fighting. He is talking of sending back into combat men who
are many of them wounded, all of them tired, hungry, thirsty;
Odysseus reminds him of the facts of life. "No soldier can
battle all day, cut-and-thrust / till the sun goes down, if he is
starved for food." Odysseus suggests not only time for the
army to rest and feed, but also a public ceremony of reconciliation: the acceptance of Agamemnon's gifts, the swearing
of the oath about Briseis. Agamemnon approves the advice
and gives orders to prepare a feast. But Achilles' reply is
brusque and uncompromising. He is not interested in cere-
monies of reconciliation which will serve to restore Agamemnon's prestige, he is not interested in Agamemnon's apology,
still less in food; he thinks of one thing and one thing only:

Hector. He is for battle now, and food at sunset, after the day's work. The corpse of Patroclus makes it impossible for him to take food or drink before his death is avenged. Only Hector's death can avenge Patroclus and reestablish Achilles' identity as the unchallengeable, unconquerable violence of war in person.

> You talk of food?
> I have no taste for food—no, no, gorge Achilles
> on slaughter and blood and the choking groans of men!

It is inhuman, godlike in fact. But the others are men, and Odysseus reminds him what it is to be human.

> We must steel our hearts. Bury our dead,
> with tears for the day they die, not one day more.
> And all those left alive, after the hateful carnage,
> remember food and drink . . .

Human beings must put limits to their sorrow, their passions; they must recognize the animal need for food and drink. But not Achilles. He will not eat while Hector still lives. And, as if to point up the godlike nature of his passionate intensity, Homer has Athena sustain him, without his knowledge, on nectar and ambrosia, the food of the gods.

When he does go into battle, the Trojans turn and run for the gates; only Hector remains outside. And the two champions come face to face at last. Hector offers a pact to Achilles, the same pact he has made before another fight long ago, the formal duel with Ajax in Book 7—the winner to take his opponent's armor, but give his body to his fellow-soldiers for burial. The offer is harshly refused. This is no formal duel and Achilles is no Ajax; he is hardly even human, he is god-like, both greater and lesser than a man. The contrast between the raw self-absorbed fury of Achilles and the civilized responsibility and restraint of Hector is maintained to the end. It is of his people, the Trojans, that Hector is thinking as he throws his spear at Achilles: "How much lighter the war would be for Trojans then / if you, their greatest scourge, were dead and gone!" But it is Hector who dies, and as Achilles exults over his fallen enemy, his words bring home again the fact that he is fighting for himself alone; this is the satisfaction of a personal hatred. The reconciliation with Agamemnon and the Greeks was a mere formality to him, he is still cut off from humanity, a prisoner of his self-esteem, his obsession with honor—the imposition of his identity on all men and all things.

> Hector!—surely you thought when you stripped Patroclus'
>   armor
> that you, you would be safe! Never a fear of me,
> far from the fighting as I was—you fool!
> Left behind there, down by the beaked ships
> his great avenger waited, a greater man by far
> that man was I . . .

He taunts Hector with the fate of his body. "The dogs and birds will maul you, shame your corpse / while Achaeans bury my dear friend in glory!" And in answer to Hector's plea and offer of ransom for his corpse, he reveals the extreme of inhuman hatred and fury he has reached:

Beg no more, you fawning dog—begging me by my parents!
Would to god my rage, my fury would drive me now
to hack your flesh away and eat you raw—

This is how the gods hate. His words recall those of Zeus to
Hera in Book 4.

> Only if you could breach
> their gates and their long walls and devour Priam
> and Priam's sons and the Trojan armies raw—
> then you just might cure your rage at last.

And as Achilles goes on, we recognize the tone, the words,
the phrases:

No man alive could keep the dog-packs off you,
not if they haul in ten, twenty times that ransom
and pile it here before me and promise fortunes more,
no, not even if Dardan Priam should offer to weigh out
your bulk in gold! Not even then . . .

We have heard this before, when he refused the gifts of Agamemnon:

Not if he gave me ten times as much, twenty times over, all
he possesses now, all that could pour in from the world's
        end . . .
no, not if his gifts outnumbered all the grains of sand
and dust in the world, no, not even then . . .

It is the same wrath now as then, implacable, unappeasable, like the wrath of Hera and Athena—only its object has changed.

Achilles lashes Hector's body to his chariot and drags it in full view of the Trojans on the walls, to his tent, where he organizes a magnificent funeral for Patroclus. After the burning of the pyre, the hero's memory is celebrated with funeral games—contests, simulated combat, in honor of a fallen warrior. Such was the origin, the Greeks believed, of all the great games—the Olympian, the Pythian, the Isthmian, the Nemean games, and in Homer himself we hear of funeral games for Amarynceus of Elis and for Oedipus of Thebes. The honor paid to the dead man is marked by the richness of the prizes and the efforts of the contestants. Here the prizes are offered by Achilles, so he himself does not compete. There are to be many contests: a chariot race (which earns the longest and most elaborate description), a boxing match, wrestling, a foot race; after that a fight in full armor, discus throwing, and an archery contest. As the events are described, we see all the great Achaean heroes familiar to us from battle scenes, locked not now in combat but in the fierce effort of peaceful contest. Homer takes our minds away from the grim work of war and the horror of Achilles' degradation of Hector's corpse to show us a series of brilliant characterizations of his heroes in new situations. But the most striking feature of this account of the games is the behavior of Achilles. This seems to be a different man. It is the great Achilles of the later aristocratic tradition, the man of princely courtesy and innate nobility visible in every aspect of his bearing and conduct, the Achilles who was raised by the centaur Chiron. It is a vision of what Achilles might have been in peace, if peace had been a possibility in the heroic world, or, for that matter, in Homer's world. "The man," says Aristotle in the *Politics*, "who is incapable of working in common, or who in his self-sufficiency has no need of others, is no part of the community, like a beast, or a god." As far as his fellow Achaeans are concerned, Achilles has broken out of the self-imposed prison of godlike unrelenting fury, reintegrated himself in society, returned to something like human feeling; he is part of the community again.

All through the games he acts with a tact, diplomacy, and generosity that seem to signal the end of his desperate isolation, his godlike self-absorption; we almost forget that Hector's corpse is still lying in the dust, tied to his chariot. But if we had forgotten we are soon reminded. Once the games are over, Achilles, weeping whenever he remembers Patroclus— "his gallant heart— / what rough campaigns they'd fought to an end together . . ."—drags Hector's corpse three times round Patroclus' tomb. But Apollo wards off corruption from the body, and on Olympus the gods are filled with compassion for Hector, all the gods, that is, except Hera, Athena, and Poseidon—a formidable combination. Apollo (the champion of Troy as the other three are its enemies) speaks up for action to rescue Hector's body. For him, Achilles is the lower extreme of Aristotle's alternatives—a beast: he is

> like some lion
> going his own barbaric way, giving in to his power
> his brute force and wild pride . . .

Hera, on the other hand, sees him as closer to the other alternative—a god: "Achilles sprang from a goddess—one I reared myself." So Zeus makes a decision designed to satisfy both sides: Thetis is to tell Achilles to surrender Hector's body to Priam, but Priam is to come as suppliant to Achilles' tents, bringing a sign of honor, a rich ransom.

When Thetis conveys to Achilles the will of Zeus, his attitude is exactly the same as his reaction to Agamemnon's renewed offer of gifts after the death of Patroclus—cold indifference. He agrees to accept the ransom, but his speech shows no relenting; his heart is still of iron. What is needed to break the walls down, to restore him to full humanity, is the arrival in his tent not of the heralds whom he evidently expected to bring the ransom, but of Priam himself, alone, a suppliant in the night. And that unforeseen confrontation is what Zeus now moves to bring about.

The god Hermes brings Priam safely through the Achaean sentries and through the gate that bars the entrance to Achilles' courtyard; Priam takes Achilles by surprise as he sits at table, his meal just finished. His appearance, unannounced, is a mystery, a thing unprecedented, and Achilles is astonished. Homer expresses that astonishment by means of a simile, one of the most disconcerting of the whole poem:

> as when the grip of madness seizes one
> who murders a man in his own fatherland and flees
> abroad to foreign shores, to a wealthy noble host
> and a sense of marvel runs through all who see him . . .

It seems to reverse the situation, as if Priam, not Achilles, were the killer. And yet it is carefully chosen. For Achilles, a child of the quarrelsome, violent society of the Achaeans we know so well from the bitter feuds of the camp, from old

Nestor's tales of cattle raids, ambush, and border war, from the tales of Achaean suppliants fleeing their homeland with blood on their hands, for Achilles the appearance of a distinguished stranger and his gesture of supplication evoke the familiar context of the man of violence seeking shelter. Achilles cannot imagine the truth. And now Priam tells him who he is—but not at once. First he invokes the memory of Achilles' father—pining at home for a son he may never see again. And then he reveals his identify and makes his plea. It ends with the tragic and famous lines "I have endured what no one on earth has ever done before / I put my lips to the hands of the man who killed my son."

And Achilles begins to break out at last from the prison of self-absorbed, godlike passion: "like the gods," Priam called him, but that is the last time this line-end formula (exclusive to Achilles) appears. He will move now to man's central position between beast and god. But the change is not sudden. The stages in his return to feelings are presented with masterly psychological insight. Achilles took the old man's hands and pushed him "gently," says Homer, away, and wept. Not for Priam but for his own aged father, to whose memory Priam has appealed and who will soon, like Priam, lose a son. He raises Priam to his feet and sits him in a chair, and speaks to him in awed admiration: "What daring," he asks, "brought you down to the ships, all alone . . . ?" It was indeed an action calling for the kind of extraordinary courage that is Achilles' own preeminent quality. He comforts the old man, with what small comfort mortals can take for their lot. From his two urns of good and evil, Zeus dispenses now evil, now evil mixed with good. So it was with Peleus, Achilles' own father, who had great honor and possessions. But then,

only a single son he fathered, doomed at birth
cut off in the spring of life—
and I, I give the man no care as he grows old
since here I sit in Troy, far from my fatherland,
a grief to you, a grief to all your children.

That last phrase is a new view of the war; he sees it now from
Priam's point of view. And moves on from pity for his own
father to pity for the bereaved king of Troy.

And you too, old man, we hear you prospered once . . .
But then the gods of heaven brought this agony on you . . .

This is a new way of thinking for Achilles; he sees himself as
another man must see him, in this case, as he must appear to
the father of his enemy, Hector.

He tells Priam to bear up and endure, but the old man, his
moment of danger past, his end accomplished, grows impatient and asks for Hector's body at once. Suddenly we are
shown that the newfound emotions have only a precarious
existence in Achilles' heart; at any moment they may be overwhelmed by a return of his anger, his self-centered rage. He
knows this himself, and warns Priam not to go too fast; he
knows how tenuous a hold his new mood has:

No more, old man, don't tempt my wrath, not now! . . .
                    Don't stir my raging heart still more.
Or under my own roof I may not spare your life, old
    man—
supplicant that you are . . .

Achilles goes to collect the ransom, and when he orders Hector's body to be washed and anointed, he gives orders to have it done out of Priam's sight:

> he feared that, overwhelmed by the sight of Hector,
> wild with grief, Priam might let his anger flare
> and Achilles might fly into fresh rage himself,
> cut the old man down . . .

He knows himself. This is a new Achilles, who can feel pity for others, see deep into their hearts and into his own. For the first time he shows self-knowledge and acts to prevent the calamity his violent temper might bring about. It is as near to self-criticism as he ever gets, but it marks the point at which he ceases to be godlike Achilles and becomes a human being in the full sense of the word.

He tells Priam Hector's body is ready. And offers him food. It will be Priam's first meal since his son's death. And he speaks to Priam as Odysseus had spoken to him before the battle; there must be a limit to mourning for the dead, men must eat and go on with their lives.

> Now, at last, let us turn our thoughts to supper.
> Even Niobe with her lustrous hair remembered food,
> though she saw a dozen children killed in her own halls . . .
> Nine days, they lay in their blood . . .
> then on the tenth the gods of heaven interred them.
>   And Niobe, gaunt, worn to the bone with weeping
> turned her thoughts to food.

It is an admission of mortality, of limitations, of the bond which unites him to Priam, and all men.

He has a bed made for Priam outside the tent, for any Achaean coming into the tent and seeing Priam would tell Agamemnon. Achilles assumes the role of the old king's protector; even in his newfound humanity, he is still a man alone—his sense of honor will not allow him to let Priam fall into the Achaeans' hands. And he promises to hold off the fighting for the twelve days Priam needs for the funeral of Hector. He has come at last to the level of humanity, and humanity at its best; he has forgotten himself and his wrongs in his sympathy for another man. It is late, only just in time, for when the fighting resumes, he will fall in his turn as his mother told him and as Hector prophesied with his dying breath. The poem ends with the funeral of Hector. But this is the signal for the resumption of the fighting. The first line of the poem gave us the name of Achilles and its last line reminds us of him, for his death will come soon, as the fighting resumes. The poem ends, as it began, on the eve of battle.

The tragic course of Achilles' rage, his final recognition of human values—this is the guiding theme of the poem, and it is developed against a background of violence and death. But the grim progress of the war is interrupted by scenes which remind us that the destruction of war, though an integral part of human life, is only part of it. Except for Achilles, whose worship of violence falters only in the final moment of pity for Priam, the yearning for peace and its creative possibilities is never far below the surface of the warriors' minds. This is most poignantly expressed by the scenes which take place in Troy, especially the farewell scene between Hector and Andromache, but the warriors' dream of peace is projected over and over again in the elaborate similes, those comparisons with which Homer varies the grim details of the bloodletting, and which achieve the paradoxical effect of making the particulars of destructive violence familiar by drawing for illustration on the peaceful, ordinary activities of everyday life. Dead men and armor are trampled under the wheels of Achilles' chariot as white barley is crushed under the feet of oxen on a threshing-floor. Hostile forces advancing against each other are like two lines of reapers in the wheat or barley field of a rich man, cutting their way forward; the two fronts in tense deadlock at the Achaean wall hold even like the scales held by a widow, working for a pitiful wage, as she weighs out her wool; the combatants fighting for possession of Sarpedon's corpse swarm over it like flies over the brimming milk buckets in spring. Menelaus bestrides the body of Patroclus as a lowing cow stands protectively over its firstborn calf; Ajax is forced back step by step like a stubborn donkey driven out of a cornfield by boys who beat him with sticks; the pain that suddenly assails Agamemnon as his flesh wound in the arm contracts is like the sharp sorrow of pain that descends on a woman in labor. These vivid pictures of normal life, drawn with consummate skill and inserted in a relentless series of gruesome killings, have a special poignancy; they are one of the features of Homer's evocation of battle which make it unique: an exquisite balance between the celebration of war's tragic, heroic values and those creative values of civilized life which war destroys.

These two poles of the human condition, war and peace, with their corresponding aspects of human nature, the destructive and creative, are implicit in every situation and statement of the poem, and they are put before us, in something approaching abstract form, on the shield which the god Hephaestus makes for Achilles. Its emblem is an image of human life as a whole. Here are two cities, one at peace and one at war. In one a marriage is celebrated and a quarrel settled by process of law; the other is besieged by a hostile army and fights for its existence. Scenes of violence—peaceful shepherds slaughtered in an ambush, Death dragging away a corpse by its foot—are balanced by scenes of plowing, harvesting, work in the vineyard and on the pasture, a green on which youths and maidens dance. War has its place on the shield, but it is the lesser one; most of the surface is covered with scenes of peaceful life—the pride of the tilled land, wide and triple-plowed, the laborers reaping with the sharp sickles in their hands, a great vineyard heavy with clusters, young girls and young men carrying the sweet fruit away in baskets, a large meadow in a lovely valley for the sheep flocks, and above all, the dance, the formal symbol of the precise and ordered relations of people in peaceful society.

Here young boys and girls, beauties courted
with costly gifts of oxen, danced and danced,
linking their arms, gripping each other's wrists.
And the girls wore robes of linen light and flowing,
the boys wore finespun tunics rubbed with a gloss of oil,
the girls were crowned with a bloom of fresh garlands,
the boys swung golden daggers hung on silver belts.
And now they'd run in rings on their skilled feet,
lightly, quick as a crouching potter spins his wheel,
palming it smoothly, giving it practice twirls
to see it run, and now they would run in rows,
in rows crisscrossing rows—rapturous dancing.

> A breathless crowd stood round them struck with joy
> and through them a pair of tumblers dashed and sprang,
> whirling in leaping handsprings, leading out the dance.

And all around the outermost rim of the shield the god who made it set the great stream of the river Oceanus, a river which is at once the frontier of the known and imagined world and the barrier between the quick and the dead.

The imbalance of these scenes on the shield of Achilles shows us the total background of the carnage of the war; it provides a frame which gives the rage of Achilles and the death of Hector a true perspective. But it is not enough. The *Iliad* remains a terrifying poem. Achilles, just before his death, is redeemed as a human being, but there is no consolation for the death of Hector. We are left with a sense of waste, which is not adequately balanced even by the greatness of the heroic figures and the action; the scale descends towards loss. The *Iliad* remains not only the greatest epic poem in literature, but also the most tragic.

Homer's Achilles is clearly the model for the tragic hero of the Sophoclean stage; his stubborn, passionate devotion to an ideal image of self is the same force that drives Antigone, Oedipus, Ajax, and Philoctetes to the fulfillment of their destinies. Homer's Achilles is also, for archaic Greek society, the essence of the aristocratic ideal, the paragon of male beauty, courage, and patrician manners—"the splendor running in the blood," says Pindar, in a passage describing Achilles' education in the cave of the centaur Chiron. And this too strikes a tragic note, for Pindar sang his praise of aristocratic values in the century which saw them go down to extinction, replaced by the new spirit of Athenian democracy. But it seems at first surprising that one of the most famous citizens of that democracy, a man whose life and thought would seem to place him at the opposite extreme pole from the Homeric hero, who was so far removed from Achilles' blind instinctive reactions that he could declare the unexamined life unlivable, that Socrates, on trial for his life, should invoke the name of Achilles. Explaining to his judges why he feels no shame or regret for a course of action which has brought him face to face with a death sentence, and rejecting all thought of a compromise which might save his life (and which his fellow citizens would have been glad to offer), he cites as his example Achilles, the Achilles who, told by his mother that his own death would come soon after Hector's, replied: "Then let me die at once . . ." rather than "sit by the ships / a useless dead weight on the good, green earth . . ."

And yet, on consideration, it is not so surprising. Like Achilles, he was defying the community, hewing to a solitary line, in loyalty to a private ideal of conduct, of honor. In the last analysis the bloodstained warrior and the gentle philosopher live and die in the same heroic, and tragic, pattern.

What Did Achilles Look Like?

Matthew Arnold pointed out in a famous passage that Homer nowhere attempts to describe Helen's beauty; rather, we apprehend it through the effect it has on the old men who sit on the Trojan wall. But this reticence about the physical appearance of his characters is characteristic of Homer throughout. What did Achilles look like, for example? We are told that he was *pelorios*, huge, that he had a *kharien*, graceful, forehead and face and *aglaa*, shining, limbs; and he himself proclaims that he is handsome, *kalos*, and big, *megas*. But Agamemnon and Ajax too are *pelorios*, Hector and Priam are *megas*, Nireus and Agamemnon are *kalos*, and Hector's head is *kharien*. As for Achilles' limbs, they are "shining" only once, and that in a passage (*Iliad* 19.383) where the overwhelming majority of our manuscripts read not *guia*, limbs,

This essay originally appeared in *New Perspectives in Early Greek Art*, edited by Diana Buitron-Oliver (Hanover, N.H., and London: National Gallery of Art, Washington; distributed by the University Press of New England, 1991).

but *dora*, gifts. How is Achilles different from other heroes? What color were his eyes, for example? This is a question the emperor Tiberius should have put to his scholars instead of asking them "what songs the sirens sang"—a question any well-read schoolboy could have answered. For about the color of Achilles' eyes we are told nothing, though Homer has epithets for both Athena and Hera that describe (in vague terms, it is true) their eyes. Achilles' hair was *xanthe*—whatever that color was, presumably the same color as his horse Xanthos—but so was that of Menelaus and Odysseus. Did he have a beard? Or was he, like Hermes in Book 24 of the *Iliad* (347–48), an ephebe with the first down on his cheeks, "appearing as a boy whose lip was downy in the first bloom of manhood, a young prince"?[1]

We might presume that he was full-bearded from the phrase used to describe his chest in Book I (189): *stēthessin lasioisi* "his shaggy breast." But the adjective *lasios* is elsewhere applied to the word *kēr*, and though a shaggy breast may be normal on a grown man, a shaggy heart would be cause for alarm. In these cases the word obviously means "manly" or "courageous," but it may mean the same thing in Book I, for *en stēthessin* elsewhere often refers not to the exterior but to the interior, the seat of the passions and of internal debate. So that this line might be telling us not that Achilles has hair on his chest (and indeed why should he be so singled out? Were Agamemnon and Odysseus smooth-chested?) but that his "heart within his manly breast was divided in counsel." In any case, the vase painters of the sixth and fifth centuries seem to

---

[1] This translation from the Robert Fitzgerald version (New York: Doubleday, 1974).

have received mixed signals from the Homeric text, for they portray Achilles sometimes as the bearded warrior (as on the Exekias vase showing Achilles and Ajax) but more often as the handsome ephebe (as on the Sosias Painter's picture of Achilles and Patroclus and on the Achilles Painter's name vase). For Achilles, as for the rest of the heroes, Homer offers us no distinctive overall vision of his physical form and figure.

This might be thought a natural corollary of the idea the late, and much lamented, Bruno Snell developed in his *Entdeckung des Geistes (The Discovery of the Mind)*[2]—that Homer's world had no concept of the human body as a unity, a form. Pointing out that Homer regularly mentions a part of the body where we would refer to the body as a whole—the spear pierces the skin, *chroa* (not the body), and sweat flows from the limbs, *guia* (not the body)—he comes to the conclusion that "the early Greeks did not . . . grasp the body as a unit." "Homeric man," he goes on, "had a body exactly like the later Greeks but he did not know it *qua* body, but merely as the sum total of the limbs." The Homeric word *soma*, as Aristarchus first pointed out, was used only of the dead body. Snell dismisses *demas*, Aristarchus' candidate for the living body, on the grounds that it is used only as an accusative of respect: "Its use is restricted to a mere handful of expressions."

Homer, then, has, according to Snell, no word for the living body. "Through Homer," he concludes, "we have come

---

[2]Translated by Thomas Rosenmaner (Cambridge, Mass.: Harvard University Press, 1953). Quotations below from pp. 7–8, ix.

to know early European thought in poems of such length that we need not hesitate to draw our conclusion, if necessary, *ex silentio*. If some things do not occur in Homer though our modern mentality would lead us to expect them, we are entitled to assume that he had no knowledge of them."

This was in its time a stimulating and one might even say creative insight, linked as it was to Snell's much more persuasive and important discussion of the Homeric mentality. But like most generalizations about Homer, Milman Parry's among them, it has lost some of its capacity to dazzle over the years. For one thing, the argument from silence is not really applicable here. It is true that we have a great body of material—"poems of such length"—but the sample consists of archaizing artificial language, limited by its exclusion of forms not compatible with its demanding metrical pattern. For another, Homer's description of physical activity—sweat ran from the limbs, the spear pierced the skin—proves only that Homer's language, like all true poetic language, prefers the concrete telling detail to the abstract general concept. Thirdly, buttressing an argument from silence by ruling out an obvious exception—the existence of the word *demas*—on the basis that it occurs only as an accusative of respect would be a high-handed procedure even if the reason given were true. But it is not. *Demas* occurs as the direct object of the verb in two places in the *Odyssey*. It is used once when Odysseus' crew is changed into swine by Circe; they had, Homer tells us, "the heads and voice and hair of swine—and the body" (10.-240–41). It occurs again when Athena transforms Odysseus from aging beggar to handsome mature man: she "increased his body and youth" (16.174).

And lastly, Snell has overlooked two other Homeric words

that, like *demas*, refer to the human body conceived of not as separate parts but as a unit—the words *phyē* and *eidos*. This is not the place to present a detailed analysis of Homer's use of these words, but a few examples will suffice to demonstrate that Homer was not the mental primitive Snell took him for.

The word *demas*, of course, is connected with *demo-*domo*; its obvious English equivalent is "build," "frame," "structure." For some of its occurrences in Homer the English word *body* imposes itself as inescapable, as for example when first Telemachus at Pylos and later Odysseus, once again master in his own home, strides naked out of the bath: "from the bath he stepped, in body like the immortals"—*demas athanatoisin homoios* (3.468, 23.163). More important than this, however, is the fact that *demas* is very often used to express the physical ensemble that is recognizable as a distinct individual. Poseidon, for example (*Iliad* 13.45) "takes on the likeness of Calchas, in bodily form," *eisamanos Kalchanti demas*, and so Apollo takes on the bodily likeness of Periphas, *demas Periphanti eoikōs* (*Iliad* 17.323). And when the gods simply assume human shape, not identified with any individual, *demas* is the word used; Poseidon and Athena, Homer tells us in the *Iliad* (21,285), take human form *(demas)*.

The word *eidos*, of course, is one that later served Plato as one of the names for the ideal forms. In Homer it is always used of the human form and seems to mean something very different from Plato's *eidos*: "appearance," "looks." This meaning, the exact opposite of Plato's *eidos*, is clear to see in Homer's description of the beggar Irus in *Odyssey* 18.4: "He had no strength or force, but, in appearance [*eidos*], he was big to look at." Here *eidos* is appearance as opposed to reality. But it is for the most part a complimentary word. Paris, for example, is blessed with *kalon eidos* (*Iliad* 3.44), and this meaning, "beauty," "comeliness," can be conveyed even without a qualifying adjective such as "beautiful"; elsewhere Paris is *eidos ariste* "most excellent in appearance." One of the gifts he has received from Aphrodite is *eidos*. "The gifts of Aphrodite," Hector tells him bitterly, "your hair and beauty [*eidos*] will do you no good when you lie in the dust" (*Iliad* 3.54). But *eidos* can also be used in a different context. Dolon, we are told, was evil in appearance, *eidos*, but he could run fast (*Iliad* II.316). Priam, on the other hand, is "admirable in build and appearance," *demas kai eidos* (24.376), and the dream Zeus sends to Agamemnon in Book 2 (58) resembles Nestor in "appearance [*eidos*] and size."

This dream also resembles Nestor in the last of the three words under discussion: *phye*. This is a difficult word for which to find an English approximation; its particular field of meaning is best understood from its contexts. In Book 8 of the *Odyssey*, one Laodamas appraises the physique of (the as yet unidentified) Odysseus. "In *phye*, he is not to be despised," he says, and goes on to specify for us what *phye* means: "in thighs and calves, his two arms above his stout neck and his great strength" (*Odyssey* 8.134–36). Here, in the detailed enumeration of the limbs, is Snell's "physical body of a man ... comprehended not as a unit but as an aggregate," but it is preceded by a word, *phye*, which *does* comprehend the aggregate as a unity. The term *phye* here obviously means something like "physical appearance," "shape," or "form," as it does in a similar passage in the *Iliad* (3.208), where Antenor remembers the visit to Troy of Odysseus and Menelaus: "I came to know their *phye* and their cunning schemes." The *phye* is defined in the following lines: "when they stood, Menelaus with his broad shoulders was taller than Odysseus . . . but when they were seated Odysseus was the more majestic." And one remembers that in Sophocles' *Oedipus the King* when Oedipus asks Jocasta, "What did Laius look like?" and gets the answer "He was tall, his hair just lately sprinkled with white and as for his shape it was just like yours," the word he uses is *physis*—a later form of *phye*.

Homer, then, had the vocabulary and the concepts necessary to give us detailed descriptions of individuals in their physical appearance. But he rarely did so. And it is interesting to see where he did.

He does so when the details of appearance and physique are necessary for the development of the action, as in the passage already quoted, where Laodamas assesses Odysseus' qualifications as an athlete—a prologue to Euryalus' challenge and Odysseus' phenomenal discus throw (the first stage in his recognition at the court of Alcinous). And again in the descriptions of Odysseus' physique transformed by Athena from maturity to old age and back again.

Homer can use a telling physical detail to intensify pathos at a climactic moment, as when Menelaus is wounded by the arrow from the bow of Pandaros: "so, Menelaus, your thighs were fouled with blood, your shapely calves and the fine ankles below" (*Iliad* 4.146–47). So when Hector's corpse is lashed to Achilles' chariot: "as he was dragged, the dust flew up, and on either side his dark hair was spread, and in the dust lay that head that was once so handsome" (*Iliad* 22.-401–3). This is the first mention of the color of Hector's hair. And the passage as a whole triggers the memory of an earlier passage—the death of Patroclus. Achilles' helmet, struck from Patroclus' head by Apollo himself, rolls in the dust. It had never done so before "but used to guard the head and handsome brow of a godlike man Achilles" (*Iliad* 16.798–99), a statement followed immediately by a foreshadowing of Hector's death. Zeus allowed Hector to wear it on his head, yet his day of destruction was near.

And Homer does give us, once, a full, unforgettable, detailed picture of a human figure. It is that of Thersites, the ugliest man that came to Troy: "He was bandy legged, and lame in one foot; his shoulders were rounded out and sunk over his chest. And above them his head came to a point, and on it the stubble was patchy" (*Iliad* 2.216–19). He looks, as Cedric Whitman pointed out in *Aristophanes and the Comic Hero*, for all the world like the Karaghiozes of the modern Greek shadow play.

These three examples are enough to show that Homer could, when he wanted to, create vivid, indeed unforgettable, images of the human form. But he used this power very sparingly, for plot development, for creation of pathos at climactic moments, or for caricature. We are left to form our images of heroes ourselves—not even, as in the case of Helen, through the reactions of others, but through the heroes' own actions and, above all, their speech.

Caviar to the General

P*indar*[1] is the first book in a series, edited by John Herington for the Yale University Press, which aims to close a gap. It is the gap between "the classical masters of Greece and Rome, those models of concision, elegance, and understanding of the human condition" and "a sort of industrial complex, processing those masters into an annually growing output of technical articles and monographs." The editor sees a need for the kind of book that will direct "the general reader not to the pyramid of secondary literature piled over the burial places of the classical writers but to the living faces of the writers themselves, as perceived by a scholar-humanist with a deep knowledge of, and love for, his subject." For his authors he looked for "men and women pos-

This essay originally appeared in *The New York Review of Books*, October 24, 1985. Reprinted with permission from *The New York Review of Books*. Copyright © 1985 Nyrev, Inc.

[1]D. S. Carne-Ross, *Pindar* (New Haven, Conn.: Yale University Press, 1985).

sessed of . . . a love for literature in other languages; extending into modern times; a vision that extends beyond academe to contemporary life itself; and above all an ability to express themselves in clear, lively, and graceful English."

That all three qualities are native to the critical writing of D.S. Carne-Ross is no secret to those who have read his reviews in this journal, his many contributions to that now defunct but sorely missed periodical *Arion*, and his collection *Instaurations: Essays in and out of Literature*,[2] which proceeds "from Pindar to Pound" by way of Sophocles, Dante, Góngora, and Leopardi. In this new volume he has tried to find the way in which a reading of Pindar's poetry can "best be proposed to today's incurious world."

That adjective is well chosen. Pindar (probable dates 518–438 B.C.) has often been called the greatest of the Greek lyric poets, but in the modern world his forty-five victory odes for athletic champions who won prizes at Olympia, Delphi, Nemea, and the Isthmus are, like the play Hamlet so much admired, caviar to the general. The modern world is not alone in this indifference; Pindar had not been long in his grave when the Athenian comic poet Eupolis spoke of his songs as "already condemned to silence by popular lack of taste." They were the exquisite products of a performing art which vanished together with the society that had called it into being: the aristocratic world of archaic Greece, a world of political stability and religious certainty, and also of patrons who could afford to celebrate an athletic triumph at the great games with an ode that was composed by a master poet such as Pindar, usually in honor of a victorious athlete returning to

[2]University of California Press, 1979.

his city, to be recited at a single performance by a dancing chorus. One of Pindar's most impressive religious personifications is Hesychia—"Tranquillity"—a concept that embraces individual calm of mind, internal political stability, and restraint in foreign relations.

As Carne-Ross points out in his discussion of Pindar's invocation of Hesychia in the opening lines of the eighth Pythian ode, this attitude was no longer at home in a Greece for which the competitive, aggressive, and egalitarian spirit of Athenian democracy set the tone. Pindar was no democrat. "There is great weight in inherited glory," he sang in the third Nemean ode, for Aristokleidas of Aegina, "while mere instruction leaves a man a thing of shadows." But his defiant celebration of aristocratic values was the swan song of a dying ideal; by the end of the fifth century BC his poetry no longer had an audience. For the Alexandrian scholars of the third and second centuries it was a bare literary text, its music and choreography long since lost, a difficult text, too, that called for editing and interpretation. Since its rediscovery in the West (the first printed edition appeared in Italy in 1513) it has served scholars as an arena for acrid controversy and the literate public as a model of the sublime which everyone admired and some, Rabelais for instance, made fun of, but few took the trouble to read.

It would seem from this description of the fate of Pindaric poetry that it was not for all time but of an age, and Carne-Ross indeed points out that unlike other Greek literary creations such as tragedy, comedy, lyric, pastoral, and epigram, the victory ode had no future.

If Homer and Virgil and Horace have (until yesterday) been household figures, it is because they lived on in our poetry through allusion, imitation, and translation. This did not happen with Pindar and in consequence he has remained a marginal figure in our tradition.

Yet few who can read him in the original have doubted that he is a great poet; even those scholars who find him full of digressions and irrelevancies admire the splendors of what Horace taught us to call "purple patches." And modern translators, the poet-scholar Richmond Lattimore leading the way, have offered the English-speaking public versions that give at least an idea of the magnificence and subtlety of Pindar's rhythms, the brilliance and originality of his imagery, and the elevation of his language, consistently noble but never pompous.[3] Yet for most readers the poems remain difficult, as anyone knows who has tried to teach them in translation. Carne-Ross addresses himself to the problem of trying "to give some impression of what it 'feels like' to read a victory ode, to suggest the way the thing works, how it moves and breathes, by means of a series of rather close readings of individual poems."

The problem is, and has been from the beginning, that of the unity of the individual ode. One scholar expresses it pointedly in a recent book: "One's first reaction to any poem by Pindar is to feel that one is confronting a series of un-

---

[3]Lattimore first published his translation of five of the Pythian Odes, *Some Odes of Pindar*, in 1942 (New York: New Directions); the complete collection, *The Odes of Pindar*, appeared in 1947 (Chicago: University of Chicago Press). A more recent translation by Frank J. Nisetich, *Pindar's Victory Songs* (Baltimore: Johns Hopkins University Press, 1980), contains a long, enlightening essay on Pindaric poetry, as well as short introductions to each of the odes.

related fragments."[4] Cryptic references, abrupt transitions, mythical themes of dazzling radiance but apparently marginal relevance, proverbial wisdom and gnomic exhortation, invocation of gods and heroes, and statements that sound like assertions in the poet's own person assault the reader's attention as they race by with the speed of the athletes these strange productions claim to celebrate. Here, for example, is Pindar, in the tenth Olympian ode, apologizing for late delivery:

> For the time ahead is suddenly here,
>   and I am deep in arrears
>   and embarrassment.
>   And yet payment
>   with interest
>   can alleviate
>   the sting of discredit.
> As the white wave washes the spinning pebble under,
> so I'll sweep my debt away gladly.
> For Honesty rules in Western Lokroi,
>   and they cultivate Kalliopa there

[4]Mary R. Lefkowitz, *The Victory Ode* (Park Ridge, N.J.: Noyes, 1976). Like Carne-Ross she "seeks to bring the reader directly into contact with the poetry itself." But unlike Carne-Ross, who cites Pindar in his own translations for the most part, she does so with constant reference to the Greek text. She offers a close line-by-line discussion of six poems, four by Pindar and two by Bacchylides, and invites the reader to "share in appreciation both of the amazing potential of the complex art form and in the innovative linguistic talent of two great poets." Bacchylides often suffers from the inevitable comparison with his greater rival but he deserves better of the critics than the lukewarm praise he is usually accorded. A fresh and convincing reevaluation of his work by an "unabashed admirer," Anne Pippin Burnett, is *The Art of Bacchylides* (Cambridge, Mass.: Harvard University Press, 1985).

and the bronze God of War. Even champion Herakles
recoiled once, in battle with Kyknos.
Let Hagesidamos, winner in boxing at Olympia,
pay his trainer Ilas gratitude
as Patroklos paid Achilleus.
With a god's favoring hand, one man
may whet another's ambition, inspire him
to prodigious feats, if glory's in his birthright.

(Translated by F. Nisetich)

Scholarly attempts to deal with these recalcitrant texts
took two main directions: to find for the individual ode one
basic concept—the *Grundgedanke*—to which most if not all of
the elements could be somehow connected (a variant was to
look for a central unifying symbol) or to renounce the idea of
unity and see the ode as a scattering of poetic gems in a
prosaic setting. The *Grundgedanke*, unfortunately, always
turned out to be some staggering banality (and the ubiquity
of a basic symbol usually had to be imposed on a reluctant
text by special pleading). The admirers of individual purple
passages fastened on the "prosaic" stretches as a base for
reconstituting Pindar's life and times. The masterpiece in this
line, Wilamowitz's 538-page *Pindaros* (1922), offers a detailed
biography of the poet, with an exploration of his beliefs, prejudices, and political attitudes, the whole towering edifice
precariously based on fanciful deductions from the text of the
poems.

No progress seemed possible; disciples of both schools simply
went on refining the arguments of their mentors. The critical

situation resembled that of Homeric studies, where the unitarians continued to smooth over anomalies in the text and the separatists to exaggerate them. In that field the rules of the game were changed by the new insights of an American scholar, Milman Parry, whose hypothesis of oral composition by theme and formula explained so many of the anomalies in the text that though the argument continued it now had to be recast along different lines. In Pindaric studies the work of another American, Elroy Bundy, produced a comparable upheaval. Parry died young, before the scholarly world at large had recognized the importance of his work; Bundy, too, died young but, in spite of initial neglect and in some cases angry dismissal, he lived to see his approach to the problem of unity in the victory ode almost universally accepted in whole or in part, either adopted with qualifications and demurrals or pushed to unacceptable extremes by overenthusiastic imitators.

Bundy suggested that the vinculum earlier scholars had tried to find in *Grundgedanken* and the like, the bond or chain that would link the apparently disparate elements of the poem, had been clearly visible from the start to anyone who paid attention to the social context of the victory ode; it was the poet's main purpose, the overriding obligation to the patron who had commissioned the ode—to praise the victor. In a pair of highly condensed articles published in 1964[5] Bundy attempted to demonstrate, in his analysis of two odes, that all those "characteristics of style and temper" usually ascribed to Pindar—"an allusiveness that would strain the powers of a

[5]"Studia Pindarica" I and II, *University of California Publications in Classical Philology*, vol. 18, no. 1, pp. 1–34; no. 2, pp. 35–92.

listening audience, . . . personal, religious, political, philosophical and historical references that might interest the poet
but do nothing to enhance the glory of a given patron, . . .
abruptness in transitions . . . gross irrelevance . . . lengthy ser-
monizing . . . literary scandals and embarrassments"—must
be creations of the modern imagination; they stem from mis-
understanding of the conventions of encomiastic poetry.
Bundy observes and catalogues "a host of these conventions"
and find that "they point uniformly . . . to one master principle: that there is no passage" in these poems "that is not in its
primary intent . . . designed to enhance the glory of a particular patron."

Bundy was not the first scholar to investigate the conventions of the genre (Schadewalt, in Germany, had made a
start), but his was far and away the most thoroughgoing and
convincing analysis of the poetic tactics of the encomium.
Public praise is a dangerous medium; it can all too easily provoke disgust if it verges on flattery, boredom if it belabors the
obvious or runs to repetition, derision if it exaggerates
beyond the limits of credibility. The only place where such
considerations do not apply is the court of a dictator where,
on the contrary, abject flattery, monotonous repetition, and
wild exaggeration are exactly what official spokesmen are expected to produce. Such qualities are omnipresent, for example, in the collection of twelve speeches in praise of Roman
emperors which have come down to us under the title
Panegyrici Latini. When I met Bundy at Berkeley in 1964 he told
me that the crude adulation and abject servility of these com-
positions had set him to reflecting on the infinitely subtle and
sophisticated techniques employed by the practitioners of the
victory ode, who had to sing public praises not of an autocrat

before his court but of a free man in the presence of his fellow citizens.[6]

The two essays in which Bundy explored the intricacies of this refined art were unfortunately written without much regard for the reader; on the contrary, the clipped and allusive prose, studded with new and repellent technical terms—"pronominal name cap," "focusing foil," "prooimial priamel," "categorical vaunt," "inverted gnome"—seemed designed to repel rather than attract; even for professional Greek scholars these essays are hard going. And some who did not welcome Bundy's conclusions seized on his style as an excuse to discount them. Yet even though he did not fulfill his promise to move on to explore "odes celebrated for their obscurity or willful irrelevance" his achievement has been generally recognized; no one will ever again interpret a Pindaric statement along biographical or historical lines without first making sure it is not an exquisitely disguised form of one of the conventions of the genre. For what Bundy found in Pindar was a "marvelous creative energy shaping and reshaping the nuances and colors of traditional form."

Of course, like most scholars with an original insight, Bundy went too far; Pindar is more than a superb technician of praise and certainly more than the shabby figure who emerges from the work of some who have adopted Bundy's approach to create, as Hugh Lloyd-Jones puts it, "a dreary scholasticism, treating the ode as a collection of common-

---

[6] The odes for Sicilian tyrants might seem an exception, but in fact they maintain the same level of decorum in this matter as the odes for less powerful victors. The tyrant's participation in the races (not in person, of course, but with a charioteer and horses running in his name) put him temporarily on a level with his competitors.

places strung together by a few stock devices." The phrase comes from Lloyd-Jones's British Academy "Lecture on a Master Mind"[7]; his choice of Pindar for such a series, justified by the claim that his poetry "communicates a distinctive vision of the world, conveyed with great imaginative power," does not imply a rejection of Bundy's results but only of the limitations they seem to impose on Pindar's creativity.

Carne-Ross, too, is emphatic on this point. "When a major artist makes use of an existing form he does not simply follow the rules. . . . He is more likely to reshape it to his own ends." To appreciate Pindar, he says, "we should master the grammar of choral lyric, learning its rules so well that we internalize them and half 'forget' them: in order to leave our attention free for what may be specially even uniquely Pindaric."

In his opening chapter he gives a swift survey of the "grammar of choral lyric" for the uninitiated but proceeds to point out that though recent studies of the form of the victory ode "have removed many old barriers to understanding" they "hardly take us beyond the level of technique." They have brought us to appreciate "a consummate virtuoso" but no closer to Pindar as a great poet or indeed to that archaic Greek world which in its values and assumptions is still alien territory to us. And yet, he goes on to claim, the sensitive reader attuned to modern poetry can react to Pindar in a way that was hardly possible for generations brought up on Wordsworth and Tennyson. "The rapid cutting from one theme to another, the ellipses and apparent lack of connections, the brilliant images imbedded in some pretty impene-

[7] *Proceedings of the British Academy*, vol. 68 (1982), pp. 139–63.

trable stuff" should present no unsurmountable barrier to the
reader who has "cut his critical teeth on Eliot's *The Waste Land*
and who is "not notably dazed by the opening of Pound's
fourth canto," which, incidentally, is a passage notable not
only for its Pindaric aura but for the quotation of the Greek
word ANAXIFORMINGES—which opens Pindar's second
Olympian.[8]

> Palace in smoky light,
> Troy but a heap of smouldering boundary stones,
> ANAXIFORMINGES! Aurunculeia!
> Hear me. Cadmus of Golden Prows!

Carne-Ross buttresses this appeal to modern sensibility as
a bridge (a fragile one he admits) to Pindaric poetry with a
reference to another "modernist poem," David Jones's *Ana-
themata* ("great if still too little read"), and Gwyn Williams's
comparison of it to medieval Welsh poetry, which is remarkable for "the absence of a centred design." That absence,
Williams says, is not a weakness, since Welsh poets were not
following the classical convention; they "were not trying to
write poems that would read like Greek temples . . . but,
rather, like stone circles or the contour-following rings of the
forts from which they fought, with hidden ways slipping
from one ring to another."

Herington wanted for his series writers with "a love for

---

[8]Pound, as Carne-Ross himself reminds us, called Pindar "the prize wind-bag
of all ages," but according to Carne-Ross, "the Pindar he disliked was the
creature of an old misreading. Had he been able to see through to the true
Pindar. . . ." Luckily Carne-Ross's comparison of Poundian with Pindaric
rapid, allusive transitions needs no such hypothetical reinforcement.

literature . . . extending into modern times"; it is fascinating to see Carne-Ross summon such contemporary masters as Pound and Jones—together with Yeats, Eliot, Wallace Stevens, Nietzsche, Hölderlin, and Dante—to bridge the chasm of the centuries which separate us from Pindar. He is not, however, "saying that Pindar is really quite modern after all"; on the contrary, he believes that his poet is "very distant" and that "this distance must be preserved and cherished." We can no more transform the victory ode into a modern poem than we can assume the mentality of archaic Greece. "To establish a true relation with a work from the past is to enter into a dialogue with it." And this he goes on to do in the succeeding chapters, as he takes the reader through twelve of the odes, a representative selection which ranges from the comparatively simple to the highly obscure, from the serene joy of the ninth Pythian (for which Carne-Ross uses a Petrarchan epigraph— *Qui Regna Amore*) to the darker overtones of Pythian 8.

One remarkable chapter—"An Ode Takes Shape"— works up to a translation of the tenth Nemean ode by way of an attempt "to trace in imagination the genesis of an ode— not the mysterious process whereby a work of art comes into being, but the way a writer observing strict conventions and with a patron to satisfy goes about his task." This peek into "the poet's workshop" sets Pindar on a tour of Argos (the home of the victor) where "shrines, altars, temples, emblems of divinity, heroic memories" stir his imagination. The song is beginning to take shape: "There must be a long rich section on Argos and the victor's great inheritance" and another on the athletic triumphs of the victor's family. A family tradition links the victor to the divine twins Kastor and Polydeukes; their story will be told, but *which* story? . . . and so on.

All this, as Carne-Ross admits, is speculation, but it carries conviction. And it is a welcome change from the kind of speculation Bundy's work relegated to oblivion, the erection of towering biographical and historical structures on doubtful inference. In its wit, imaginative insight, and graceful exposition it is typical of the book as a whole; Carne-Ross has written, for the modern reader of poetry, an introduction to Pindar's strange world "of straddling energy and splendor" which might even succeed in moving Pindar some little way from the margin of our poetic tradition toward the center.

One other quality Herington looked for in his authors was "a vision that extends beyond academe to contemporary life itself." A passionate concern for the present state of our culture in the widest sense of that term has been characteristic of Carne-Ross's writing from the first, and it is not lacking even in this introduction to a poet whose majestic celebration of archaic and aristocratic virtues seems at first, and for that matter at second, glance to have little or no relevance to the way we live now.

Yet Pindar draws for the themes of his poems on timeless constants of human existence, and there is one recurrent burden of his song that, though it would have seemed outdated to our grandfathers, now strikes our ears more persuasively with every day that passes. It is his acceptance of the bounds set to human endeavor, his vision of human prowess and glory contained within limits set by divine power and natural law. In that same third Nemean ode which championed "inherited glory" against "mere instruction" the victor is hailed as one who "has reached the peak of manliness" and told that "to go on from there is no light matter." He has reached a limit—like Herakles, who, great hero though he was, turned back on his westward journey when he reached the Atlantic and at the straits we call Gibraltar raised on both sides the rocks the ancients called the Pillars of Herakles. They were "the world's boundary." (In another ode Pindar says of the Atlantic, in words whose rhythm suggests its chop and swell: "beyond Cadiz into the dark of the West no man may go.")

Carne-Ross sees the third Nemean as a poem that "if we contrive to station ourselves before it in such a way that it can address us," poses "a question or choice that is starting to take shape." The choice is whether or not to abandon what George Steiner calls "the conviction centrally woven into the Western temper, at least since Athens, that mental enquiry must move forward, that such motion is natural and meritorious in itself"[9]—even if it leads us to open the last door in Bluebeard's castle which, in Carne-Ross's words, "gives on to realities wholly beyond our control." These are, as he points out, our terms, not Pindar's, whose acceptance implies not retreat but a society's choice "to endure round its immemorial truths rather than advance." Those pillars of Herakles Pindar sees as constructive not restrictive, "a grace of containment providing man's energetic nature with the space within which it can flourish in the manner that is proper to it." It is proud affirmation not craven submission. But "it may be too late to hear those words as Pindar speaks them."

[9]*In Bluebeard's Castle* (New Haven, Conn.: Yale University Press, 1971).

The Poet as Prophet

Euripides was a many-sided poet; even in the fraction of his work that has come down to us—about one-fifth—we can hear many different voices: the rhetorician and iconoclast of Aristophanic travesty; the precursor of Menandrian comedy; the realist who brought the myths down to the level of everyday life; the inventor of the romantic adventure play; the lyric poet whose music, Plutarch tells us, was to save Athens from destruction when the surrender came in 404; the producer of patriotic war plays—and also of plays that expose war's ugliness in dramatic images of unbearable intensity; above all, the tragic poet who saw human life not as action but as suffering. The essays of this collection explore in detail many different aspects of this Protean dramatist's work; this introductory note is concerned with one aspect of Euripides' tragic mood, its prophetic vision.

This essay originally appeared in *Directions in Euripidean Criticism*, edited by Peter Burian (Durham, N.C.: Duke University Press, 1985), pp. 1–12. Copyright © Duke University Press. Reprinted with permission of the publisher.

We have nineteen of his plays—almost three times as many as the seven of his contemporary and competitor Sophocles, the seven of his predecessor Aeschylus. We know him better than the other two and yet we find him more difficult to understand, to accept, to love. He seems unable or perhaps unwilling to resolve the discords his plays inflict on our ears; even his masterpieces leave us full of disturbing questions. If he were not so great a dramatist we would suspect him of lack of direction, of faulty construction, of exploitation of dramatic effect without regard to structure, of rhetoric without regard for character; in fact many critics have tried him and found him guilty on some or all of these charges. But a man who could conjure up out of iambic lines and a mask such awesomely living figures as Medea, Phaedra, and Pentheus, who could round off the action of a play with final scenes like those of the *Trojan Women* or the *Hippolytus*, clearly knew his business as a dramatist. He must have intended to produce this unsettling effect, which disturbed his contemporaries as it disturbs us: to leave us with a sense of uncertainty, painfully conscious now, if not before, of the treacherous instability of the world in which we live, its utter unpredictability, its intractability. It might be said of him what the Corinthians in Thucydides say of the Athenians, that he was born never to live in peace himself and to prevent the rest of mankind from doing so.

Nearly all the plays we have were written in the last twenty-five years of his life, the years of the Peloponnesian War. One of the most famous, and shocking, of them, the *Medea*, was first produced at the very start of that disastrous war, in the early spring (end of March—beginning of April) in the year 431 B.C. This was the spring festival of the god

Dionysus, and the Athenians looked forward to it eagerly, for it marked the end of winter.

It had been a tense winter. Thucydides, who watched carefully the events of those months, intent, as he tells us, on writing the history of the war that was in the making, describes the atmosphere of that spring of 431 B.C. "Although war was imminent, the contending powers maintained diplomatic relations and exchanged representatives, but without confidence. For the preceding events were in fact a renunciation of the thirty years' peace treaty and anything now might provoke open hostilities" (I.146). We know this atmosphere very well; we lived in it from the end of World War II to the breakup of the Soviet Union—the Cold War, we called it. It did not, mercifully, turn into a hot one, a full-scale general conflict. In Greece it did, and the spark that set off the explosion was, as usual, an insignificant episode in itself—the Theban attack on the small city of Plataea on a rainy night in March 431 B.C., the month and the year in which the *Medea* was produced.

This spring was the last spring of peace, of the Golden Age of Athens, the Periclean age, that period of enormous creative activity in every field of endeavor, political, scientific, intellectual, artistic. This was the last spring: two years later Pericles, speaking of those who died in the opening battles, was to say, "the spring has gone out of the year."

In the *Medea* the chorus sings the praises of that Athens of the great, the Golden Age. "The Athenians . . . rich and happy from of old, sons of blessed divinities, inhabitants of a land which is holy, and undamaged by enemies; their diet is wisdom, which brings them honor; they walk luxuriously through air which is brilliantly clear, a land where once, the story goes, the nine Muses were born to golden-haired Harmony" (824–32). This description of an ideal Athens, set in a play in which a husband cynically betrays a wife and a mother murders her children, was sung in the theater of Dionysus at the very moment when what it described was about to disappear forever. "Rich and happy"—the wealth of Athens stored as golden plates on the Phidian statue of Athena in the Parthenon was to be poured down the sink of nearly thirty years of war; the happiness, the Periclean sense of mastery of the environment, of control and balance, of unlimited horizons—all this was to go up in smoke, the smoke of the burning farmhouses and orchards in the Attic countryside. The "land undamaged by enemies" was to feel the ax of the Spartan invader chopping down the olive trees. And wisdom was to go too—that sense of proportion, that bold initiative which yet recognized proper limits, the moderation of real understanding—all this was to die and fester in the plague that swept through the besieged, crowded city. The "brilliantly clear air" was to be clouded not only with the smoke from burning trees and houses but also with passionate hatred, anger, greed, partisan accusation, ambitious demagoguery—"golden-haired Harmony" was to be replaced by serpent-haired Discord.

And this is what the *Medea*, the *Hippolytus*, and Euripidean tragedy in general are about. It is a vision of the future. In it we can see at work the poet as prophet, as seer: *vates* the Romans called him, a word that means both poet and prophet.

The prophet is not a familiar figure in our modern civilization, but ancient Greece had many prophets human and divine who foretold the future, Apollo at Delphi the greatest among them. In the museum at Olympia one can see, among the figures on the pediment showing Oenomaus and Pelops about to run their chariot race, the figure of the prophet—a bearded old man whose tense and tragic face shows that at this very moment he foresees all that is to come from that fatal charioteering: the children eaten by their father, the husband slaughtered by his wife, the mother cut down by her son. Though prophets play a prominent role in Greek art and literature, as they did in everyday life, all this seems foreign to us. Yet we have our prophetic writers too, not only those who deliberately try to foretell the future, like Huxley in his *Brave New World* or Orwell in his *1984*, but also those greater writers who, without consciously trying to, create in their writing the shape of things to come—such as Dostoyevsky, who, in his nineteenth-century novel *The Possessed*, creates a character who describes with terrifying accuracy and with apparent approval the theory and practice of Stalin's rule by terror and purge.

The writer as prophet is not someone with a lucky gift of foresight but someone who foresees only because he sees, sees clearly, unmoved by prejudice, by hopes, by fears, sees to the heart of the present, the actual situation. He knows where he is. And if you really know where you are, you can see where you have been and also where you are going. The poet as prophet is no vague, dreamy seer but on the contrary a man of hard analytic vision who sees the here and now truly and exactly for what it is. His face is not that of the young Shelley in the idealized portraits but the face of the prophet on the Olympia pediment, worn, sad, and loaded with the burden of terrible knowledge. The poet as prophet lives not in the past, as most of us live—our attack on reality made with weapons that are already out of date—nor, as others live, in dreams of the future which turn away from the world as it is, but in the present, really in the present, seeing the present.

And this is what another poet-prophet, Arthur Rimbaud, meant when he said, *"Il faut être absolument moderne"*—one must be absolutely modern. This is what Euripides was, as he still is: absolutely modern.

But it is a dangerous thing to be. Rimbaud gave up poetry, left France to become an unsuccessful gun-runner in Abyssinia, and died of gangrene in a hospital in Marseilles, unknown, unrecognized. Euripides left his beloved Athens and went to spend his last years in the half-savage kingdom of Macedonia, where he died. The trouble with being absolutely modern is that you are ahead of all your contemporaries. You are, in fact, like all prophets, rejected and scorned by the present, to be acclaimed and understood by the future. It is the story of the Trojan princess Cassandra again: the divine gift of true prophecy and the condition that the prophet will not be believed. The prophet is rejected. With Euripides, in fact, begins the tradition of the poet not only as prophet but also as outcast and rejected. His career is a modern career. Unsuccessful throughout his life (he rarely won first prize and was the constant target of the comic poets), he became after his death the most widely read and most frequently performed Greek dramatist, eclipsing, and on the stage at any rate almost entirely extinguishing, the fame of his competitors. Euripides was understood not by his own generation but by the next and the generations that came after. Stendhal, when he published *La Chartreuse de Parme* in 1839, said, *"Je serai lu vers mille huit cent quatre-vingts."* He was right. It was just around 1880 that the modern adoration of Stendhal began.

This was the fate of Euripides too. The tragic world he

created in the *Medea*, the *Hippolytus*, the *Trojan Women*, and many other plays is an image of the world in which he lived, but few recognized the accuracy of that image. It shocked his contemporaries because they had not come to realize the nature of the world they lived in; still less could they imagine what sort of a world their sons and their sons' sons were to live in. One can forgive their dismay. The world Euripides created in the theater of Dionysus is one of disruption, violence, subversion, uncertainty, discord. The keenness of his vision of reality cut him off from his fellow citizens. He "saw beyond," as Aeschylus says of the prophet Calchas. "You cannot see them, but I can," says Orestes to the chorus—he is talking about the Erinyes. And the chorus replies to Cassandra's visions of the future: "We seek no prophets in this place at all."

The democratic regime established in Athens at the close of the sixth century had emerged triumphant from its trial by fire and sword, the Persian invasions of 490 and 480–79; the next half century saw the system consolidated at home on an increasingly egalitarian base and supported by the tribute from an Aegean empire which made Athens the dominant power in Greece. These were the years of confidence, of an outburst of energy, political, military, intellectual, and artistic, which astonished the world. There seemed to be no limits to what Athens—and Athenians—could achieve. It was in these years that Aeschylus produced his final masterpiece, the *Oresteia*, and Sophocles moved into his place to succeed him as the foremost poet in the theater of Dionysus. They spoke, through their actors and chorus, to a citizen body which, for all its diversity of income, status, and opinion, was fundamentally united on essentials; it was not until a long war had taken its toll and a disastrous defeat in Sicily had inflicted enormous losses that the democratic regime was overthrown in 411 B.C. It was soon restored, but Athens was never the same again; the ideal city of the Periclean funeral speech, a vision of creative order, tolerance, and freedom, was now a fading memory.

And Euripides is the poet of the crackup: the *Medea*, the *Hippolytus*, the *Orestes* are visions of a divided city, a disordered universe, the nightmare in which the dream of the Athenian century was to end. Small wonder that Euripides was rejected by the majority, passionately admired by a few, but liked by no one. No nation, no society, welcomes the prophet of its own disintegration, any more than Belshazzar, at the feast, welcomed the writing on the wall.

> They drank wine and praised the gods of gold and silver, of brass, of iron, of wood and of stone. In the same hour came forth fingers of a man's hand and wrote over against the candlestick upon the plaster of the wall of the king's palace; and the king saw the part of the hand that wrote. Then the king's countenance was changed and his thoughts troubled him. . . .
> (Daniel 5.4–6)

The words on the wall were words of a language the king did not understand: MENE MENE TEKEL UPHARSIN. The prophet Daniel interpreted them: "Thou art weighed in the balances and found wanting." Euripidean tragedy is the writing on the Athenian wall. It numbers and weighs; it understands and pities. It does not condemn, for the situation is beyond judgment; it does not propose reform, for it is beyond action. Euripides attempts to understand and to sympathize; but he offers no comfort, no solution, no explanation, only sympathy. And this quality is perhaps what made Aristotle say that in spite of his defects he was the most tragic of the poets.

In his time and place he was a man apart. Sophocles served as general, as ambassador, as one of the treasures of the Delian League, and even on the emergency committee set up to guide the democracy after the Sicilian disaster. For Euripides we have not the slightest hint that he ever held political office or took part in political activity. Aeschylus fought at Marathon and probably at Salamis too; for Euripides we have no record of military service. Like the incomprehension of his audiences, this apparent withdrawal hints at a modern situation: the alienation of the intellectual writer. And many passages in his plays suggest that he was familiar with that situation. Medea, for example, defends herself against the charge that she is *sophe*, an intelligent woman. Such a reputation, she says, is a dangerous thing to have, and she goes on to claim that no one should have his children too highly educated; it will only earn them the hatred of their fellow citizens. Young Hippolytus, an ascetic and religious intellectual, explains himself to his father along similar lines. "I don't have a talent for explaining myself to the crowd; my intelligence is best displayed in converse with a small group, men of my own generation. That's quite natural. The people who charm a crowd usually make a poor showing among intelligent people" (*Hippolytus* 986–89). The tone is familiar; and so is the reaction to it. "Go on," says his father, Theseus, the public man. "Go on, sing your own praises, pick and choose your vegetarian food, claim Orpheus as your mystic priest and study the cloudy doctrines of those many books of yours. But I have seen through you" (*Hippolytus* 952–55). We can recognize in these characteristic passages a modern phenomenon, that alienation which seems to be the inevitable mark of the artist and intellectual in modern society. In fact Euripides is the first European to whom the modern term "intellectual" could with some exactness be applied. We know for example that he had a private library (perhaps the first in European history); he read many books and this was rare in fifth-century Athens, where literature and even philosophy were an oral, rather than a written, affair; where Homer was recited by professional rhapsodes, not read, dramatic and lyric poets performed, not read; where Socrates talked incessantly but wrote nothing. The library of Euripides could almost have been deduced from the titles of his plays—many of the plots come from out-of-the-way stories, legends from the periphery of the Greek world, local myths that deal with minor figures rather than the great heroes of the central Greek tradition. The Thessalian story of Alcestis is one example and the tale of Iphigenia as a sacrificial priestess among the barbarous Taurians another, but there are even more striking examples in the tragedies that have been lost. The *Aeolus*, for example, dealt with the love of brother for sister in the strange family of the king of the winds on his floating island; its high point was a lyric aria by the heroine which was interrupted by cries of pain as her birth pangs came on. The *Pasiphae* dealt with the passion of a Cretan queen for a bull and the *Auge* with one of the many loves of Heracles, but one who happened to be a priestess and who gave birth to his child in the temple precincts (a place where birth and death were taboo). The choice of subjects we can recognize as modern too. They seem to have been chosen, like those of Faulkner or Sartre, for their shock value.

One feature we know did shock his contemporaries was the predominant role in his drama of what the Greeks called Eros, the irresistible force of sexual passion. The chorus of the *Hippolytus* finds it strange that this powerful deity ("tyrant over mankind") has no cult at Olympia and Delphi; in the play Eros brings about the deaths of Phaedra and Hippolytus, and in many another Euripidean tragedy it "comes down on mortals with destruction and every shape of disaster." In the debate between Aeschylus and Euripides in Aristophanes' *Frogs* the elder dramatist is made to claim that he never put on stage a woman in love; he accuses Euripides of producing women "who act as go-betweens, who give birth in temples, sleep with their brothers—and say life is not life." Aeschylus had, of course, created the powerful figure of Clytemnestra, who conspired with her lover to murder her own husband, but, though her speeches are shot through with sexual imagery, no emphasis is placed on her feelings for Aegisthus. And in the scheme of the trilogy, though she is victorious in the first play, she is in the end defeated, rejected by gods and men. In the *Hippolytus* there is no such rejection of Phaedra; in the *Medea* it is Jason who appeals in vain to men and gods. Conservative expectations are disappointed, traditional relationships reversed, and this reversal is not confined to the domestic sphere. In the *Trojan Women*, for example, there is no question about where our sympathy is directed— it is to the defeated, the enslaved. In Euripidean tragedy old certainties are shattered; what seems solid cracks and melts, foundations are torn up, direction lost. "The waters of the holy rivers flow uphill," sings the chorus of the *Medea*. "Justice and everything in the world is turned upside down."

The subversive force turning the world upside down was something the intelligent moderation of the Periclean funeral speech had failed to reckon with, which the belief in human progress under divine tutelage built into the fabric of the *Oresteia* had relegated to the past, which Socrates, as we see him in the early Platonic dialogues, underestimated: the blind passions and ambitions native to the human soul which reason may for a time control but never entirely subdue. For Socrates, man's ethical and political problem is an intellectual one: if a man knows what is really good he will do it—goodness is in essence knowledge, evil merely ignorance. Euripides seems to have no such belief in the human capacity to make the right choice. Phaedra in the *Hippolytus* states the human dilemma in words that have been considered a specific Euripidean critique of the Socratic program: "We know what is right, we distinguish it clearly, but we don't achieve it" (380–81). The irrational elements in our human nature can overwhelm our reason.

Among those forces Eros has pride of place. But Euripides studies them at work not only in individuals but also in groups—war fever in armed mobs, as in *Iphigenia in Aulis*, Dionysiac frenzy in the Maenads of the *Bacchae*. Eros, in any case, is not a deity confined to the loves of men and women. When Achilles in *Iphigenia in Aulis* describes the mood of the army which demands immediate departure for war, he says: "So fierce a desire [*erōs*] for this expedition has fallen on the Greeks" (808–9). Writing, probably, at just about the same time, Thucydides (6.24) proposed an identical explanation of the Athenian expedition to Sicily: "a passionate desire fell upon them all [*erōs enepese tois pasin*]." The historian who had so meticulously explained the causes, real and professed, of the outbreak of the war could find no other word to describe this irrational and, as it turned out, fatal decision.

Thucydides cites *erōs* as a psychological factor, a human impulse, but Achilles, in his speech at Aulis, is careful to qualify his explanation. To the statement that *erōs* for the expedition has fallen on the Greeks he adds the words (809) "not without the gods." The gods are in fact regularly adduced, in Euripidean tragedy, as wholly or partly responsible for irrational behavior in human beings. This is, of course, a commonplace of Greek epic and tragic motivation, but in Euripidean tragedy it is given such impressive dramatic form that it must be taken as more than metaphor. Aphrodite begins the *Hippolytus* (28) by explaining how she has driven Phaedra mad with love for her stepson—"her heart was seized with a terrible passion for Hippolytus—it was my decision [*tois emois bouleumasin*]"—and, when Phaedra comes on stage, we see the goddess at work in her victim, Racine's *"Venus toute entière à sa proie attachée."* In the *Heracles* we see Hera's deadly ministers, Iris and Madness, appear onstage on their way to take possession of the hero's mind and direct his murderous hands against his wife and children. And in the *Bacchae* we watch Dionysus himself transform Pentheus into a simpering transvestite victim, crazed with megalomaniac visions as he dances off to his hideous death.

Pentheus' fate might be considered no more than the appropriate punishment for his opposition to the god's cult and the insults offered to his person. But no such defense can be offered for the unspeakable calamity that falls on Heracles;

Hera has hated him from the moment of his birth and now chooses the point at which he has completed the great labors for mankind to bring him to ruin. Hippolytus has offended one great goddess by the purity of his devotion to another, but even if his attitude exhibits a reprehensible pride, there is no moral justification possible for the destruction of Phaedra, and in fact Aphrodite announces: "she is noble—but she shall die just the same." Agave, too, is cruelly used by Dionysus as an instrument of divine revenge, and Cadmus, whose offense was venial and who begs for mercy, is driven into exile together with his wife and daughter. There seems to be no correlation between divine intervention and human ideas of justice.

Divine intervention, in fact, is always, in Euripidean tragedy, motivated by considerations of personal prestige. The gods act like jealous sovereign states, which will go to any lengths to maintain that prestige, no matter what the cost in human life. In the *Trojan Women* we see Athena and Poseidon, bitter opponents in the Trojan War, negotiate an alliance against the Greeks; Athena's change of sides is in retaliation against the whole Greek fleet, for an insult offered her by one Greek chieftain. And in the *Hippolytus* we learn from Artemis that she cannot intervene to save her favorite because of the rules of the game: "This is law and custom [*nomos*] for the gods; no one is willing to oppose the will of another who has a wish; we stand back always" (1328–30). All she can do is destroy some human favorite of Aphrodite, which she promises to do at the first opportunity. Mortal lives count for little or nothing in the alternating friendships and enmities of the powers that rule the universe. These powers are in their relationships no more rational than the human beings in whose destinies they intervene so cruelly; the creatures whose passions are too much for their reason are in any case unwitting victims of tyrannical, amoral forces intent only on manifesting their power. In such a world there is little place for heroic action: what is called for is heroic endurance—Heracles' resolve to go on living (*enkarterēsō bioton*, *Heracles* 1351), Talthybios' advice to Andromache to bear pain and sorrow with nobility (*eugenōs*, *Trojan Women* 727) and be silent.

Even in his own time some of his audience must have felt that his plays were images of a new Greek world in the making. But to the audiences and readers of the next century Euripides spoke directly, as if he were their contemporary; the world had finally caught up with his vision. The Greek city-states exhausted their material resources and their spiritual potential in endless, indecisive struggles for hegemony—all Greece became the theater for the mindless violence of the *Orestes*, the irreconcilable hatred of the brothers in the *Phoenician Women*. Too weak and too divided to resist successfully the pressure of Macedon, the city-states lost that jealous independence which had been the source of their creative energy and also led to their downfall. As Alexander's conquest opened up the East for Greek settlement, the cities, no longer sovereign states, became the cultural and administrative centers of the huge Hellenistic kingdoms. And as the Hellenistic kings, like Euripidean gods, fought out their everlasting dynastic disputes with sublime indifference to the fate of the victims sacrificed in a quarrel not their own, men faced the unpredictable with Euripidean attitudes: the Epicurean withdrawal from the world of action, foreshadowed in Hippolytus and Amphion; the Stoic acceptance of suffering and the will to endure whatever comes that Heracles proclaims as he renounces suicide. All through the Hellenistic and Roman centuries, in the theaters of Asia Minor, Palestine, Egypt, and farther east, it was Euripides who held the stage—even in the non-Greek court of Parthia there was a performance of the *Bacchae* going on when a general arrived from the battlefield of Carrhae carrying the head of Marcus Licinius Crassus. Even the triumph of Christianity did not put an end to Euripides' presence in the minds of men. The writings of the Greek Fathers of the Church, Clement of Alexandria especially, are studded with quotations from Euripides. And the reason is not hard to understand. They found exposed in his tragic plays the desperation of the human spirit, the misery of the human condition, in a civilization which had reached the end of its spiritual reserves and, as it looked forward, saw, like the prophet on the Olympia pediment, nothing but disaster to come.

Passion and
Playfulness

Yeats's poem about Catullus, "The Scholars," published in 1919, speaks of "lines / That young men, tossing on their beds, / Rhymed out in love's despair / To flatter beauty's ignorant ear." Charles Martin, in his book on Catullus in the Yale Press's Hermes series,[1] is fully aware of the poet's "unimpeded spontaneity and uninhibited self-expression," but he is interested also in presenting him to modern readers as "a masterful ironist practicing a highly sophisticated art." Martin, like Yeats, is a poet; the difference in emphasis is in part due to the gap between their generations.

There might well have been no text of Catullus for them to differ about, for his work came within a hair's breadth of perishing forever in the centuries

This essay originally appeared in *The New York Review of Books*, December 3, 1992. Reprinted with permission from *The New York Review of Books*. Copyright © 1992 Nyrev, Inc.

[1]Charles Martin, *Catullus* (New Haven, Conn.: Yale University Press, 1992).

that saw the disintegration of the Roman Empire and the foundation of the European kingdoms. The production of books was the province of the Catholic Church and its monastic scriptoria; they preserved, partly for educational purposes, the classic works of the Augustan and later ages. They even had copies made of Juvenal, who could be just as scabrously obscene as Catullus, and on occasion more so. But Juvenal wore the mask of a harsh moralist, while Catullus' mask was that of a fashionable, loose-living young man about town.

From the second century until the ninth, the only citations of Catullus that turn up in the literature are fragments preserved by grammarians and encyclopedists. One poem, our number 62, a dialogue between choruses of youths and maidens at a wedding ceremony, appears in a ninth-century anthology, and in 965 Bishop Rather of Verona, a contentious Fleming, wrote in one of his sermons: "I am reading Catullus . . . [whom I] never read before." It was in Verona, Catullus' hometown, that early in the fourteenth century a complete text of the poems came to light; its discoverer, one Benvenuto Campesani of Vicenza, claimed, in an enigmatic Latin poem he wrote on the manuscript, that it had been "shut up under a bushel." This reminiscence of the New Testament suggests that the phrase may be metaphorical; Campesani probably found the manuscript lying neglected in the library of the cathedral at Verona, where Rather had left it when, at odds with the ruling dynasty and the local clergy, he was forced out of office in 968.

Campesani's manuscript soon disappeared, and has never resurfaced. Fortunately copies had been made; on them depends the text of what Catullus, in the dedicatory poem that opens the collection, calls his *libellus*, his "little book." It consists of 113 poems,[2] in lengths ranging from two lines to 408. They are arranged in three sequences of roughly the same size. The first consists of fifty-seven poems, most of them short, in different meters; the second is a group of longer poems, also in a variety of meters, with the longest, number 64, its center; and, lastly, a run of poems in elegiac couplets, most of them short, many of them epigrams.

Catullus' word *libellus* cannot be a reference to the book that has come down to us. A papyrus roll large enough to contain the entire collection would have been too bulky for use and too liable to tear. The word probably refers to the first sequence of short poems in different meters; the rest would have been accommodated in two more rolls. The poems were presumably organized in one book when, in later centuries, the codex, a volume of folded sheets sewn together, became the standard book form. We do not know whether the arrangement of the poems in the book reflects the intentions of the poet; it may be the work of an editor who assembled the collection from the poet's manuscripts after his death, at the age of thirty, probably in 54 b.c. There are what look like fragments of unfinished poems in the manuscripts and missing lines here and there; opinions differ on whether these phenomena are the result of accidents in the transmission or the decision of an editor to include everything he found in the poet's papers.

[2]Modern editions number the poems 1 to 116 but numbers 18, 19, and 20 are omitted. These three items, mistakenly attributed to Catullus, were inserted by Muretus in his influential edition of 1554, printed in Venice. They were later, in the nineteenth century, expelled from the text. But the numbering had become standard for reference and so is retained to this day.

The three earliest copies (now in Oxford, Paris, and Rome) suggest that if Rather in the tenth century was reading the same manuscript found by Campesani in the fourteenth, he must often have scratched his tonsured head in despair of making sense of it. It has been calculated that it contained at least a thousand errors, some of them so compounded as to produce garbled nonsense that was changed into metrical and meaningful Latin only by the magic wand of scholars on the order of Scaliger, Bentley, and Housman. But the state of the text was not the only thing that must have disturbed the bishop of Verona. The content of many of the poems is explicitly sexual (and not all of it heterosexual) and, at times, flagrantly, if often wittily, obscene. We do not know what Rather's reaction was, but Catullus has proved too hot a brew for more than one modern editor. A recent English edition (1961), with a valuable commentary by C. J. Fordyce, professor of Humanity at the University of Glasgow, would have been even more valuable if he had not omitted "a few poems which do not lend themselves to comment in English."[3] That "few" amounted to thirty-one items out of the total of 113. "Tropic of Cancer," so ran a review in the Glasgow University Magazine, "has been published in vain; Lady Chatterley has tiptoed through the bluebells to no avail."[4]

The book also contains some of the most exquisite love lyrics ever written, equaled in their passionate intensity only

[3] See C. J. Fordyce, Catullus: A Commentary (New York: Oxford University Press, 1961).
[4] See T. P. Wiseman, Catullus and His World: A Reappraisal (New York: Cambridge University Press, 1985), p. 242. The review was signed "Asinius Pollio," and Professor Wiseman was reliably informed that the author was "a student in Fordyce's own department."

by those of Sappho. Catullus acknowledges his debt to her by
adapting for Latin verse her characteristic meter and stanza,
even going so far as to translate the first three stanzas of the
famous poem in which she details the physical symptoms
produced by the fearsome combination of desire and jeal-
ousy. Sappho, however, is not the only Greek poet so honored; poem 66, as Catullus tells us himself, is a translation of
Callimachus' courtly compliment to Berenice, wife of King
Ptolemy II of Egypt. It celebrates the disappearance from the
temple of the lock of her hair she had dedicated when her
husband went off to war and its reappearance as a constella-
tion in the night sky where, neighbor to Bootes and Virgo, it
still shines, known to stargazers and astronomers as the *Coma
Berenices.*

Callimachus was the Alexandrian scholar-poet par excellence, the arbiter of literary elegance, the scourge of long-
windedness, the high priest of subtle allusion. He had become
the New Model for a whole generation of Roman poets of
the last days of the Roman republic, the age of Julius Caesar
and Cicero. These are the poets whom Cicero—himself a
gifted poet-translator, though known to posterity mainly as
the author of one superbly fatuous line[5]—referred to with
the Greek word *neoteroi* and the Latin words *novi poetae*, words
that in his mouth and in their context were not entirely com-

---

[5]*O fortunatam natam me consule Romam,* "O happy Roman state born in my con-
sulate!" Cicero is boasting about the drastic measures (later indicted as illegal
by his enemies, among them Clodius Pulcher, Clodia's brother) to save the
republic from the *coup d'état* planned by Catiline. The translation is that of W.
V. Clausen in *The Cambridge History of Classical Literature,* vol. 1, *Latin Literature*
(New York: Cambridge University Press, 1982), p. 178.

plimentary. The two members of this group best known to later generations were Licinius Calvus (affectionately addressed by Catullus in poems 14 and 50), whose work has not survived, and Catullus, whom later Roman poets described as *lascivus*—"playful" but also "licentious"; *argutus*—"clever, witty"; and, most frequently, *doctus*. This word—"learned, sophisticated"—is a clear reference to his adherence to the Alexandrian program. He avoided undue length; his nearest approach to an epic is only 408 lines long. He favored exotic subject matter; poem 63, for example, features a young Greek devotee of the goddess Cybele who in a wild frenzy of devotion castrates himself in order to become one of her eunuch priests and then bitterly regrets his action. And he rejoiced in near-pedantic mythological allusions: "maiden of Amarynthus," for example, is Artemis, a puzzle that must have sent many an older Roman reader in search of his equivalent of Lemprière's classical dictionary.[6]

This poetry, as Cicero realized, was a radical break with the Roman epic tradition of Ennius that he himself admired, and it is appropriate that Charles Martin, introducing Catullus to modern readers, should set his poet in a similarly neoteric context. He mentions William Carlos Williams, Ezra Pound, and Henry Miller on page 4, quotes Archibald MacLeish and Wallace Stevens on pages 6–7, Pound on page 8, and Williams on pages 9 and 10; he goes on to cite Ivor Winters,

[6]Unless the correct text is *Rhamnusia*, in which case the goddess referred to is Nemesis—an only slightly less arcane allusion.

W. H. Auden, Frank O'Hara, and Marianne Moore, as well as writing, on pages 20–21, a "neoteric manifesto" for Catullus and his friends, "based on a similar document concocted by Ezra Pound and F. S. Flint at the instigation of Harriet Monroe, who wished, in 1913, to explain Imagism to the readers of her new magazine *Poetry*." Martin is aware that "this may be too facile an analogy" but claims that there are "similarities between these ancient modernists and ours." And he proceeds to explore them, in what must be the liveliest, most consistently interesting and rewarding introduction to the poetry of Catullus that the general reader could ever hope for.

One of the reasons for its brilliance and effectiveness is that, unlike many critics who undertake to introduce ancient authors in translation, he doesn't have to wrestle with the deficiencies, inadequacies, and even outright errors in an English version that, for all its shortcomings, is the best one he can find. Martin relies on a translation that successfully re-creates in English the wit, the lyric exaltation, the playful banter, the despair, the scurrilous invective, and the dramatic flair of the original, all of it moving easily in artfully contrived and skillfully controlled English equivalents of Catullus' many and varied meters. This translation is his own.[7]

Not the least of its virtues is that, as might have been surmised from the mention of Henry Miller in the opening pages, Martin is not one for whom Lady Chatterley has tiptoed through the bluebells to no avail. The opening hendecasyllable lines of poem 16

[7]Charles Martin, trans., *The Poems of Catullus* (Baltimore: Johns Hopkins University Press, 1990). The original publisher was Abbatoir Editions, University of Nebraska at Omaha, in 1979.

Pedicabo ego vos et irrumabo,
Aureli pathice et cinaede Furi . . .

appear as

I'll fuck the pair of you as you prefer it,
oral Aurelius, anal Furius . . .

This is slightly milder than the original, but that is no fault
of Martin's. "The English language," he explains, "provides
the groaning translator with no exact equivalent for most of
the terms Catullus uses." These two lines, and many others
like them, certainly justify Ovid's description of Catullus as
lascivus in the letter he wrote to Augustus from his place of
exile in Romania apologizing for his own risqué *Art of Love*.
But besides meaning "free of restraint in sexual matters," *lascivus* can also mean simply "playful, frolicsome." *Pedicabo ego
vos et irrumabo*—"Does he really mean it?" Martin asks himself
and the reader. It is a good question, for in another poem,
(number 11), one of the most famous in the book, Catullus
addresses the very same pair in very different terms.

Aurelius and Furius, true comrades,
whether Catullus penetrates to where in
outermost India booms the eastern ocean's
    wonderful thunder;

whether he stops with Arabs or Hyrcani
Parthian bowmen or nomadic Sagae;
or goes to Egypt, which the Nile so richly
    dyes, overflowing;

            . . .

> you're both prepared to share in my adventures,
> and any others which the gods may send me.
> Back to my girl then, carry her this bitter
> message, these spare words . . .

Did he really mean it? If these two are his "true comrades," ready to go to the ends of the earth with him or for him, to take his message to Lesbia, how can he make the degrading threats that open poem 16?

Anyone who has ever served time in an enlisted men's barracks knows, of course, that startlingly obscene and even threatening language is common coin between acquaintances and even friends (though the specific threats made by Catullus would in any real situation be regarded as fighting words). For that matter, I have heard Washington luminaries of the legal, medical, and musical worlds exchange, in the sauna of a health club, insults they would be appalled to see reproduced in print. There is an element of play in such threatening exchanges, and Martin explores this aspect of Catullan invective, drawing on Gregory Bateson's theory of metacommunicative discourse, in which signals are exchanged that carry the message "This is play." These signals constitute a "frame separating play from reality," and one of the key signals is exaggeration. Martin suggests the example of a father who playing with his three-year-old son "strikes an exaggerated posture of threat and says: 'I'm gonna getcha!' " The child understands that this is a play situation.

The "frame" of the Catullan threats is of course poem number 16, the artificial construct in which they are embedded and which distinguishes them from the random and formless obscenities of the barracks latrine and the sports locker room. The intricate patterning of those opening lines, so sophisticated in their arrangement of the Latin verbs, nouns, and adjectives (something "Alexander Pope would have appreciated"), acts "as a counterbalance" to the horrendous threats and keeps "the playful frame intact." And as the poem proceeds it becomes clear that the precise terms of the sexual threats have been carefully chosen. Aurelius and Furius think they have detected indications of effeminacy in Catullus' poetry; these threats are the classic response of the virile male to such a charge. But the exquisitely artificial form of the threats undermines this assumed persona of hairy-chested, outraged masculinity, and in any case, it turns out, the offense of Aurelius and Furius is literary—they have misunderstood, or misinterpreted, one of Catullus' poems.

The poems, then, especially those of the first section of the book, are to be read with the caution firmly in mind that "for Catullus the poet's responsibility lies within the poem rather than outside it" and that, for the poet, "exaggeration in the service of persuasion is no vice." These are formulas that, as Martin himself admits, are "getting close . . . to modernist notions of the self-referential work of art." They may be useful guides to our understanding of passages like the ribald onslaught on Aurelius and Furius, but what about Lesbia? How much play is at work in the poems that have made Catullus famous, the triumphant lyrics of love returned and the despairing elegies of love betrayed, the apparently unrestrained outpouring of desire and ecstasy, of hatred and contempt, that have encouraged Romantic critics and romantic readers to accept the Lesbia poems as slices of life, to construct a history, even a chronology, of the love affair of Caius Valerius Catullus and Clodia Metelli? For Clodia, we are told by a later writer, Apuleius, was the real woman to whom Catullus gave the name Lesbia in his poems.

She was the most notorious and talented of three aristocratic sisters who were all, in the Roman patriarchal fashion, named Clodia—the name of the family—until they could assume in addition the name of a husband and become "somebody's Clodia," as Catullus' Lesbia became "the Clodia of Metellus," the wife of Quintus Metellus Celer. Information about Roman wives of the Republican period is not usually abundant, but Clodia is an exception. Unfortunately for her reputation, she was a key witness in 56 B.C. for the prosecution of one Caelius, who had persuaded Cicero to undertake his defense. Cicero had good private grounds for hating Clodia and even stronger grounds for hating her brother Clodius Pulcher. In the masterly speech he delivered in court he set out to blacken her name. He started by calling her a prostitute, proceeded to hint broadly at the truth of rumors that she was her brother's mistress ("that woman's husband—excuse me, I meant to say brother—I always make that mistake"), and suggested that she had poisoned her husband Metellus, who had died in 59 B.C. How much truth there may have been in Cicero's allegations and innuendos we cannot estimate, but he obviously counted on their effectiveness in the courtroom. Nevertheless, Clodia was a member of one of the most distinguished families of the Roman aristocracy; she was wealthy and also cultured. Catullus must have been just as flattered and overwhelmed by her initial acquiescence as he was humiliated and embittered by her later infidelity.

In the Lesbia poems, Martin warns us, we should remem-

ber that Lesbia is not Clodia; she is "that complex fiction to
which Catullus gave the name of Lesbia," a "theme running
through many" of the poems, "an emblem abstracted and
idealized from the poet's experience, the projection of his
erotic expectations and disappointments." The play factor is
not to be entirely discounted. The numbers game in poem 5,
for example,

> Give me a thousand kisses, then a hundred,
> another thousand next, another hundred,
> a thousand without pause & then a hundred . . .

is, like the threats to Aurelius and Furius, a case of playful
exaggeration, and, as Martin reminds us, literary play is at
work in disconcerting fashion in one of the poems (number
60) that has often been taken as Catullus' last, perhaps even
dying, word to Lesbia.

> Either a lioness from Libya's mountains
> or Scylla barking from her terrible bitch-womb
> gave birth to you, so foul & so hard your heart is:
> the great contempt you show as I lie here dying
> with not a word from you! Such a beastly coldness!

In 1983 George Goold pointed out in his edition and translation of Catullus something "that had been overlooked for
at least the past seven hundred years" of scholarly commentary and interpretation: in the Latin text, the initial letters of
the lines reading downward, followed by the terminal letters
of the lines reading upward, form the words NATU CEU AES—

"by birth like bronze."[8] The lover's last agonized cry is encased in an Alexandrian acrostic straitjacket.

Yet, though Lesbia is not Clodia, the ecstatic happiness and the racking torments of the poet's love for her are brought to life in lines that for emotional impact and immediacy have no parallel in ancient literature. And many of the elegiac epigrams of the book's third section seem, as Martin puts it, "to have been written as antidotes" to the playfulness of so many of the polymetric poems of the first. "They are satirical or analytical instruments of discovery and correction," and they are aimed not only at others but also at Catullus himself and his "lapses in self-awareness." It is a process that culminates in the renunciation of his love in poem 76.

> Now I no longer ask that she love me as I love her,
> or—even less likely—that she give up the others:
> all that I ask is for health, an end to this foul sickness!
> O gods, grant me this in exchange for my devotion.

Martin finds the poet's obsession with Lesbia not only in the first and last sections of the book, where she is named, but also in the central section, the long poems (61–68), where she is not (though she is clearly the woman referred to in poem 68). Here, however, the illusion of conversation with and criticism of a real woman in a variety of social situations is abandoned for a strategy of "mythologizing their relationship and projecting its drama onto a larger screen than the lyric can provide, thus transforming his passion and her infidelities into something beyond the reach of praise or blame." In

[8]G. P. Goold, *Catullus* (London: Duckworth, 1983), p. 248.

poem 68, a reminiscence of the lovers' meeting in a house provided by Allius, to whom the poem is addressed, Lesbia appears as "my radiant goddess," who came to him "stepping / lightly and paused to stand with the sole of her sandal / on the well-worn threshold as her bright foot crossed it." Since she is one of the immortals, Catullus must put up with her infidelities and be grateful for what she grants him, but, as Martin says, the immortal with whom Catullus chooses to compare her comes as something of a shock:

> . . . often Juno herself, the greatest of goddesses,
>   gulps back her passionate rage at the sins of her husband,
>   knowing the countless tricks of promiscuous Jove!

Lesbia is Jove, and Catullus, as Juno, must play the silent, acquiescent wife to a philandering husband.

Martin sees an even more drastic mythological image, of Lesbia as a cruel and dominating goddess, in poem 63, in which Attis' passionate devotion to the goddess Cybele drives him to the extreme of castrating himself to become a priest in her service. When he comes to his senses and tries to return to his home, the goddess sends one of her lions to drive him back into the forest. "The impetuous and ferocious *domina* wills both the emasculation of her slave and his exile in the forest, an endless separation from the rational and supportive society he willingly abandoned to join her service." And he finds another echo of Catullus' doomed love for Lesbia in poem 64, the epyllion, the minor epic that describes the wedding of Peleus and Thetis; it is the long, pathetic lament of Ariadne as she stands in the shore eddies watching Theseus' ship vanish in the distance on its way to Athens—another instance, says Martin, of "thematic cross-dressing," like the casting of Lesbia as Jove and Catullus as Juno in poem 68.

For most readers, the most puzzling and alien poem in the whole collection is this minor epic that is clearly one of Catullus' major offerings, an Alexandrian compact, allusive narrative, exquisitely crafted, and probably, like the lost *Smyrna* of his friend Cinna,[9] the end product of many years of work (Cinna's epic, we are told in poem 95, took nine). Catullus' poem 64 is a narrative with no real action, hardly any characterization (Ariadne is the only figure that leaves an impression of a real personality), and in which almost half of the lines are devoted to a description of an embroidered coverlet on a couch in the palace where the guests for the wedding of Peleus and Thetis are gathering. This coverlet illustrates Ariadne's abandonment on the island of Dia off Crete and her lament as she sees Theseus' ship leaving without her, Jove's consent to her prayer for vengeance, Aegeus' instructions to his son to hoist a white sail if he returns safely, Theseus' forgetfulness in hoisting a black sail and Aegeus' suicide[10] on learning of the supposed loss of his son, and, finally, the arrival of Iacchus (Dionysus) to comfort Ariadne.

[9]Probably the Caius Helvius Cinna who was torn to pieces by the mob at the funeral of Julius Caesar; he was a friend of Caesar but they took him for one of the conspirators who had the same name. Shakespeare's "Tear him for his bad verses" has no ancient authority.

[10]Readers familiar with the topography of Athens will be surprised to read that Aegeus, when he sees the black sails, "flings himself from the heights of the Acropolis into the sea" (he does so in the translation as well—"his father, keeping vigil on the Acropolis . . . threw himself down into the ocean"). Catullus does not mention the sea, for the very good reason that Aegeus could

Martin's analysis and justification of the poem invokes the structural feature already seen at work in the two lines addressed to Aurelius and Furius—chiasmus, a pair of balanced sequences in which the elements of the second reverse the order of the first. As in Pope's line "Prose swell'd to verse, Verse loitering into prose." Martin divides the poem into eight unequal sections to which he gives titles that point up their complicated relationship. They are: (1) The courtship of Peleus and Thetis. (2) The Wedding Feast, Part I. (3) Ariadne's search. (4) Ariadne's lament. Bridge: the judgment of Jove (almost central in the poem, a bridge between the two halves). (5) Aegeus' lament on seeing the black sail. (6) Iacchus' search for Ariadne. (7) The Wedding Feast, Part II. (8) Conclusion.

This neat scheme, like many of the similar tables constructed by structuralist critics of mythology, loses some of its cogency when compared with the text on which it is based. It is hard to find any passage in which Ariadne is engaged in a "search," except for two lines in which she climbs a steep mountain to "scan the ocean's wide expanse"; for the rest of the long episode she is standing at the water's edge. And it is not easy either to find the "lament" of Aegeus that will parallel the sixty-nine lines of Ariadne's denunciation of Theseus.

---

only have negotiated the five kilometers or so that separate the Acropolis from the nearest salt water with a pair of wings made by Daedalus. Martin has probably confused the story with another, which placed Aegeus' lookout on Cape Sounion; his plunge into the sea gave it its name—Aegean. If, however, the "acropolis" of Sounion is marked by the ruins of the temple there, a plunge into the sea would be out of the question for an aging Athenian king; it might just be done by an experienced stunt man in a hang glider with a brisk offshore wind behind him.

Though Aegeus' speech, delivered as Theseus departs for Crete, does contain some lines of self-pity, it is mainly concerned with his instructions (*mandata*) to Theseus about changing the sails; the speech is followed by an account of Theseus' neglect of these instructions and his father's suicide.

As for the section headed Wedding Feast Part II, it consists mainly of a long prophetic chant by the Fates, who foretell the martial glory and early death of Achilles, the offspring of the marriage of Thetis and Peleus, concluding with a violently realistic picture of the sacrifice of Polyxena, a blood offering demanded by the ghost of Achilles (who was treacherously killed by Paris just as he and Polyxena were about to be wed). Wedding Feast I, its chiastic counterpart, consists of a mere eighteen lines, three of which introduce the couch on which is spread the coverlet that tells the story of Ariadne and Theseus, the subject of the next two hundred lines.

Still, Martin makes a good case for the intricate correspondences in the poem—"the multiplicity of viewpoints we now recognize as polyphonic"—and adds significantly to our appreciation and understanding of it. Equally interesting is a different approach he takes to its subtleties of construction, a comparison with "developments occurring in the work of the visual artists" of the period, especially those still preserved for us in the frescoes on the walls of Roman late-Republican houses. These "artists invited gods, goddesses, and heroes into the homes of their patrons, mingling mortals and immortals in the same way Catullus does in poem 64." They created the illusion of depth by placing some figures higher on the picture's plane and scaling their size down; they also created lines of perspective converging "on a vertical axis (or axes) at or near the center of the painting."

Martin's analysis of poem 64 studies Catullus' attempt to arrange words "in lines and then in scenes that would give the illusion of depth." He emphasizes the visual immediacy of the scenes that are presented to us as the poem moves from broad seascape to rich palace interior, and back to Ariadne standing half-naked on the shore, scenes composed "with a painterly eye" and set in a frame that re-creates in words the mural artists' illusion of perspective. "The center of the poem, the vertical axis on which all sight lines converge, is the mast of Theseus' ship as it disappears over the horizon." This is a valuable insight, which strengthens and enriches the reader's appreciation of the basic chiastic structure. And it is a remarkable coincidence that this proposal to elucidate the structure and meaning of poem 64 by a comparison with contemporary work in the plastic arts appears in the same year as its mirror image: an attempt to solve the perennial mystery of the figures on the Portland Vase by identifying one set of them as Peleus, Tethys, the mother of Thetis, Oceanus, her father, and Jove, which goes on to claim also that "the structure, mechanics, and the theme of the frieze . . . are drawn directly from Catullus 64."[11]

Martin ends his book with a chapter called "Lifting the Poet's Fingerprints." Here he tentatively claims to "have found the poet's fingerprints on the arrangement of his Book," and attempts to demonstrate the existence of a unifying pattern in the group of longer poems, 61 to 68, that presumably constituted the contents of the second of the three papyrus rolls in which Catullus' complete works were first is-

[11]Randall L. Skalsky, "Visual Trope and the Portland Vase Frieze: A New Reading and Exegesis," *ARION,* Winter 1992, p. 57.

sued. According to Martin, poems 61–68 form a sequence, even "a single poem in eight parts, each of which may be read as a poem by itself, and each having its place in the sequence as a function of its relations with the other poems in the sequence." Briefly summarized, his thesis is that the themes of poem 64—"unsanctified passion (Theseus and Ariadne) and the erotic fulfillment possible in marriage (Peleus and Thetis)"—recur in the poems that surround it, contrasted in the same chiastic pattern that governs the relation of parts to whole in 64 itself. Thus 61 and 62 are marriage hymns, while 67 and 68 deal with adultery; 63 (Attis) presents us with "destructive erotic obsession" and 65–66 (one poem, not two) with "the devoted and faithful bride of her royal husband."

Martin develops these connections with a wealth of striking corroborative detail, to make a case that, though it may not convince everyone, will certainly enrich everyone's reading of the poems, which have usually been treated as an editor's omnium-gatherum of long poems that would have been out of place among the short polymetric poems or the elegiac epigrams. And, of course, if Martin's thesis is correct, we can dispense with that posthumous editor and see, as everyone would wish to see, the poet's fingerprints in the arrangement of his poems. "Most poets," says Martin, "arrange their own poems for publication: they know their own work best and who else would do it for them?"

Martin sees Catullus as "not just a poet of unimpeded spontaneity and uninhibited self-expression" but also one whose "intentions and accomplishments have much in common with those of our modernist and late-modernist masters." He hopes to "offer the common reader access to the art, the artifice, and the matchless intelligence behind the maker's impassioned intensities." That he has done, and brilliantly; his "little book" should send the reader back to Catullus with a fresh eye, to the Latin if he can handle it, but if not, to Martin's own superb translation, which provides the English-speaking reader with an equivalent of the spontaneity and artifice of the original.

The Poet in Exile

Writers have often had to do their work in exile. Thucydides, Dante, Machiavelli, Byron, Heine, Hugo:
the list is long and illustrious, and our century has
seen it swollen to gigantic proportions by the mass
emigration of German intellectuals in the 1930s, and
by the flight of the dissidents from the Soviet empire in recent decades. Most of these writers exchanged a tyranny that could tolerate them no longer for a relatively free society; the exile could hope
to obtain, in Gibbon's words, "in a happier climate,
a secure refuge, a new fortune adequate to his merit,
the freedom of complaint and perhaps the means of
revenge." Such opportunities were denied those condemned to internal exile: Lenin in Siberia under the
czar, Trotsky in Alma Ata under Stalin, Sakharov in
Gorky under Brezhnev. Lenin and Trotsky eventually found their way to Western Europe, and even

This essay originally appeared in *The New Republic*, August 20 and
27, 1990.

for Sakharov there remained the possibility that he might in the end, like Solzhenitsyn, be expelled (though he would probably have refused to go.)

For a citizen of the Roman empire, however, banishment was a dead end. "The empire of the Romans," Gibbon again, "filled the world, and when that empire fell into the hands of a single person, the world became a safe and dreary prison for his enemies." Beyond the frontier lay death at the hands of hostile barbarians; on the frontier itself, primitive conditions and constant danger. And it was to a troubled frontier that the emperor Augustus, in A.D. 8, banished one of the most famous citizens of Rome, the poet Publius Ovidius Naso— Ovid, to the English-speaking world, though in his poems, because of metrical constraints, he always refers to himself as Naso.

Ovid was not an exile, technically speaking, for *exsilium* normally involved loss of citizenship and confiscation of property. He was "relegated" *(relegatus)* to a particular place in the empire, where he was to stay at the emperor's pleasure. Others—some unruly members of the imperial family, for example—had been "relegated" to the Mediterranean islands close to Rome, but Ovid's fate was to languish, for the remaining nine years of his life, at Tomi, site of the modern Romanian city of Constanta. It was situated on the Danubian frontier of the recently pacified province of Moesia, facing east on the Black Sea. Moesia was the Siberia of the Roman empire. "I've stopped for a drink," Ovid writes, in David Slavitt's brilliant adaptation,[1]

[1] David Slavitt, trans., *Ovid's Poetry of Exile* (Baltimore: Johns Hopkins University Press, 1990).

> . . . and hardly even remarked
> as the innkeeper peeled away the wineskin to leave the wine
> standing, frozen, in what was the wineskin's shape.
> He hacked me a chunk of wine to drink or, rather, suck on
> as it thawed in my mouth.

The emperor's choice of the place for Ovid's banishment was exquisitely cruel. The playboy of Augustan Rome, who had written the *Amores*, a witty, audacious chronicle of his fictitious love life with Corinna (not to mention her maid), who had followed that with the even spicier *Ars Amatoria*, a handbook for the seducer of Roman wives, and had recently used the epic hexameter of Ennius's *Annals* and Virgil's already classic *Aeneid* to sing the loves and changed shapes, the *Metamorphoses*, of legendary heroes and heroines—this was the man condemned to spend the last years of his life in a Roman equivalent of Fort Apache:

> The country here is grotesque, the people savage,
> the weather awful, the customs crude, and the language a
> garble . . .
> . . . Tomi was once a Greek city
> but the Greeks are not stupid and most of them left.
> Then the Getae moved in, barely pacified, barely
> civilized. One sees them scamper about,
> bareback, quivers and bows on their backs, their arrows
> dipped
> in venom, their faces covered over with hair . . .
> . . . They all carry knives at their belts and you never know
> whether they're going to greet you or stab you.
> . . . Among such people your old friend, Ovid, the
> dancing-master of love,
> tries to keep from hysterical laughter and tears . . .

The reasons for Ovid's punishment are still a mystery, a favorite theme for scholarly speculation. We have no information except what Ovid himself tells us, or rather, hints at cryptically, in the poems he wrote at Tomi and sent back to Rome: the *Tristia* (*Sorrows*) and the *Epistulae ex Ponto* (*Letters from the Black Sea*). He speaks of two reasons: *carmen*, a song, and *error*, a word that can mean a simple mistake, a moral lapse, or a temporary derangement of the mind. The song, for which he often apologizes at length in the poems from Tomi, is the *Ars Amatoria*. It was a saucy defiance of Augustus's program of moral reform, his vain attempt to restore, by propaganda and legislation, the legendary family virtues of the early Roman republic. (The closing lines of the poem, for example, give explicit directions to the ladies on the position for intercourse best suited to their complexions and figures; and the preceding lines make it clear that the last person for whose delectation these positions are to be assumed is the lady's husband.)

But this poem cannot have been the immediate cause of Augustus's harsh sentence; the *Ars Amatoria* had been in circulation for ten years or so. It must have been the *error* that brought the emperor's resentment to the boiling point and launched Ovid on the long journey to Tomi. All we know, from the poet's vague hints, is that his *error* was not anything that he did: it was something he saw, should have reported, and failed to do so. In the year that Ovid's sentence was pronounced, A.D. 8, a conspiracy in high places against Augustus had been exposed. Ovid may have been tangentially involved. Whatever the nature of his *error*, it was clearly one that mortally offended the imperial ruling family; Augustus remained deaf to Ovid's eloquent appeals until his death in A.D. 14, and his successor, Tiberias, left Ovid to live, die, and be buried in the frozen snow of Tomi.

These poems of Ovid, the *Tristia* and the *Epistulae ex Ponto*, are unique in the literature of exile. They contain no protest against the regime that has imposed so cruel a penalty, no disclosure of its shameful secrets, no satire of its ruler or his ministers. The poems are all, from first to last, appeals, in one form or another, for clemency, or for help in obtaining it. They ask at first for permission to return to Rome, and later, as hope wanes, for removal to some more civilized place of exile. They contain fulsome compliments to Augustus and other members of the imperial family, contrite admissions of guilt (discreetly worded so as to conceal whatever state secret Ovid had stumbled on), and detailed rehearsals of the hardness of his lot in the brutal life of a barely pacified province.

The verdict of the critics has not been enthusiastic. Gibbon speaks of Ovid's "just, but unmanly lamentations." According to the authoritative Teuffel-Schwabe *Geschichte der römischen Literatur*, "His flattery and adulation surpass all bounds." A *"délire d'adulation,"* says Boissier; and Mackail finds the poems "a melancholy record of flagging vitality and failing powers." But these complaints about flattery and adulation do not sit well on the lips of scholars comfortably at home in their studies. "Our century," as Slavitt points out in his prefatory note, "has, to our shame, better prepared us to understand capriciousness and violence." And though Ovid's themes do sound repetitious in the later letters from the Black Sea, as hope for reprieve dims and finally dies, the verses are still elegant, and the matter often fascinating—as, for example, his account of the poem he wrote in the local Getic language and recited to an audience of tribesmen, who greeted it with prolonged murmurs and a rattling of the arrows in their quivers.

In the earlier poems, the *Tristia*, there are some of the best things Ovid ever wrote. Here he is no longer the dashing rake of the *Amores*, the drill sergeant of seduction of the *Ars Amatoria*, or the epic singer of changing shapes of the *Metamorphoses*. He writes in his own suffering person to friends in Rome, to Augustus himself (a poem of 578 lines), and, in compassionate tones of consolation and encouragement, to the wife, who had stayed in Rome, at his insistence, to safeguard his property and work for his return. Among the many jewels of the collection are Ovid's account of his last night in Rome (*Tristia* 1.3), his autobiography (4.10), and his many graphic descriptions of the climate, flora, fauna, and inhabitants of Tomi.

These poems are not just complaints and appeals for clemency. They are Ovid's weapons, the only weapons he has in his campaign for reprieve, or at least for mitigation of his sentence. Dispatched to Rome at intervals, they were copied and widely circulated. Ovid was on the imperial blacklist—his books were removed from the three great public libraries of Rome—but he was still Rome's most famous and admired living poet. His hope must have been that public opinion would eventually influence Augustus in the direction of clemency, and in this he may have been successful, for he tells us (*Epistulae ex Ponto* 4.6.25) that Augustus had begun "to forgive the fault that I committed in error." If so, Augustus died before he could act on his change of mood. But there is something more, in these exquisitely stylish poems, than a strategy to win public support and an imperial reprieve. There is a pride in the supremacy of poetry, in its indepen-

dence of power, of time and change—a sort of quiet defiance
of earthly power, even the power in Rome that ruled the entire civilized world, that had sent him to the end of that
world, and that could, if it so desired, take his life at any moment:

> . . . It's only the blessings of heart and mind
> that ever endure. In those you should put your trust.
> I offer my own example. You know how much
> I lost when I was sent away into exile. Ruined!
> But see what I still have, my mind, my work.
> Unless he put me to death, not even Caesar can take
> this from me or banish me from this.

"The *Tristia*," wrote E. J. Kenny in his splendid chapter on
Ovid in the *Cambridge History of Classical Literature*, "have been
criticized as abject; in some respects they show Ovid as bold
to the point of foolhardiness."

Ovid wrote his poems from exile in the same meter that he had
used for the *Ars Amatoria*, the characteristic elegiac couplet of
Latin erotic elegy, the meter of Tibullus and Propertius. It is
a meter that poses difficult problems for a translator: a hexameter followed by a shorter line, the pentameter, the feet
defined not by the incidence of stress but by length of syllable. Length of syllable is not a significant factor in English
versification, and attempts to reproduce the Latin metrical
pattern by marshaling stresses result in verses of mechanical
rigidity. Coleridge's imitation of Schiller's famous elegiac
couplet uses stress to accent the Latin metric:

In the hexameter rises the fountain's silvery column.
In the pentameter aye falling in melody back.

This is ingenious, but a succession of even twenty of such couplets (and Book 2 of the *Tristia* has over two hundred) would produce the effect of a phonograph tone arm stuck on the same musical phrase. In the Latin, the pattern of long and short syllables is played off against the natural stresses of the words. In the hands of Ovid, the elegiac's grand master, the couplets are a virtuoso series of rhythmic variations. English translators, forced to work with stress alone, must at all costs avoid the lockstep of Coleridge's paradigmatic couplet.

Pound's *Homage to Sextus Propertius*, parts of which were first published in 1919, took the bull by the horns. Two elegiac couplets of Propertius emerged as

When, when and whenever death closes our eyelids,
Moving naked over Acheron
Upon the one raft, victor and conqueror together,
Marius and Jugurtha together, one tangle of shadows

Magnificent as it is, this preview of the free verse of the *Cantos* is no solution; the Propertian spirit is there, but no lingering trace of the form. In any case, Pound's creative adaptation was greeted with such contempt and vituperation by the classical establishment that subsequent translators of elegy retreated to the eighteenth-century Augustan standby, the rhymed heroic couplet, which, as Guy Lee remarked in his 1968 translation of the *Amores*, "lacks the variety of elegiacs and is haunted by the ghosts of Dryden and Pope—not to mention the Pantomime Good Fairy." Lee chose what he

calls "free verse." Sometimes he catches the tone and suggests
the form with remarkable success, as in the opening distich of
Amores IIixb:

> Offered a sexless heaven I'd say *No thank you*
>   women are such sweet hell.

But often the lines are much too short, and he even goes so
far as to ignore at times the brute fact that in the Latin couplet the first line is always, and must always be, longer than
the second. In 1982 Peter Green, with warm acknowledgment
of Lee's pioneering effort, improved on the model in his *Ovid:
The Erotic Poems*, a masterly translation of the *Amores*, the *Ars
Amatoria*, and some shorter poems in the same category. He
used a first line with "a loose six-beat (occasionally five-beat)
line," representing the pentameter with "a variable, short-
stopped line with anything from five to three main stresses":

> It was you, no doubt about it, Graecinus. I always
>   remember
> How you said no man could possibly fall in love
> With two girls at once. I believed you. I dropped my
>   defenses.
>   Result—double love-life. Embarrassing. All your fault.

David Slavitt uses a similar metrical pattern of two lines
with eleven stresses. It is, he says in his introduction to his
earlier, separate version of the *Tristia* (1986), "the adaptation
Auden used" (in "Prospero to Ariel," for example). Slavitt is
comfortably at home in this verse form (he used it before in a

translation of five elegies of Tibullus), and from the beginning to the end of the 250 pages of this version of Ovid's poems from Tomi, the lines retain their suppleness and variety. The voice of the speaker, moreover, remains consistent. This is a real, and fascinating, human being we are listening to.

Slavitt has assumed large powers as Ovid's twentieth-century voice, however. "Ovid's habit of piling up mythological examples and parallels," he says, "can get wearisome for the modern reader, and when this happens I invent what I need, usually reducing the number of references or sometimes enlarging upon something else in the poem." In order to achieve "urbanity and modernity," he claims, "a translator must have at least the illusion of parity, must suppose himself to be the collaborator if not an actual pal of the poet who wrote the original work." Sometimes, however, the collaborator (perhaps it is the pal) grabs the ball and runs far ahead of his partner as he races toward modernity. As in this version of part of *Tristia* 1.3, the account of Ovid's last night in Rome:

> The nimble hours skittered, turning us all clumsy
> and the simplest menial task onerous. Packing
> was either a nightmare itself or one of those cruel jokes
> you sometimes find in your worst dreams. Papers
> hid and even after we'd found them refused to stay put.
> We blamed ourselves for having wasted time
> trying to talk it out and ourselves into understanding
> what was going on, and not to impose what
> we were feeling. I'd made lists of clothing, equipment . . .
> But who had the composure? And pitiless time
> nudged us along, forcing our minds to these cruel
> questions.

> Or was it, perhaps, a mercy? We managed to laugh
> once or twice, as my wife found in some old trunk
>   odd pieces of clothing. "This might be
> just the thing this season, the new Romanian mode . . ."
>   And just as abruptly our peal of laughter would catch
> and tear into tears as she dropped the preposterous
>   shepherd's cloak
>   and we held each other . . .

The only basis in Ovid's text for this admittedly moving passage, however, is the four lines 7–10, which run, in a bare prose version: "There had not been time for getting ready what was suitable, nor the mind for it, either; our hearts had been numbed by the long delay. I took no thought for the slaves, for selecting companions for the journey, or for the clothes and equipment a banished man would need."

Yet, though no one should quote this version as Ovid without checking the Latin text, Slavitt has done Ovid a service. He has brought back from the limbo to which insensitive critics had relegated it a book that cries out for translation. His version will win new readers for the poet who even in the depths of despair never lost his elegant facility, his virtuoso touch for the rhythms of his medium, or, above all, his proud conviction that his poetry would survive him:

> Now I have done my work. It will endure
> I trust, beyond Jove's anger, fire and sword
> Beyond Time's hunger . . .
> I shall be read, and through all centuries
> If prophecies of bards are ever truthful
> I shall be living always.

This prophecy, from the closing lines of the *Metamorphoses,* may well have been one of the final touches that Ovid added to his great poem in exile at Tomi.

§ix of the letters from the Black Sea (and possibly two in the *Tristia*) are addressed to one Maximus Cotta, an admirer and close friend of the poet. He is the principal character of Christoph Ransmayr's strange and haunting novel *The Last World,*[2] which describes a fictional journey by Cotta to Tomi in search of Ovid, rumors of whose death have reached Rome. This is not, however, a conventional historical novel, as its deliberately flaunted anachronisms make clear. Slavitt allows himself an occasional playful modern touch—the Tomi Chamber of Commerce, for example, and Ovid expecting galley proofs—but in *The Last World* we very soon come up against billboards, firing squads, newspapers, sauerkraut, diesels, projectors, and can openers; ships on the Black Sea have smokestacks, Jason's *Argo* has a gun deck, and Thiess, one of the inhabitants of Tomi, is a German veteran of the Wehrmacht's campaign in the Crimea who remembers the people crowded into the gas chambers.

Ransmayr, born in Wels, Austria, in 1954, sees the Roman world of Ovid through the dark filter of Eastern Europe's twentieth-century agony. In the fifteen chapters of his novel (Ovid's *Metamorphoses* has fifteen books), past and present are fused in a timeless blur—just as they are at the end of Ovid's epic, when the transformations of primeval Greek and later Roman mythical figures culminate in the near-contemporary

[2]Christoph Ransmayr, *The Last World* (New York: Grove Weidenfeld, 1990).

murder of Julius Caesar and the transformation of his spirit into a comet that blazed for seven nights while his adopted son Octavius, later to be Augustus, presided over the games that honored his memory in 44 B.C.

Cotta is searching not only for Ovid, but also for his magnum opus, the *Metamorphoses*. Roman audiences had so far heard only enigmatic excerpts read aloud by the poet himself; they had no conception of the work as a whole. And Ovid had burned the manuscript during his last night in Rome. (In fact, though Ovid does speak of burning the manuscript, he also mentions the existence of copies in circulation and claims only that they lack the author's final touches.) All Ransmayr's Cotta finds, in the end, are fragments of the poem, written on rags and inscribed on stones that are covered with slugs, but long before he makes any sense of these fragments, he comes to know the inhabitants of Tomi, a town that consists of crumbling, rusting ruins.

He never does find Ovid (who is presumably dead), but, though he does not immediately realize it, he has found in the strange characters that haunt the stones and hovels of Tomi the originals of the figures that appear in Ovid's poem. Ransmayr is playing games with his readers here. Cotta never finds more than tiny fragments of the poem, but we have it all, and can see that Ransmayr is transforming Ovid's mythical figures into denizens of his timeless, nightmare city. Pythagoras, for example, the Greek philosopher who in Ovid's poem proclaims the doctrine of eternal change and of the soul's passage through different shapes, is here a half-crazed man who used to be Ovid's servant and now stands outside the town butcher's shop preaching abstinence from meat. The brutal Thracian king Tereus becomes the town butcher; he drives

Pythagoras away by pelting him with sheeps' hearts and guts. His fat wife, Procne, is stuffing sausages when she recognizes her raped sister Philomela. And so on.

In his stunning re-creation of this tale of Philomel—"so rudely forced. / Tereu"—Ransmayr gives new and lurid life to the figures of what is perhaps Ovid's most influential story. Tereus still rapes his wife's sister and cuts out her tongue, Procne still discovers the truth and avenges her sister by killing his son Itys, and Tereus tracks the two sisters down through the ruins of Tomi, only to see them change into birds, swallow and nightingale, and to turn bird himself as he pursues them through the air. But Ransmayr's version is grimly realistic. The raped and tongueless woman who stumbles down from the mountains is mocked and tormented by the town children until Procne "recognized the disfigured, fly-covered face. It was her sister Philomela." Ransmayr does not, however, try to sidestep the tale's fantastic ending:

> Tereus lifted his ax. . . . But the two women did not raise their arms to fend off the blows—instead, two startled birds spread their wings. . . . Yet even before they shot through the broken window into the open air and were lost in the blue night sky, the curved handle of the ax had become yet another beak. Tereus's arms had turned to wings, his hair to brown and black feathers. A hoopoe lifted in easy, billowing flight and sailed off in pursuit of the two escaping birds. . . .

This smooth blend of gritty detail and high fantasy, the essence of the novel's method, resembles the magic realism of García Márquez and may indeed have been influenced by the Colombian writer's work, especially *One Hundred Years of Solitude.*

The novel's translator has added an "Ovidian Repertory," which, in parallel columns, poses the lives, loves, and transformations of the mythical characters against those of Ransmayr's world. Since this repertory was compiled on the principle of an index, only those figures named in Ransmayr's text are included. As a result, readers unfamiliar with Ovid or Greek mythology will search in vain for an explanation of the appearance of a white cow (Io), a herdsman with eyes all over his body (Argus), and a silent killer (Mercury), who slips into the room, slits the herdsman's throat, and leads the white cow away.

Ransmayr has transformed not only the mythical persons of the *Metamorphoses*, but also the world in which Ovid lived and died. In this world Ovid's exile is the result not of a *carmen* or an *error*, but of the workings of a repressive bureaucracy, the members of "the society of power, families whose pomp and luxury, safeguarded by dogs, glass-studded walls, armed sentries, and barbed-wire barricades, reflected the splendor of the emperor." Invited to be one of eleven speakers at the dedication of a gigantic new stadium, before an audience of 200,000 people and the emperor Augustus, Ovid forgot to preface his speech with the mandatory fulsome compliments to the emperor.

As if that were not scandalous enough, his speech described, in hideous detail, the death from plague of the entire population of the island of Aegina and their replacement by ants that appropriated the organs of the dead to assume human form. This new race, said Ovid, was

> docile and asked no questions and followed their new leaders, who were of the same descent, into the triumphs and miseries of

time—without complaint . . . an army of workers wherever ditches were to be dug, walls razed, or bridges built. In time of war they were a nation of warriors. . . . And yet, through all these transformations, they proved more tractable than any other race. . . .

Ovid went on to prophesy that the new stadium would also be "a place of transformation and rebirth, a stone caldron in which from hundreds of thousands of the abandoned, the subjugated, and the helpless a new nation will be cooked. . . ."

The story of the plague is based on a long narrative in the *Metamorphoses*, but the import and the emphasis of the original have been transformed. The ants in Ovid become the famous Myrmidons, the warrior hordes of Achilles (the Greek word *myrmex* means "ant"). In Ransmayr's parable they become the docile, tractable working class of the bureaucratic state and in the vision of the future the dispossessed and abandoned who will finally come into their own.

Quite apart from the omission of the compliments to the emperor and the ill-omened content of the speech, Ovid's final words would have been enough to provoke the emperor's wrath. But Augustus had not heard a word the poet said. He was asleep. At the imperial court, however, there was set in motion the next morning "an apparatus of whispers, dossier entries, hints, and recommendations." Its movements "were slow, dispassionate, and void of . . . anger," but it "was not to be placated, nor could it be shut down. And so information concerning the poet Publius Ovidius Naso, verified now in files, gradually began to flow," ending in an indictment of the

Metamorphoses, "the work of an enemy of the state, an affront to Rome, the document of a deranged mind."

There followed a visit of a functionary to the emperor, who, fascinated by the spectacle of a rhinoceros that had been sent him by the procurator of Sumatra, waved the visitor away with "an abrupt, curt motion of his hand, hardly more vigorous than if he were shaking off a housefly." The gesture was variously interpreted as it moved along the bureaus of the apparatus: prison, labor camp, Sicily, and the stonecutters; an injunction against literary activity for a year; a forfeiture of royalties; merely a warning. When the emperor's sign finally "reached the bottom level—where the blows are actually inflicted and not simply decreed, where the cell doors really clicked shut," a judge gave a decision. "A wave of His hand meant *Begone. Out of my sight.* Out of the sight of the emperor, however, meant to the end of the world. And the end of the world was Tomi."

We are in Kafka country here. Or perhaps in Ceauşescu's Romania, where, in fact, before the fall of the regime, a German-language periodical in Bucharest was denied permission to publish an extract from Ransmayr's novel. The sections of the novel that are set in Rome, under Augustus and his successor Tiberius, are a chilling vision of what happens when the "empire falls into the hands of a single person" and the world becomes "a safe and dreary prison for his enemies."

But Ransmayr's Rome and Tomi are also the "last world." In Tomi, metamorphosis is a phenomenon not experienced by human beings alone. The basic matter of the earth is being transformed. The iron town is turning to rust. "Iron shutters . . . crumbled like cardboard and disintegrated. Wrought-iron fences buckled. The decoration of metal lilies, spear-headed leaves, even the railings on the footbridges across the brook broke loose. Gratings rotted like plaited grass." The landscape too begins to disintegrate. "The landslides had not spared a single upland valley. Like primeval monsters clad in uprooted pines and heather, flows of gravel and mud had come down . . . creeping over meadows, deserted huts, and the entrances to abandoned mine shafts."

In Ovid's great poem similar changes are described by Pythagoras in Book 15:

> Nothing, no nothing, keeps its outward show
> For golden ages turn to years of iron . . .
> I've seen land turn to miles of flood-tossed waters,
> Or land rise up within a restless sea . . .

But in Pythagoras' famous speech the context of these changes is optimistic:

> Nothing retains the shape of what it was,
> And Nature, always making old things new,
> Proves nothing dies within the universe
> But takes another being in new forms.

The process is one of continuous renewal and rebirth. In Ransmayr's book, however, the emphasis is on loss, on ruin, on decay. The world is running down, and it is the last world, *die letzte Welt*. We are not likely to be given another.

II

Men, Gods,
and Cities

The Athenian
Century

My title, as you may have realized, is an echo of the
slogan "The American Century," which Henry
Luce, from the pages of *Time* and *Life*, announced to
a world emerging from the trials of World War II
to face the atomic age. It was a claim that the United
States, in the immortal phrase of the authors of *1066
and All That*, was now Top Nation. The century is
not quite over yet, and there are other candidates for
the title, but the fifth century B.C. might well be
called the Athenian Century, since throughout its
course the city-state of Athens was not only the predominant power in the Greek world, it was also that
world's cultural and artistic center. It was, to cite the
proud claim of Pericles, the leader of its democracy
at the height of its power and influence, "an education for all Greece." And it was also, in the phrase
Plato put in the mouth of the sophist Hippias, "the

This essay originally appeared as the text of an address to the
Circle of the National Gallery of Art in Washington, D.C., on
November 19, 1992, in connection with the opening of the exhibi-
tion "The Greek Miracle."

center and shrine of Greek wisdom," the intellectual center that attracted thinkers, writers, and teachers from all over the Greek world: Anaxagoras from Clazomenae, Herodotos from Halicarnassus, Protagoras from Abdera, Gorgias from Leontini—they all came to Athens, some of them to stay for long periods. Athens was also the literary center of the Greek world, the home of the first theater in the West and of its three great tragic poets. It was the site of new buildings, the Parthenon, the Erechtheum, the Propylaea, that won the admiration even of those who feared and hated the imperial city. And it was the workshop for those red-figure vases that men in countries where no Greek was spoken treasured in life and took with them to their graves.

It had not always been so. Athens came to the fore very late in the fierce Greek competition for dominance and glory. Neither of the two great poets of the eighth century, Homer and Hesiod, was an Athenian. The first philosophers were Ionians from the city of Miletus on the coast of Asia Minor and western Greeks from the Greek cities of Sicily and South Italy. The lyric poets of the seventh and sixth centuries came from all over the Greek world except from Athens—Sappho and Alcaeus from Lesbos, Archilochus from Paros, Alcman and Tyrtaeus from Sparta, Mimnermus from Colophon, Callinus and the iambic poet Hipponax from Ephesus.

And Athens took no part in the great enterprise of colonization of the eighth to sixth centuries, the expansion of Greek language and culture to the coasts and islands of the central and eastern Mediterranean as well as to the costs of the Black Sea. It was the work of desperate men, driven by poverty, who took to the sea in search of new land, close to the sea but fertile enough to grow their staple crops—grain, the olive, and the vine—where they could found their own new city. Sparta and Corinth on the mainland, Eretria and Chalcis on the long island of Euboea, and Miletus on the Asia Minor coast were among the many cities whose colonists built new cities such as Massilia, Antipolis, and Nike (now known as Marseilles, Antibes and Nice), Siracusa, Gela, Taras (now Taranto), and Neapolis (now Naples) in Sicily and southern Italy, Cyrene on the coast of what is now Libya, Sinope on the northern coast of what is now Turkey, Tomi on the west coast of the Black Sea on the site of the modern city of Constanta, and Olbia on the southern coast of Russia at the mouth of the Bug River. By mid-sixth century there were Greeks settled around the coasts of the two inland seas, "like frogs," as Plato put it, "sitting around a pond."

Athens, which had taken no part in the great enterprise, was not, of course, immune to the social unrest created by an increasing population and scarcity of arable land that had elsewhere driven men to take to the sea. But, unlike many other Greek cities, Athens had in early times consolidated its political hold on a comparatively large hinterland—the peninsula of Attica—and so, unlike the island cities and those confined between the sea and a mountain range, the Athenians were able to stave off the crisis for a century or so. By the beginning of the sixth century the crisis had arrived. Many small independent farmers had fallen into debt to the hereditary aristocratic landowners; unable to pay, they had lost their farms and some their freedom—they had been enslaved and sold. The specter of civil war, that endemic disease of the Greek city-state, hung over the land.

The usual outcome of such a situation was the advent of what the Greeks called a *tyrannis*, a word that was not, initially, loaded with the evil connotations of our word "tyr-anny." It meant simply the rule of a single individual, who, by a combination of political skills and the threat or the actual use of a body of loyal armed followers, took advantage of the civil disorder and the faction fights of the great landed families and their supporters to seize power and rule as an autocrat. The tyrant usually championed the common people against the aristocratic clan leaders; he developed programs of public works to give employment to the poor and prestige to his regime; he engaged in an active foreign policy, designed to enhance the commercial interests of his merchant class; typically, too, he invited to his court poets and artists who would celebrate his achievements.

Such a tyranny was almost a normal phase in the development of a Greek city-state, but in 590 B.C., when Athens seemed ripe for its advent, the two sides came to an extraordinary agreement. They appointed one of their citizens to a year in office with full powers to reform the laws and restore stability and peace in Athens. His name was Solon. He is the first Athenian we really know anything about, and most of it we know from his own poems, some of which defend and explain the program he wrote into law during his tenure of office. It was called the *Seisachtheia*, the "shaking off of burdens"; it included the cancellation of mortgages, the liberation of the enslaved, and even the liberation and repatriation of those who had been sold abroad. But it drew the line at one of the revolutionary demands of the poor, the redistribution of the land. "My purpose," he wrote,

> was to bring my people back together. . . . Had someone else
> . . . taken the reins, some ill-advised or greedy person, he would

not have held the people in. . . . Had I agreed to do what pleased
their adversaries at that time or what they themselves planned to
do against their enemies, our city would have been widowed of
her men. . . . I put myself on guard on every side, and turned
among them like a wolf inside a pack of dogs.

Solon saved Athens from civil war but not from tyranny,
which came in 546 B.C. when Pisistratus, after two false starts,
finally established himself in power with the aid of a force of
mercenaries paid from the revenue derived from his operation
of gold and silver mines in Thrace. Pisistratus was a classic
tyrant. His regime favored the poorer citizenry against the
aristocrats (one wealthy and prestigious family, the Alcmaeonidae, spent most of the years of his tyranny in exile); he
encouraged commerce and through an expansive foreign policy secured markets and bases abroad, while at home
Athenian black-figure pottery became the most popular ce-
ramic ware of the Greek world and the silver coinage of
Athens one of the most respected Greek currencies. He carried on a building program; the temple of Olympian Zeus—
some of its tall pillars still stand in modern Athens—was one
of Pisistratus' projects. And it was during his regime that the
Dionysia, a festival of the rural god Dionysus, developed into
the first theater of the Western world, when a man called
Thespis added lines for an actor to the song of the chorus.

Pisistratus died in 527, leaving the reins of government in
the hands of his sons Hippias and Hipparchus. Perhaps because, as so often elsewhere, the tyrant's sons lacked the political skills and experience that had brought their father to supreme power, the regime soon ran into trouble. Hipparchus,
the younger brother, was assassinated in 514, and four years

later Hippias was driven out of Athens by his opponents, who were backed by an expeditionary force from Sparta, then the predominant military power in Greece, and one which did not approve of the innovative policies of tyrants. Hippias went to the court of the Great King of the Persian empire and schemed for his restoration.

In Athens things went back to normal. Pisistratus had not abolished the traditional organs of Athenian government— the archons, annually elected magistrates who were the executive arm of the Council, that might, on occasion, call a meeting of the full citizen assembly to endorse an especially important decision. Pisistratus had simply filled the offices and the Council with his relatives and supporters. And now, with the expulsion of Hippias, the great aristocratic families resumed their control of the offices of state and also renewed their fierce rivalries, those faction fights that had enabled Pisistratus to seize power in the first place.

But in 508, during the archonship of Isagoras, head of one of the warring families, something absolutely unprecedented happened. His main opponent, Clisthenes, head of the clan of the Alcmaeonidae, facing isolation and defeat in the power struggle between aristocratic factions, made a revolutionary move. Our earliest authority for his crucial decision that in fact created the world's first democracy is the historian Herodotus, who was writing some sixty years after the event. His words have been translated in various ways: "Clisthenes made friends with the popular party"; "managed to win popular support"; "called to his aid the common people." These versions, though they convey the general sense, give no idea of the peculiar flavor of the verb Herodotus uses to express the idea translated as "made friends with, "called to his aid," and so on. The Greek word he uses is an almost technical term of aristocratic infighting, *prosetairizeto*. It means to make someone your *hetairos*, your comrade, your drinking companion in the aristocratic symposium, to enlist him in the ranks of the young bravos who will harass and on occasion draw the sword against the young ruffians on the other side; the word conjures up an atmosphere like that of the warring families and their young champions in Shakespeare's *Romeo and Juliet.*

But there is nothing aristocratic about the people Clisthenes decided to enroll in his faction; they are the *demos*, the common people, small farmers, fishermen, craftsmen—the people who so far in history had had no voice. A voice was what Clisthenes promised them: the citizen assembly as the supreme organ of government. The response was enthusiastic. Alcmaeon, one of Clisthenes' family, was elected archon for the following year to pass the laws establishing the new regime.

But Isagoras, who had friendly connections with the Spartans, called on them for help, and King Cleomenes came in 507 with a small detachment of the famed Spartan infantry to restore order in the streets of Athens. He had made a bad miscalculation; the people of Athens rose up against him, and he was forced to surrender before they let him go home. And Cleisthenes went on with the work of creating democracy.

We know very little about this man, but one thing is clear: he must have been a political genius of the first rank. He realized that simply changing the laws would not be sufficient; in the Athens of turbulent aristocratic clan leaders, strong in their ancestral and financial hold over their dependants, democracy was not going to work. The assembly of citizens would find it difficult to produce a majority vote based purely on the merits of the proposal before them—it would simply become the battleground for electoral blocs reflecting the old divisions. To make sure this did not happen, Clisthenes had to change not only the political but also the social and religious contexts of the citizen's life. His was one of the most radical reforms ever attempted. The fact that the new regime lasted, with only two short oligarchic interruptions, for nearly two hundred years is some measure of the brilliance of his design.

He had two main problems to deal with. One was the fact that Athenians were born into and enrolled as citizens in four hereditary Ionian tribes, and these tribal units, with their separate religious rites and festivals, were presided over by hereditary aristocrats who held family priesthoods and claimed descent from the four mythical sons of Ion. Clisthenes abolished these tribes and assigned citizens to ten new tribes, named after legendary Athenian heroes—Erechtheus, for example, an early Athenian king whose shrine, the Erechtheum, would one day be built on the Acropolis. These tribes were the base of the tribal regiments in which Athenians from now on took their place in the battle line or served the state in peacetime. The annually elected Council of Five Hundred that sat in permanent session and prepared business for the full Assembly was composed of fifty men from each of the ten tribes. The tribes were no longer ancestral units of separation and division but corporate entities that affirmed and strengthened the citizen's loyalty to the city-state.

Clisthenes' other problem might be described as topographical. Athenians had been divided not only by aristocratic tribal tradition but also by the economic constraints and interests of the part of Attica they lived in. The inhabitants of the long coastline of Attica—fishermen, boat-builders, boatmen—had different wants and concerns from the peasant farmers of the upland interior, and both of these differed in outlook from those who lived in the city and its expanding suburbs. Exploitation of these divisions had in fact been one of the keys to Pisistratus' seizure of power—he had championed the cause of the farmers from the hills against the city-dwellers and the men of the coast.

Clisthenes' solution for this problem was a complicated system designed to eliminate local insularity from the political machinery. Each of the ten new tribes, for example, was made up of communities from all three areas. A citizen from the coast would find himself serving in the tribal regiment or on the Council or a jury side by side with citizens from the other two regions.

Such a radical reorganization of the traditional religious, social, and political fabric has rarely been attempted, and in this case the attempt hardly had time to get under way before its home base was faced with a mortal danger. Spartan kings were not accustomed to capitulating to an armed citizenry, and Cleomenes came back in 506 with the full army of the Peloponnesian League, to restore Isagoras to power. There were two other invading forces, the Thebans from the north and the men of Chalcis from the long island of Euboea that hugs the eastern coast of Attica. But the Corinthians, who had not been informed of the objective of the expedition, withdrew when they found out, and Cleomenes' colleague in the Spartan joint kingship also protested; the Peloponnesian forces went home. And Athens decisively defeated the other two invading armies. On this victory Herodotus has a famous comment:

> Thus Athens went from strength to strength, and proved, if proof were needed, how noble a thing freedom is. . . . for while they were oppressed under a despotic government, they had no better success in war than any of their neighbors, yet, once the yoke was flung off, they proved the finest fighters in the world. This clearly shows that, so long as they were held down by authority, they deliberately shirked their duty in the field, as slaves shirk working for their masters; but when freedom was won, then every man . . . longed to distinguish himself.[1]

The word here translated as "freedom," *isegorie*, means literally "equal right to speak." it was one of the two words Herodotus used to characterize the new regime. *Isegorie* meant that in Athens now the opinion of a small farmer, a fisherman, or a charcoal burner was just as worthy of consideration as that of an aristocrat who through his ancestors claimed descent from the gods. Every male citizen in the Assembly had the right to be heard: all though the long history of Athenian democracy, the herald would ask, after one speaker had finished, *tis agoreuein bouletai?*—"Who wishes to speak?" The other word that Herodotus uses, *isonomia*, means something like "equality of political rights." Through his participation in the meetings of the Assembly and his service on the Council, not to speak of his presence in the large juries that often dealt with cases at law that had political significance, the

[1]Translated by Aubrey de Sélincourt (Harmondsworth, U.K.: Penguin Books, 1954).

poorest citizen was now as fully enfranchised as the wealthiest or most nobly born of the Athenian upper class. This word appears in the drinking song that became, so to speak, the *Marseillaise* of the democratic revolution, a song that (quite unhistorically) attributed the establishment of equal rights to Harmodius and Aristogeiton, the two men who had killed Hipparchus back in 514: "*En myrtou kladi to xiphos phoreso* . . . In a branch of myrtle I'll hide my sword / Like Harmodius and Aristogeiton / When they killed the tyrant / And made Athens a city of equal rights. . . . *hosper Harmodios k'Aristogeiton / hote ton tyrannon ktaneten / isonomous t'Athenas epoiesaten.*" Nobody called it "democracy" yet; that word meaning "power in the hands of the common people" does not make its appearance for some decades. But the reality was there.

The new Athens had survived its first ordeal by battle; a greater challenge was to come. In 499 the Ionian Greek cities of the Asia Minor coast revolted against their Persian conquerors and Athens sent a small force that joined them in the sack and burning of the Persian provincial capital of Sardis. The Ionians' revolt was eventually suppressed, and the Great King Darius, so Herodotus tells us, ordered one of his servants to say to him three times, whenever he sat down to dinner: "Master, remember the Athenians." Athens was on the periphery of Darius' enormous land empire that stretched from Afghanistan to the Aegean; Darius did indeed need to be reminded. And in 490 he sent an expeditionary force with instructions to punish the Athenians and install Hippias as tyrant of Persia's latest acquisition. The Persians landed at Marathon, and the Athenians went out to meet them in their new tribal regiments under ten elected generals who were to exercise overall command day by day in rotation. It sounds like a recipe for disaster, but, to the astonishment of both sides, they drove the Persians back to their ships.

It was Athens' most glorious hour. She had defeated the troops of the huge menacing power that was obviously intent on adding Greece to its already enormous empire. The dramatist Aeschylus fought in the battle, and when, many years later, he died at Gela in Sicily, the epitaph he had written for his tomb made no mention of the tragedies he had produced in the theater of Dionysus; it recorded only the proud claim that he had fought at Marathon.

In 1851, Sir Edward Creasy published the Victorian classic *The Fifteen Decisive Battles of the World.* He included some that only a Victorian Englishman would have regarded as decisive—Hastings, for example, and Blenheim (though he did have the grace to include Saratoga)—but he headed the list with Marathon. To the Great King in far-off Susa, Marathon (if he ever heard the name) must have seemed merely a temporary setback on a distant frontier. The English poet Robert Graves wittily explored this aspect of the situation in his poem "The Persian Version":

> Truth-loving Persians do not dwell upon
> The trivial skirmish fought near Marathon.
> As for the Greek theatrical tradition
> Which represents that summer's expedition
> Not as a mere reconnaissance in force
> By three brigades of foot and one of horse
> (Their left flank covered by some obsolete

Light craft detached from the main Persian fleet)
But as a grandiose, ill-starred attempt
To conquer Greece—they treat it with contempt;
And only incidentally refute
Major Greek claims, by stressing what repute
The Persian monarch and the Persian nation
Won by this salutary demonstration:
Despite a strong defence and adverse weather
All arms combined magnificently together.

And yet Creasy was right to call Marathon decisive. A base at Athens would have enabled Persia to take over a disunited Greece piecemeal; even if there had been united resistance, without the Athenian fleet there would have been no victory like Salamis. With Greece part of the Persian empire there would have been no Greek miracle; the astonishing explosion of creativity in art, literature, and thought that marked the next two centuries would have been strangled at birth.

The Persians came back ten years later, in overwhelming force, led by the Great King himself, Xerxes, successor to Darius. But in the meantime Athens, under the leadership of Themistocles, had become a sea power, with a fleet of two hundred fast warships. When the Persian land forces broke through what was then the narrow passage between sea and mountain at Thermopylae, the city of Athens could no longer be defended. So the Athenians took to the sea. We have a copy, on stone, of the decree of the Council and the assembly that authorized the evacuation. It was made many years later and has clearly been rephrased in the language of a later time, but though it does not always preserve the letter it recreates the spirit of that heroic resolve. "Decided," it runs,

by the council and the people. Themistocles son of Neokles
moved the proposal. The city shall be entrusted to Athena,
Protector of Athens, and to the other gods, all of them, for
protection and defence against the barbarian on behalf of the
country. The Athenians in their entirety and the aliens resident
in Athens shall place their children and their women in
Troezen. . . . the elderly and the movable property shall be
deposited at Salamis. The Treasurers and Priestesses are to remain on the Acropolis and guard the possessions of the gods.
The rest of the Athenians in their entirety and those resident
aliens who have reached young manhood shall embark on the
200 ships that stand ready and they shall repulse the barbarians
for the sake of freedom, both their own and that of the other
Greeks, together with the Spartans, Corinthians, Aeginetans,
and the others who wish to have a share in the danger.[2]

Athens was taken and burned, the temples on the Acropolis demolished, their statues mutilated; but at Salamis the Persian fleet was defeated and Xerxes went home, leaving a land
army to carry on the campaign. That army was defeated at
Plataea in the following year, and mainland Greece was free.
But the Greeks carried the war across the Aegean, intent on
liberating the Greek islands and coastal cities that had been
annexed by the Persians in the preceding decades. Though
the nominal commander of the Greek forces was a Spartan,
the principal constituent of the Greek fleet was Athenian, and
it was Athenian energy and initiative that drove the enterprise
forward. Sparta soon withdrew from the campaign; Athens
organized the newly liberated cities in a league against Persia.

[2]Russell Meiggs and David Lewis, *A Selection of Greek Historical Inscriptions to the
End of the Fifth Century B.C.* (New York: Oxford University Press, 1969), no. 23.

The Athenian allies, as they were officially termed, could contribute either manned warships or money; many of them chose the second alternative, and their tribute money, used to build ships and pay crews, added to the strength of the Athenian fleet. As the prospect of a Persian counteroffensive faded, some of the allies who had retained their ships decided to resign from the league, only to find that Athens refused to let them go and, when defied, reduced them to obedience by armed force. The league had become an empire, and in succeeding years, as the danger of Persian retaliation vanished, the tribute money was used for projects that had little to do with Persia or the former allies—among other things, it financed the replacement of the temples destroyed by the Persians and the construction of the Parthenon, the Erechtheum, the Propylaea, and the Temple of Victory.

Before long, Athens found itself at war not only with Persia but also with some of the Greek cities by whose side she had fought at Salamis and Plataea. The Spartans and Corinthians, afraid that Athens was on the path to hegemony over the whole Greek world, intervened in an attempt to cut her down to size. Thucydides gives us a remarkable estimate by Athens' enemies, the Corinthians, of the heroic, almost demonic, militancy deployed by the city that had, by its invention of democracy, liberated the creative energies of its own population and saved Greece.

"You have never fully considered," they say to their Spartan allies,

what manner of men these Athenians are. . . . They are innovators, equally quick in the conception and in the execution of every plan. . . . They are audacious beyond their strength; they run risks which policy would condemn; and in the midst of dangers they are full of hope. . . . When conquerors, they pursue their victory to the utmost; when defeated, they give as little ground as possible. They devote their bodies to their country as though they belonged to other men, and their minds, their dearest possessions, to action in her service. . . . To do their duty is their only holiday, and they think peaceful repose is as much a misfortune as incessant fatigue. If a man should say of them, in a word, that it is their nature never to live in peace themselves and to prevent the rest of the world from doing so, he would just speak the simple truth.[3]

This is, of course, a hostile assessment, rhetorically height-ened since it is an attempt to spur the Spartans to action, but there is more than a little truth in it, as we can see from an independent record, an inscription on a stone now in the Louvre in Paris. It is a monument for the Athenians of one of the ten tribal regiments who fell in battle in the year 460–59, when Athens was fighting not only against the Persian empire but also against its former allies in Greece. It is, like our own Vietnam Memorial, a simple list of the names of the dead, 179 of them, who were lost in six campaigns, three in Persian territory, three on land and in waters not far from Athens. "Of the Erechtheid tribe," it says, "these men died in the war—on Cyprus, in Egypt, in Phoenicia, at Halieis, at Aegina, at Megara, in the same year."[4]

It is about this time, in midcentury, that the Greek word *demokratia* seems to have been coined to describe the form of

[3]Translated by Benjamin Jowett; revised and abridged by P. A. Brunt (New York: Washingon Square Press, 1963).
[4]Ibid., no. 33.

government that Athens had created. In a play of Aeschylus that was produced in Athens in 464, *The Suppliants*, the chorus of suppliant women asks about the result of the voting in the Argive assembly on the proposal to grant them asylum. The concentrated metaphorical phrase they use means something like "On what side was the show of hands that rules the people in the majority?" The Greek words are *demou kratousa cheir*. We also have from around this time notice that an Athenian citizen named his son Democrates, who thus qualifies as the world's first Democrat.

It was also in these middle years of the century that Athenian democracy, through some important modifications of the original Clisthenic model, found, as Aristotle might have put it, its natural form, the full democracy that, with two short intervals of antidemocratic reaction in wartime, was to be the context of Athenian life for the next hundred years.

The institutions established by Clisthenes, though revolutionary in their time, were still a creation of the Archaic age, the years before Athens, in 480, became a fleet without a city. The key element of the "people" that Clisthenes enlisted in his faction was the class of citizens who were prosperous enough to equip themselves with the expensive bronze armor—breastplate, shield, helmet, and greaves—without which no man could take his place in the line of interlocking shields that faced the enemy on the battlefield. These were the men who had saved Athens when the new regime was hardly a year old and also, more spectacularly, at Marathon. And Clisthenes' political arrangements reflect the conservative as well as the reformist tendencies of his new constituency. Although election to office was now dependent on the vote of the people as a whole, a vote that could no longer be manipulated by the aristocratic families, the high office of archon could be filled only by members of the two highest of the four income groups into which Solon had divided the population. Furthermore, the Court of the Areopagus, composed of men who had served in the high office of archon, had powers of supervision and review that could halt any movement toward broader democratization.

But by midcentury the defense of the state, now a maritime empire, depended not so much on the courage of the middle-class landsmen who formed the infantry line as on the skill and discipline of the crews—two hundred per ship—that rowed and sailed the galleys of the fleet. And they came from the lowest of the four income classes. Leaders soon came forward to represent this new power factor in the community, to press its claim for recognition of its services. One of them was an Alcmaeonid, a member of the same aristocratic family that had played so great a role in the overthrow of the tyranny, the family of Clisthenes. His name was Pericles, and, together with his ally Ephialtes, he ran a successful campaign to restrict the powers of the Areopagus to what may have been its original function, the trial of cases of homicide. This paved the way for the emergence of the full democracy that is the context of the great age of Athenian architecture, art, and literature, the age of Ictinus and Phidias, of Sophocles, Euripides, and Aristophanes, and of Socrates.

This was a much more egalitarian city than the Athens of Clisthenes. The archonship was now opened to the third of the income classes, and the lowest class was involved in the day-to-day business of the state by payment offered for service on the annually elected Council of Five Hundred as well as on the huge juries that sat in permanent session and often

tried cases that had political consequences. The money came
from the tribute still paid by the former allies, now subjects
of the empire; from the same source came the money for the
materials and labor that went into the construction of the
great buildings rising on the Acropolis.

We have two contemporary assessments of this democracy. One
is hostile; it is a sort of political pamphlet written by an un-
named author, usually referred to today as the Old Oligarch.
He admits that for a power dependent on naval crews rather
than on armored infantry, democracy is the proper form of
government.

> It is right that the poor and the ordinary people there should
> have more power than the noble and rich, because it is the
> ordinary people who man the fleet and bring the city her power;
> they provide the helmsmen, the boatswains, the junior officers,
> the look-outs, and the shipwrights; it is these people who make
> the city powerful much more than the armored infantrymen and
> the noble and respectable citizens. This being so, it seems to me
> just that all should share in public office by lot and by election,
> and that any citizen who wishes should be able to speak in the
> Assembly.[5]

Not that he approves of the results: "I cannot commend their
present method of running the state, because in choosing it
they preferred that the masses should do better than the respectable citizens." And he soon reveals his true beliefs:

[5]This and other quotations of Old Oligarch from J. M. Moore, *Aristotle and
Xenophon on Democracy and Oligarchy* (Berkeley, Calif.: University of California
Press, 1975).

If you are looking for an admirable code of laws, first you will find that the ablest people draw them up in accordance with their own interest; secondly, the respectable will punish the masses, and will plan the city's affairs and will not allow men who are mad to take part in planning or discussion or even sit in the Assembly. As a result of this excellent system the common people would very soon lose all their political rights.

In Athens, however, this is unhappily not the case. In fact, according to him, in Athens, resident aliens and—what is the world coming to?—even slaves have rights:

Slaves and resident aliens at Athens lead a singularly undisciplined life; one may not strike them there, nor will a slave step aside for you. Let me explain the reason for this situation: if it were legal for a free man to strike a slave, a resident alien, or a former slave, an Athenian citizen would often have been struck under the mistaken impression that he was a slave, for the clothing of the common people there is in no way superior to that of slaves and immigrants, nor is their appearance.

There is some propagandistic exaggeration here, of course, but it is certainly true that Athenian domestic slaves were better off than the Helots at Sparta, agricultural laborers in bondage to the masters, against whom the chief magistrate, in an unusually frank admission of political realities, annually declared war.

The other picture of Athenian democracy is that of the great statesman Pericles, a speech put in his mouth by Thucydides in his *History of the Peloponnesian War*. It was a funeral speech, eulogizing the men killed in the first year of the war that, beginning in 431 B.C., was to last twenty-seven years and in the end strip Athens of its fleet, its empire, and for a few months even its democracy. When Pericles delivered this speech he could not know and could hardly imagine that the war would last so long and end that way, still less that he himself would in two years die of the plague that took such a toll of Athenian lives.

In his reconstruction and adaptation of Pericles' speech, Thucydides pictures Athens at the height of its power and influence, the golden years between the signing of the Thirty Years Peace Treaty in 446 and the outbreak of the war in 431, the years that saw work under way on the Temple of Hephaestus below the Acropolis and above, on the summit, on the Parthenon and the Propylaea.

Pericles takes the occasion "to show by what manner of institutions and manner of life our empire became great" (Jowett; Brunt). He stresses the originality of the Athenian experiment. "We do not copy our neighbors; rather, we are an example to them." He proudly accepts the name "democracy"—a word which seemed to many other Greek cities a self-contradictory absurdity. "Our system," he says, "is called a democracy, for it respects the majority and not the few." But it is not, he is at pains to point out, an egalitarian society. "While the law secures equality to all alike in their private disputes, the claim of excellence is also recognized, and when a citizen is in any way distinguished, he is generally preferred to the public service . . . not by mechanical rotation, but for merit." Athens is not a timocracy either, a state in which individual wealth determines political status and privilege. "Nor again is there any bar in poverty and obscurity of rank to a man whose action can be of benefit to the community." De-

mocracy is tolerant of a wide variety of opinions and attitudes. "We conduct our public life as free men, and in our
relations with each other we avoid mutual suspicions; we
don't feel angry with our neighbor if he does what he likes,
we don't even put on disapproving looks, which, though
harmless, are unpleasant." Athenian tolerance of individual
eccentricity was proverbial among their neighbors; "At
Athens, anything goes" was a contemptuous Spartan saying.
This tolerance in everyday relationships did not, however,
generate lawlessness. "While we give no offence," Pericles
continues, "in our private intercourse, in our public actions
we are prevented from doing wrong by fear—for we obey the
magistrates and the laws. . . ."

This is a speech honoring men who have died in battle; it
is not the place for a recital of the rich programs of public
entertainment and celebration that democracy provided for
its citizens: the tragic and comic productions at the Dionysia
in the spring and at the winter festival of the Lenaea; the
spring festival of the Pithoigia, the opening of the casks,
when the new wine was poured and drunk; the summer festival of the Panathenaea, with its procession (the one depicted
on the Parthenon frieze); and its athletic, poetic, and musical
contests. Athens was famous all over Greece for the brilliant
program of communal events that brought the whole citizen
body together in celebration throughout the year. The Old
Oligarch, in fact, grumbles sourly about the difficulty of getting anything done in Athens; if you want a ruling from the
Council or the Assembly you may have to wait for a year or
even longer. The reasons are not only that, as he puts it, "they
handle more public and private lawsuits and judicial investi-

gations than the whole of the rest of mankind," but also that "they celebrate more festivals than any other Greek city, during which there is even less possibility of transacting public business." Pericles' reference to all this is brief: "No one has provided more relaxation for the spirit from toil; we have regular games and sacrifices throughout the year." But everyone in his audience knew how magnificent and how envied by the rest of the Greek world were the cultural amenities Athenian democracy provided for its citizens.

Pericles goes on to make the proud claim that the record of Athenian success in battle is not the product of lifelong training in military exercises (as at Sparta, which he does not need to name); "We prefer to meet danger with a light heart and without laborious training." Athens, unlike Sparta, did not need to transform itself into an army in permanent mobilization, to suppress all forms of cultural activity, all signs of individual initiative, in the pursuit of military efficiency. On the contrary, the Athenian can perform as well in combat as the enemy he confronts and still enjoy the refinements of civilized life: "We are lovers of beauty" he says, "without extravagance, and of learning without loss of vigor." As for wealth, "Wealth," he says, "we employ less for talk and ostentation than when there is a real use for it. . . . To avow poverty with us is no disgrace; the true disgrace is doing nothing to avoid it." But democracy, which gives freedom, demands participation. "If a man takes no interest in public affairs, we alone do not commend him as quiet, but consider him useless, and if few of us are originators, we are all sound judges of a policy." And he sums up his praise of democracy with the famous statement: "The whole city is an education for Greece and

... each individual citizen in our society would seem capable of the greatest self-reliance and of the utmost dexterity and grace in the widest range of activities."

Athenian democracy had, of course, its limitations, which modern critics have not been slow to emphasize. Its political freedoms were the exclusive privilege of male full citizens; at the meetings of the Assembly there were no women, resident aliens, or slaves. But these deficiencies have to be seen in their historical context. Modern democracies too exclude resident aliens from the voting booth (though they may draft them for military service in time of war); modern democracies were very slow to give women the vote—England, France, and the United States were democratic states for centuries before they reluctantly, under pressure, made this concession. And as for slavery, I do not need to remind you that many of those who, at risk of their lives, signed the Declaration of Independence, the only modern statement of democratic ideals worthy to be compared with Pericles' speech, were slaveholders and that freedom for the slaves was won only through a bloody and calamitous civil war. In its historical context, an ancient world in which slavery was universal and authoritarian rule by royal dynasties or aristocratic elites the political norm, Athenian democracy was nothing less than a miracle.

The war that took the lives of the men commemorated in Pericles' speech was an effort on the part of the Greek mainland powers to arrest the steady growth of Athenian power before it was too late. Ten years of fighting brought no decision; Sparta and Athens signed a peace treaty. In effect, it was an Athenian victory; all Athens had to do now was to build up its financial and military resources, consolidate its hold on its empire, and, in due time, reassert its claim to hegemony of the Greek world. But it was not to be. Dazzled by the charm and brilliance of Alcibiades, the darling and evil genius of the democracy, the Athenians, in despite of the treaty, engaged in hostilities against Sparta and her allies; worse still, in 415, they sent a powerful expedition—"No armament so magnificent or costly had ever been sent out by any single Greek power," says Thucydides—against the rich Sicilian city of Syracuse. "By adding Sicily to our empire," Alcibiades told them, "we shall probably become masters of all Greece." The campaign was a disaster; a second fleet sent out as reinforcement fared no better than the first. "Fleet and army," says Thucydides, "perished from the face of the earth; nothing was saved, and of the many who set out few returned home." Sparta and her allies now took the offensive, and though it took them another seven years, they forced Athens to surrender in 404. Backed by a Spartan army, a committee of thirty, later known as the Thirty Tyrants, abolished the democracy that had presided over Athens' emergence from obscurity, its ascendance to preeminence in the Greek world, and its spectacular fall. Like one of the heroes of its own tragic stage, Athens had fallen in love with the impossible, defied the limits set to human achievement, and come to grief through the full exercise of those same qualities—courage, energy, initiative—that had made it great.

The Athenian century was over. Democracy was soon restored, and Athens even managed to play its part in the power struggles of the fourth century as the warring states of Greece exhausted themselves, to fall victims to the new power of the Macedonian kingdom to the north. Yet though Athens could no longer claim, with Pericles, that it was an example to all Greece, it was in this century of diminished political power that it fully justified the title Hippias conferred on it in Plato's dialogue: "the center and shrine of Greek wisdom." It was in this century that Plato established, in the precinct of an obscure Attic hero called Academus, his philosophical school that continued to train philosophers until the Christian emperor Theodosius suppressed it in A.D. 529, and that Plato's pupil Aristotle established the world's first research center, with a library and a scientific collection, in the grove of Apollo Lyceius. Plato died in 347 and Aristotle in 322, and in that year too the democracy that both great philosophers disapproved of came to an end. Athens had joined an unsuccessful revolt against Macedonian rule; a Macedonian garrison was installed and no less than twelve thousand citizens of the poorer classes were removed from the voting lists. Democracy, after its first brief and glorious appearance, vanished from the face of the earth, not to be seen again for more than two millennia.

The God as Prophet

In spite of the gigantic buses parked end to end just below the Castalian spring, the schoolmarm voices of guides retailing potted information in all the languages of Europe (not to mention Japanese), the almost solid masses of camera-hung, foot-weary humanity in slow movement along the immense conveyor belt of the Greek tourist machine—in spite of all this, Delphi can still work its awesome magic. The visitor feels its spell as he looks up to the reddish rocks which tower over Apollo's temple and, higher still, to the outworks of Parnassus, or downward to the sheen of the olive trees that fill the Pleistus River gorge hundreds of feet below. In antiquity, though it lived off visitors as it does today, this was a holy place, the religious center of the Greek world. Of all the many shrines at which Apollo gave advice and prophecy—Didyma, Claros,

This essay originally appeared in *The American Scholar*, Autumn 1979. Reprinted by permission of the publishers.

and many another—this was the most famous, the most eagerly consulted. Apollo's priestess, the Pythia, seated on a tripod in the inner recesses of his temple and deep in an ecstatic trance, answered the questions put to the god. His priests interpreted her mouthings to produce—usually in hexameter verse and often in obscure, riddling terms which hedged the divine bets—oracular prophecies which were the wonder of the world. Apollo foretold the future to individuals and to states, whose policies he thus determined; he gave instruction in the sphere of constitutional reform as readily as in that of religious cult, and, in the seventh and sixth centuries B.C., it was he who, through his oracle at Delphi, guided the Greek colonial expansion which dotted the coasts of the Mediterranean and Black seas with cities—from Marseilles in the west to Olbia, between the mouths of the Bug and Dnieper, in the east.

So, at any rate, the ancient Greeks and Romans believed; and so, outside specialist circles, does the modern world. Joseph Fontenrose does not. In fact the only two items in the preceding paragraph which he would be willing to accept are, first, that the Pythia sat on a tripod and, second, that she delivered instructions (which were not only in prose but also extremely prosaic) on matters of religious cult. His book is a thoroughgoing demythification of Apollo's oracle at Delphi.[1]

On the details of the consultation procedure we have little evidence, but Fontenrose is on firm ground when he dismisses

[1]Joseph Fontenrose, *The Delphic Oracle: Its Responses and Operations (with a Catalogue of Responses)* (Berkeley, Calif.: University of California Press, 1978).

what Yeats called "the Delphian Sybil's trance." Ancient accounts of intoxicating vapors rising from the earth have long since been discredited by geological surveys; and although it was once thought that the Pythia raised her consciousness by eating Apollo's laurel, Professor T. K. Oesterreich, as E. R. Dodds puts it in his great book *The Greeks and the Irrational*, "once chewed a large quantity of laurel leaves in the interests of science and was disappointed to find himself no more inspired than usual." Few will question the conclusion Fontenrose draws from his careful review of the evidence—that "the Pythia was not seized with a frenzy; she spoke coherently."

Fontenrose's main concern, however, is with what the Pythia said. The task he sets himself is "to find out just what sort of a response was verifiably spoken at Delphi." This calls for "a careful examination of the whole corpus of extant Delphic responses." Such a corpus has already been assembled in the second volume of Parke and Wormell's *The Delphic Oracle*, in which the Greek (and occasionally Latin) texts of 615 Delphic oracles are printed. Fontenrose excludes ninety-five of these and adds fifteen from other sources. The 535 items in his *Catalogue of Responses* are paraphrased or summarized in English, set in their context (Consultant, Occasion, etc.), keyed to their ancient sources, and critically assessed. Unlike Parke and Wormell, who arranged the responses in historical order (historical order, that is, of primary sources; the oracle given to Laius, for example, turns up in the Fourth Period, 419 to 431 B.C., since it occurs in Sophocles), Fontenrose arranges the responses in four categories: Historical (75), Quasi-Historical (267), Legendary (176), and Fictional (16). The main argument of his book is that the largest class, the Quasi-Historical, is in fact not historical at all but, in one sense or another, legendary.

Fictional are those oracles obviously invented by a comic poet for a joke or a late novelist for his plot. Legendary oracles are those which, like the famous oracle given to Laius, have no historical context and, even by mythical chronology, antedate the foundation of the Delphic oracle by many centuries. Historical responses are defined as those with an "accepted probable date" which "fell within the lifetime of the writer who attests it . . . or not long before the date of the inscription which records it." And Quasi-Historical are those responses "allegedly spoken within historical times" but "first attested by a writer whose lifetime was later than the accepted or supposed date of the response."

Fontenrose's analysis of the characteristics of these categories produces devastating results. "Historical responses are commonplace pronouncements, mostly clear commands and sanctions on religious matters, occasionally on public or private affairs"—unlike the Legendary responses, which of course contain "extraordinary predictions, warnings and commands, often ambiguously expressed." But "when the Quasi-Historical responses are analyzed in the same manner many of them turn out to have the characteristics of legendary responses"; they "conform in theme and expression to the oracles and prophecies of folktale and legend"; they "are integral constituents of narratives which . . . have a legendary character"; some of them turn out to be "riddles and proverbs given an oracular origin in tradition." The obvious conclusion is that most of the Quasi-Historical oracles are in fact legendary; they come from the collections of oracles belonging to professional prophets and were attributed to Delphi by their authors or by later writers.

This is hard doctrine. The results "demand a rejection as nongenuine of almost all responses said to have been spoken in the first three centuries of the Delphic oracle, roughly 750–450." The oracles directing the colonists to Syracuse, to Cyrene, Croton, and Sybaris; the famous ambiguous reply to Croesus, as well as the equally famous reply to the Athenians, that safety lay in their wooden wall—all these are to be rejected. For most of these prophecies our authority is Herodotus; "the issue in effect," says Fontenrose, "reduces itself to the trustworthiness of the Delphic oracles Herodotus reports." Fontenrose's verdict on this point is wholly negative. In earlier times, as "from the fifth century onwards," the oracles' responses must have consisted of "commonplace sanctions of sacred laws . . . cult foundations, proposed festivals . . . prescriptions of sacrifices or offerings," and "residues of safe statements about the past, present and future in answer to specific questions."

Fontenrose's whole argument obviously depends on the definition of the category "Historical." His formula limits it to seventy-five responses; over half of these are extant, in whole or in part, on inscribed stones; the rest come from writers contemporary with the response. The inscribed responses are indeed extremely prosaic. They concern, for example, the sacrifice of an ox to Apollo and the construction of altars to Ares and Athena, and they all date from after 450 B.C. But they may not be a safe criterion. They show, indeed, that Delphic responses could be commonplace, prosaic instructions, but they do not exclude the contrary. True, state expenditures of various kinds were normally (especially at Athens) exposed for public scrutiny in this way, but there would have been no reason why the Pythia's reply about the wooden wall, for example, should be so recorded on stone, and even less reason for an inscription recording the Delphic reply to Croesus. The second category—responses recorded by a contemporary writer—is very limited: most of the writers who quote Delphic responses were, naturally, historians, and historians generally deal with the past. The obvious exception is Thucydides, who wrote the history of his own time. But it is remarkable that of the five Delphic responses he refers to, not one is "commonplace." One advised the Epidamnians to hand over their city to Corinth, thus precipitating a war. Another advised the Spartans to make war on Athens, and promised victory and Apollo's help, invited or not. Another advised the Athenians to restore the people of Delos to their homes, from which they had been removed. Another approved the Spartan proposal to found a colony in Trachinia. Yet another, in highly poetical language even in Thucydides' paraphrase, urged the Spartans to bring back their exiled king—"otherwise they will plow with a silver plowshare." (In this case the Pythia, so the Spartans claimed, had been bribed by the king, but that does not affect the form and manner of the response.) These five responses, reported by a proclaimed skeptic on the subject of oracles, give us a picture of a Delphic oracle advising on colonial settlement, intervening decisively in Greek politics, using poetic (and obscure) language which suggests verse as the original form, and, in two cases, weighting its advice with what amounts to prophecy. This is a far cry from Fontenrose's vision of its "commonplace" activity.

There is another well-attested (and even more famous) Delphic response that can hardly be described as "commonplace." Socrates, in Plato's version of his speech in his own defense in court, says that one of his young enthusiastic admirers, Chaerophon, had the effrontery to ask the god if any man was wiser than Socrates. The Pythia replied that there was no man wiser. This riddling answer, as Socrates describes it, was, he explains to the jury, the reason for his perpetual questioning of his fellow citizens; he was trying to find out if the god was right. The explanation has more than a dash of the customary Socratic irony, but given the circumstances in which he was speaking, it is hardly likely that the oracular response was his own invention. Nor is it likely that it was invented by Plato, or, as Fontenrose surmises, that it was a "pious fiction of the Socratic circle." Plato had been in attendance at the trial; his *Apology* was written for an Athenian public that included many of the 501 jurors who had heard Socrates speak as well as many of the numerous spectators. It seems beyond the bounds of possibility that he could have attributed so sensational a statement to Socrates if he had not in fact made it.

Furthermore, Socrates' reaction to what he regards as a riddle, his attempt to divine its true meaning, exactly parallels Themistocles' interpretation of the oracle's declaration that for Athens safety lay in its wooden wall as a reference to the fleet and not to the wooden wall on the Acropolis. It is also a direct contrast to Croesus' unthinking acceptance, in a favorable sense, of the oracle's prophecy that he would destroy a great kingdom. The Pythia's pronouncement and Socrates' acceptance of it as a riddle to be understood and acted upon are not only well attested historical facts, they also conform to the pattern of riddle and interpretation that is, for Fontenrose, a sure sign that the oracular response in question is "doubtful" or "not genuine."

Fontenrose's criteria of trustworthiness are neither as relevant nor as exclusive as he claims; the Delphic answers recorded by Herodotus cannot be so easily dismissed. Some of them few would now defend as authentic in exactly the form Herodotus reports (certain instructions to colonists, for example, seem all too prescient), but the Delphic oracles of the Persian War period are another matter. Herodotus cannot have been more than a child at the time of their supposed delivery, but there were Athenians alive when he gave readings from his book who could remember Salamis and the epic struggle against the Persian invasion. The two famous oracles given to the Athenians before the sea battle are dismissed by Fontenrose as "doubtful." But the grounds of this judgment are themselves a little doubtful; one example will suffice. The first oracle (the advice to "fly to the ends of the earth") was not, in Herodotus' account, an answer to a question but a spontaneous response, and "only among Legendary and non-genuine Quasi-Historical oracles do we find spontaneous responses." It so happens that we have an inscription recording just such a response; it uses a very unusual verb, *automatizo*, to specify that Apollo spontaneously instructed Battos and the people of Thera to found the colony of Cyrene. What is more, this passage occurs in a fourth-century inscription which claims to reproduce the text of a seventh-century agreement. The latest editors (Meiggs and Lewis, in *A Selection of Greek Inscriptions to the End of the Fifth Century B.C.*), though they "assume a long and complex moulding of a genuine original within the tradition of Thera," still "think it not unsafe to assume that we have before us genuine elements of what was said and done in seventh century Thera." A more serious objection to Fontenrose's dismissal is that this particular oracle shows Delphi in a very bad light—convinced that Persia is irresistible and counseling panic flight or surrender. The Delphian priesthood would have no conceivable motive to invent or preserve such a text; moreover, the fact that Herodotus, an author solidly biased in Delphi's favor, believed this oracle was genuine speaks volumes for its authenticity.

But there is one larger question raised by the results of Fontenrose's assessment which he does not satisfactorily answer. If the oracle at Delphi gave nothing but commonplace answers of the type contained in his "Historical" section, how was it that this particular oracle of Apollo surpassed and almost eclipsed the others? Why did foreign kings make such rich donations? Why did so many Greek states—Athens, Corinth, Sicyon, Thebes, and others—build their own separate "treasuries" on the site, to house the trophies and dedications made in their name? Fontenrose explains that extraneous verse prophecies began to be attributed to the oracle "as Delphi's fame increased, and especially after Delphi had surpassed other oracles in prestige." But, on his showing, it is very hard to see how it could ever have done so.

The Delphic Oracle is a book which demands and stimulates controversial argument; it is no less admirable for that. It will lead the fascinated reader through many a legendary and historical maze, and he will learn much by the way. Whether or not he is convinced by the learned and acute discussions, he will be well advised not to quote any Delphic oracle as "historical" without first consulting Fontenrose's *Catalogue*, the evidence assembled there, and the discussion of it in the main text.

How Should We Live?

"There is an ancient quarrel between philosophy and
poetry," says Plato's Socrates, as, in Book 10 of the
Republic, he reconfirms his decision to banish Homer
and the tragic poets from his ideal city. And indeed
it is true that long before Plato such philosophers as
Xenophanes and Heraclitus had inveighed against
the poets for, among other things, their presentation
of gods engaged in unjust or immoral activities.
Poets working in what Plato called the imitative poetic media, epic and tragedy, were of course unable
to reply in kind (though some passages of tragic
lyric reflect a critical reaction to current philosophical speculation), but Pindar complained that the
natural philosophers *(tous physiologous)* were "harvesting the fruit of wisdom unripe."

Later on, Aristophanes put onstage a scurrilous
caricature of Socrates, and Plato himself was a fa-

This essay first appeared in *The New York Review of Books,* December
4, 1986. Reprinted with permission from *The New York Review of
Books.* Copyright © 1986 Nyrev, Inc.

vorite target of the comic poets when his Academy became a philosophical center in Athens. We have a fragment from a play of Epicrates, for example, which presents Plato and his students trying, without much success, to "distinguish" (a Platonic technical term) between "the life of animals, the nature of trees, and the species of vegetables." And in a comedy by Amphis a slave says to his master: "What good you expect to get from this, sir, I have no more idea of than I have of Plato's 'good.'"

This "quarrel" between poetry and philosophy tends to manifest itself also in modern scholarly and critical approaches to the two adversaries. Literary surveys of classical Greek culture usually pay too little attention to philosophical texts—and vice versa. Scholars who are not philosophically trained or inclined usually confine their reading of Plato (as Martha Nussbaum slyly remarks)[1] to the early and middle dialogues, where dramatic and poetic elements are given full play; as for Aristotle, they rarely venture outside the *Poetics*, the *Rhetoric*, and the *Nicomachean Ethics*. Students of philosophy, on the other hand, often seem unaware that many of the problems discussed by ancient philosophers, especially in the ethical field, are also posed, in a different but no less valid form, by lyric and especially by tragic poets.

An extreme case of such disciplinary tunnel vision is the second volume of Michel Foucault's *Histoire de la sexualité*, published in English translation under the title *The Use of Pleasure*. Its subject is the "problematization" of sexual behavior in classical Greek culture but its evidence is drawn exclusively

[1] Martha Nussbaum, *The Fragility of Goodness: Luck and Ethics in Greek Tragedy and Philosophy* (New York: Cambridge University Press, 1986).

from the writings of Plato, Xenophon, Aristotle, and the Hippocratic physicians. It does not seem to have occurred to Foucault that for an understanding of the ways sexual behavior was conceived of in classical Greece, tragedies such as Sophocles' *Women of Trachis* and Euripides' *Hippolytus* and *Medea*, to cite only three of the relevant examples, might be just as revealing as the strictly homosexual erotic theorizing of Plato's *Symposium*.

Foucault's Olympian indifference to the evidence of tragedy is perhaps unique, but it is nevertheless "customary," as Nussbaum puts it, to regard tragic and philosophical texts as "of quite different sorts, bearing in quite different ways on human ethical questions." But this, as she goes on to point out, "was clearly not the view of the Greeks." Homer, Hesiod, and the poets of the tragic stage were in fact thought of as ethical teachers and Plato's indictment of them sprang from his conception of them not "as colleagues in another department, pursuing different aims, but as dangerous rivals." Nussbaum proposes to study the "works of the tragic poets as Plato studied them: as ethical reflections in their own right."

She is, of course, primarily a distinguished student of Greek philosophy, editor of a difficult Aristotelian text, *On the Motion of Animals*, and author not only of the first full-length commentary on that text to be published since the thirteenth century but also of a series of essays on the philosophical problems it raises.[2] But she is also the author of a remarkable

[2]Aristotle; *De Motu Animalium*. Text with translation, commentary, and interpretive essays (Princeton, N.J.: Princeton University Press, 1978). Paperback edition with corrections, 1985.

article entitled "Flawed Crystals: James's *The Golden Bowl* and Literature as Moral Philosophy" as well as a penetrating essay on Sophoclean tragedy, "Consequences and Character in Sophocles" *Philoctetes.*"[3] She comes, then, well equipped for a book which opens with chapters on Aeschylus and the *Antigone* of Sophocles, proceeds to discussion of Plato's *Protagoras, Republic, Symposium,* and *Phaedrus,* follows this with five chapters on Aristotle, and ends with an epilogue devoted to Euripides' *Hecuba.* This long, intellectually, demanding, and richly rewarding book must be almost unique in its expert analysis of both tragic and philosophical texts.

Nussbaum's argument is complex, occasionally technical, but always intelligible even for those who, like the reviewer, read Plato with pleasure as far as the *Phaedrus,* find the going tough in the *Parmenides* and *Politicus,* but get a second wind in *The Laws.* She recognizes that her chapter "Rational Animals and the Explanation of Action" may "seem rather technical for the nonspecialist reader, who might prefer to turn directly to the chapter's concluding section (v), where the ethical implications of the explanatory project are described." In a short preface she gives the reader a choice: "This book can be read in two ways." Since after the introductory chapter, which identifies the problems to be discussed, each chapter is devoted, except in the case of Aristotle, to a single work—tragedy or Platonic dialogue—"readers can . . . feel free to turn directly to the chapter or chapters that seem most pertinent to their own concerns." But the reader is also advised that "there is . . . an overall historical argument, concerning the

---

[3]*New Literary History,* vol. 15 (1983), pp. 25–50; *Philosophy and Literature,* 1976–1977, pp. 25–53.

development of Greek thought on our questions; this is closely linked to an overall philosophical argument about the merits of various proposals for self-sufficient life."

"Our questions" are those raised by the author's stated purpose: to examine "the aspiration to rational self-sufficiency in Greek ethical thought: the aspiration to make the goodness of a good human life safe from luck through the controlling power of reason." The word "luck" is a rough equivalent of the Greek word *tuche*—"rough" because *tuche* does not necessarily refer to "random or uncaused" events; *tuche* means simply "what just happens to a man" as opposed to "what he does or makes." Goodness, on the other hand, is used by Nussbaum in a double sense: the ethical quality of a human life and also the happiness, the enviability, of that life. Clearly, goodness of the second kind is vulnerable to luck; the Greeks in general believed, contrary to modern Kantian ideas, that the first—the ethical quality of life—was vulnerable also. For one thing, the constituents of a happy life—love, friendship, attachment to property—may be "capable, in circumstances not of the agent's own making, of generating conflicting requirements that can themselves impair the goodness of the agent's life." And secondly there can be an inner conflict between a person's aspiration to self-sufficiency and the irrational forces in his own nature—"appetites, feelings, emotions"—sources of disorder, of what the Greeks called *mania*, "madness."

The attainment of complete immunity to luck would seem therefore to call for a renunciation not only of those vulnerable components of the good life that set it at risk but also a total suppression of the appetites and passions that might undermine a personal dedication to self-sufficiency. Even if such rigid self-control were possible for mere human creatures, the resultant life would seem, to most of us at least, limited and impoverished. And in fact it is only Plato, at the vertiginous height of his argument in *Phaedo*, *Republic*, and *Symposium*, who proposes "a life of self-sufficient contemplation, in which unstable activities and their objects have no intrinsic value."

The tragic poets, however, especially Aeschylus and Sophocles, present us with human characters exposed to fortune through their pursuit of those genuine human values that put us at risk—responsibility to others, loyalty to a community, devotion to the family. Nussbaum offers an impressive analysis of the tragic dilemmas of two Aeschylean heroes, Agamemnon at Aulis and Eteocles at the seventh gate of Thebes: in each case a "wrong action [is] committed without any direct physical compulsion and in full knowledge of its nature, by a person whose ethical character or commitments would otherwise dispose him to reject the act." Agamemnon, if he is to do his duty as commander of the expedition, must sacrifice his daughter; Eteocles, to save his city from destruction, must engage his brother in mortal combat. Agamemnon is placed by Zeus in a situation in which there is open to him no "guilt-free course." Modern critics have found contradiction and illogicality in the Aeschylean view of tragic necessity, a criticism for which Nussbaum has scant sympathy. "Such situations," she says, "may be repellent to practical logic; they are also familiar from the experience of life."

In Sophocles' *Antigone* the two principal characters attempt to avoid such dilemmas by "a ruthless simplification of the world of value which effectively eliminates conflicting obligations." Creon rules out all loyalties except that to the city; since Polynices, though a member of Creon's own family, has led a foreign assault on the city, he does not hesitate to order the exposure of his corpse, in spite of the fact that custom and religion assign him, as the only surviving male relative, responsibility for Polynices' proper burial.

Antigone too has her strategy of "avoidance and simplification"; her exclusive loyalty is to family obligations, specifically "duty to the family dead." Both of them come to grief, and though our sympathies are with Antigone the play clearly rejects the kind of rigid simplification of issues which inspired their actions. As Antigone is led off to her underground tomb, the chorus sings about others who have been similarly imprisoned, a song which Nussbaum, in a sensitive and convincing interpretation, sees as a repudiation of human action, a blind acceptance of passivity under the blows of fortune. The play seems to offer no escape from the choice between "Creon's violence against the external and complete helpless passivity before the external."

But this "paralyzing vision" is not the last word. In the speeches of Haemon and Tiresias a third possibility emerges, a prudent and intelligent moderation that makes it possible "to be flexibly responsive to the world, rather than rigid . . . a way of living in the world that allows an acceptable amount of safety and stability while still permitting recognition of the richness of value that is in the world." Creon concludes in the end that "it is best to keep to the established conventions (no-mous)." These are "the traditions of a community, built up and established over time" which "offer a good guide to what, in the world, ought to be recognized and yielded to." They "preserve a rich plurality of values" though they "offer no solution in bewildering tragic situations—except the solution that consists in being faithful to or harmonious with one's sense of worth by acknowledging the tension and disharmony."

The second choral ode of the *Antigone* begins with a famous celebration of the *technai*, the arts and sciences which have brought man, step by step, from helplessness to mastery of his environment and his crowning achievement, the creation of the state. *Techne*, the song seems to suggest, is the instrument by which man can make himself immune to *tuche*. In the event this proves to be a delusion; the messenger who announces the deaths of Antigone and Haemon proclaims the omnipotence of *tuche*—"Luck raises and luck humbles the lucky and the unlucky from day to day"—and the only successful *techne* mentioned in the play is that of the prophet Tiresias, who reads the signs of divine wrath and comes to warn Creon that he stands "on the razor-edge of luck."

Discussion of *techne* and *tuche* was not a monopoly of the tragic poets, it was a major preoccupation of intellectual circles in Periclean Athens. The Sophists, the West's first professional educators, taught *technai*, especially the arts of persuasion, claiming they were the key to political advancement in democratic Athens; Protagoras, perhaps the greatest of them, says, in the Platonic dialogue that bears his name, that he can teach political *techne* and make men good citizens. This dialogue, one of Plato's greatest creations from the literary and dramatic point of view, is full of stumbling blocks for the admirers of Plato the philosopher; not only does Socrates use arguments that border on the fallacious, he also proposes an identification of pleasure and goodness which is specifically repudiated in nearly every other Platonic dialogue. Nussbaum's analysis of the dialogue is a subtle, finely argued attempt to set Plato's thought squarely in the context of her leitmotif: the aspiration to rational self-sufficiency.

Protagoras' science of practical reasoning can claim it is a *techne* that "increases our control over *tuche*" but, though it will go far toward "training the passions . . . it will not completely render them innocuous." Above all it will not eliminate the conflict of values and the possibility of tragedy since, against the argument of Socrates, it recognizes "a plurality of distinct values." Socrates' insistence on the unity of the virtues Nussbaum sees as a necessary base for his ethical science (*episteme*) of measurement which would remove the possibility of "serious value conflict." For instead of choosing, under circumstantial pressure, to neglect a distinct value with its own separate claims, one will merely be giving up a smaller amount of the same thing. His adoption of pleasure is "the single measuring-stick of value" Nussbaum sees as a temporary expedient, which is "undefended, even unexplored" and in effect discarded at the end of the dialogue. What is important is the formulation of a science of "deliberative measurement."

This reading of the argument of *Protagoras* is no more likely to win universal acceptance than any of its predecessors, but it is presented with persuasive skill and buttressed by footnotes addressed to professional colleagues dealing in depth with possible objections and conflicting interpretations. What is interesting about it from the point of view of the nonprofessional is the link to tragedy. Protagoras' program of practical reasoning is a *techne* which, as Nussbaum points out, "follows Tiresias' advice"; it is a "practical wisdom that bends responsively to the shape of the natural world, accommodating itself to, giving due recognition to, its complexities." It might be added that Socrates, in his insistence on a single value, seems to be following the pattern of Antigone and Creon, whose exclusive loyalty to one value armored them against normal human feelings that might conflict with it.

In later dialogues of the middle period Socrates abandons pleasure as the measuring stick but continues the search for a science concerned with "rendering diverse particulars qualitatively homogeneous and interchangeable" which will "undo several problems at once, transforming troublesome conflicts," and "cutting away our motivations for passional excess." The search leads in the *Republic* to the total rejection of passions and appetites in favor of the life of the philosopher, who "stands apart from human needs and limitations," and whose viewpoint is "detached and extra-human"; and in the *Phaedo* it leads to the creation of a model life that is "practice for the separation of the soul from the body." This is, as a doctor might put it, a heroic remedy, and Nussbaum might have pointed out that Plato's Socrates owes more than a little to tragedy's conception of the hero: he rejects compromises and goes to his death rather than change his way of life. In the *Apology*, Plato's version of his speech at his trial, Socrates compares himself to, of all people, Achilles, and even claims he is looking forward to conversing, in the next world, with the most stubborn, bloody, and revengeful of the heroes, Ajax son of Telamon.

Nussbaum's emphasis, however, is on the difference, not the resemblance. The tragic hero's single criterion of value has its roots in the passions; it involves him fatally in a nexus of human needs and interests—family, community, love of another person—which breeds conflict. Plato's hero, on the other hand, reaches his criterion through the exercise of reason, rejects the passions and appetites completely, and lives a life spent in contemplation of eternal unchanging truths, free from internal value conflicts and immune to luck.

Plato's intellectual heroism denies the premises of tragedy but, as Nussbaum reminds us in a brilliant interlude between chapters—"Plato's Anti-tragic Theater"—the medium he invented for the presentation of his ideas was much indebted to that tragic drama which he was eventually to banish from his ideal state. Not only did he develop along new lines the ethical themes that tragedy had embodied in its heroic protagonists, he also adapted for his own literary and philosophical ends tragedy's dramatic means—character, dialogue, and plot. The dramatic form of his philosophical treatises is a radical departure. Previous philosophers, whether they wrote verse like Parmenides and Empedocles or prose like Anaxagoras and Democritus, addressed their readers in their own persons and in a didactic tone; as Nussbaum observes, Parmenides claims that he is an initiate and Empedocles that he is a god on earth. These are the books that Socrates (so Plato tells us in the *Phaedrus*) compared to figures in paintings: "For if you ask them a question, they keep a solemn silence." The Platonic dialogue "puts before us the responsiveness of dialectical interaction, as tragedy has also shown us concerned moral communication and debate." Unlike the *ex cathedra* pronouncements of the philosophers or the artful rhetoric of the Sophists, the dialogues "might fairly claim that they awaken and enliven the soul, arousing it to rational activity rather than lulling it into drugged passivity. They owe this to their kinship with theater."

They are theater, but "theater purged and purified of theater's characteristic appeal to powerful emotions"; they are "a pure crystalline theater of the intellect." Like tragedy, the dialogues move toward recognition of the truth through *elenchos*, testing and refutation; they "share with tragic poetry its elenctic structure." But there is a fundamental difference between the tragic and the Platonic *elenchos*. Creon rejects the arguments of Antigone, Haemon, and Tiresias; it takes the death of his son, "the sudden rush of grief, the tug of loss to make him see an aspect of the world to which he had not done justice." Recognition of the truth comes through the emotions; it was his intellectual conviction that led him to disaster. For Plato, on the other hand, learning comes through the intellect alone; it "takes place when the interlocutor is enmeshed in logical contradiction." His emotions are not to be aroused; "the ascent of the soul towards true understanding, if it uses any texts at all, will . . . avoid any with an irrational or emotive character."

The most powerful and dangerous of the emotions is what the Greeks called Eros, an irrational, passionate attachment to another human being. If the philosophical life can be lived only with passions and emotions totally subdued, Eros is clearly the most formidable adversary to be faced.

Plato recognizes this; he devotes to the problem of Eros the most richly dramatic of his dialogues, the *Symposium*. At a banquet in the house of the tragic poet Agathon, six speakers deliver an encomium of Eros; the last to speak is Socrates. Claiming that he is handing down the doctrine of the seer

Diotima, he describes the progress of the lover, under the teacher's guidance, from love of an individual body and mind to contemplation of the beautiful itself, "unalloyed, pure, unmixed, not stuffed full of human flesh and colors and lots of other mortal rubbish" (211E, Nussbaum's translation). Anyone who can reach such a stage of unworldliness is obviously immune to luck, impervious to the sorrow that loss of the beloved person can inflict.

But to reach such heights is no easy matter. We shall be given later, when Alcibiades, an uninvited guest, speaks about Socrates, a picture of a man who has started to make the ascent. He is a man who, as Nussbaum puts it, "has so dissociated himself from his body that he genuinely does not feel its pain, or regard its sufferings as things genuinely happening to him." He is impervious to cold, to fatigue, to hardship of any kind; he can drink without fear of intoxication and he can resist "the most immediate and intense sexual temptation." This is a man "in the process of making himself self-sufficient," and it is not an inviting prospect. Socrates, as Alcibiades truly says, "is not like any human being."

When Alcibiades bursts in on the party just as Socrates concludes his exposition of Diotima's teaching, we are faced suddenly with the incarnation of everything Diotima, or rather Socrates, would have us renounce. Crowned with the ivy of Dionysus and the violets of Aphrodite, Alcibiades is a vibrant image of the splendors of this fleshly world—a man of extraordinary physical beauty, a rich aristocrat, a brilliant wit and forceful speaker, and also, at the dramatic time of the dialogue, 416 B.C., indisputably the most admired man in Athens, the political leader who was shortly to persuade the Athenian assembly to send him in command of a fleet and army to conquer Sicily. The speech he makes is not, like those of the dinner guests, an encomium of Eros; it is a tragicomic account of his unsuccessful wooing of Socrates, this strange, fascinating, but incorruptible man.

Nussbaum sees in this speech more than a reluctant encomium of Socrates; it offers, she claims, an alternative to Diotima's progress from love of an individual to contemplation of universal truth. Her cogent analysis of the implications of the speech must be read in full for a real understanding of her thesis. Roughly speaking, she sees in Alcibiades a spokesman for the lover's understanding—an understanding "attained through the subtle interaction of sense, emotion, and intellect" and "yielding particular truths and particular judgments as a form of practical understanding." This is a position which has an affinity with that of Tiresias, Haemon, and Protagoras, as well as that of Socrates in the *Phaedrus*. But its spokesman is himself, as every reader of Plato knew, a terrible example of lack of practical wisdom, a man "who will live, to the end, a disorderly, buffeted life, inconstant and wasteful of his excellent nature," to die at last in exile, murdered by order of the victorious Spartans or, according to another account, by the brothers of a girl he had seduced. On this reading, the *Symposium* does indeed seem to us "a harsh and alarming book. . . . We see now that philosophy is not fully human; but we are terrified of humanity and what it leads to."

This comfortless vision of the human dilemma was something Plato himself was later to find too extreme; he tempered and modified it—so Nussbaum's argument proceeds—in the *Phaedrus*. In this dialogue Socrates first makes an attack on "erotic passion as a form of degrading madness" and denies the passions any "role to play in our understanding of the good." Later on, however, he makes another speech, which begins with a quotation from the palinode of Stesichorus, the poet's recantation of his censure of Helen:

> This story is not true.
> You did not board the benched ships,
> you did not come to the towers of Troy.

It is a prelude to his own recantation of his first speech, a defense of the benefits of madness (*mania*). *Mania* is a word that up to this point Plato has used to designate "the state of soul in which the nonintellectual elements—appetites and emotions—are in control and lead or guide the intellectual part," a state which Socrates has always rejected in favor of *sophrosune*, "the state of soul in which intellect rules securely over the other elements."

Socrates now finds some good in *mania* after all. It is a necessity for the inspired seer as also for the poet; it is also, he goes on to say, necessary for the lover. From the poetic speech that follows, famous because of its image of the soul as a charioteer with two horses, one good and one bad, there emerges a view of the role of the passions quite different from the total rejection of them characteristic of the earlier dialogues. It makes us, Nussbaum says,

> see human sexuality as something much more complicated and deep, more aspiring, than the middle dialogues had suggested; and, on the other hand, to see intellect as something more sexual than they had allowed, more bound up with receptivity and motion.

This is not, of course, an endorsement of Alcibiades' position (though he too uses the word *mania*); the noblest lovers will stop short of sexual intercourse. Yet those who occasionally lose control of the bad horse are not condemned outright, and in any case Plato's acceptance of love for a particular person exposes the lover to luck, to the possibility of loss, to all those human emotions to which the Socratic lover of the *Symposium* has made himself immune. This dialogue, Nussbaum claims, is a work in which Plato "admits that he has been blind to something, conceived oppositions too starkly," a work in which "he seeks, through recantation and self-critical argument, to get back his sight," as Stesichorus did when he wrote his palinode to Helen. "In the *Phaedrus* philosophy itself is said to be a form of *mania*, of possessed, not purely intellectual activity, in which intellect is guided to insight by personal love itself and by a complex passion-engendered ferment of the entire personality."

Obviously such a dramatic volte-face cries out for explanation—"We feel like asking, what happened to Plato?" Nussbaum looks for it in the historical circumstances in which the work was composed. She has in fact been conscious of this element throughout her discussion of Plato. It was put to brilliant use in her evocation of what Alcibiades meant to the Athenian readers of the *Symposium* and provides the fascinating suggestion that the reason Protagoras can adopt a "conservative," compromising position is "satisfaction." He

has lived the prime of his life in the greatest age of Athenian political culture. He still seems to us to be a part of this glorious, relatively happy past. . . . He is not gripped by the sense of urgency about moral problems that will soon characterize the writing of younger thinkers.

In the case of the *Phaedrus*, the background factor is personal: it is Plato's love for his pupil Dion, the man who was to overthrow the tyranny in his native city of Syracuse, only to be assassinated later on by political rivals.

It has often been noticed that when Socrates in the *Phaedrus* speaks of the ideal lovers he juxtaposes two words that mean "of Zeus" and "brilliant" and in their original Greek form *dios dion* suggest a punning reference to Plato's pupil; the great German scholar Wilamowitz regarded the allusion as "beyond reasonable doubt." Nussbaum adds that Phaedrus' name also means "brilliant," and since she has suggested that we are to think of Socrates and Phaedrus as representing the ideal lovers of Socrates' speech she can go on to see them as "standing in for Plato and Dion." This gives the dialogue "the character of a love letter, an expression of passion, wonder, and gratitude." She is not of course saying anything as simpleminded as that love made Plato change his mind; she recognizes that "his experience of love was certainly also shaped by his developing thought." But she does claim firmly that the dialogue asks "us to recognize experience as one factor of importance."

Here, however, she may be carrying her legitimate and even admirable attempt to ground the Platonic arguments in the contemporary scene too far. An allusion to Dion there may well be, but, though Dion was Plato's pupil and the close relationship between the two men extended over a quarter of a century, the evidence for an erotic attachment is weak. Plutarch's very full biography of Dion, for example, gives no hint of it; the argument for it rests principally on the testimony of one Diogenes Laertius, whose gossipy compilation *The Lives and Opinions of the Philosophers* was put together sometime in the third century after Christ. He cites from Book 4 of Aristippus' *The Luxury of the Ancients* an epitaph for Dion written by Plato which concludes with the line "O Dion; you who drove my soul mad with love." But since this same Aristippus announces that Plato was also in love with a boy named Aster ("Star") and produces a love poem addressed to him as well, following this up with the information that Plato was in love with Phaedrus too, many scholars, including the late Sir Denys Page, the most recent editor of these poems, have concluded that like the other Platonic love poems collected by Diogenes—addressed to Phaedrus, Alexis, Agathon, and two professional ladies called Archeanassa and Xanthippe—the Aristippus love poems, including the epitaph for Dion, are typical Hellenistic forgeries.[4]

Whatever may be thought of Nussbaum's tentative reconstruction of the emotions that prompted the composition of the *Phaedrus*, there can be no doubt that she offers a challenging new reading of it. When she moves on to Aristotle, whose "conception of ethical theory . . . is," she says, "roughly" her own, she presents us with an Aristotle whose vision of the

[4]Aristippus of Cyrene was a contemporary of Plato, so it is not likely that he would have included Plato's love affairs in a book called *The Luxury of the Ancients*. Even Wilamowitz, who accepts the Dion epitaph as genuine, assigns Diogenes "Aristippus" to the second century B.C.

good life has more affinity with the *Phaedrus* than with the middle dialogues. Her Aristotle

> develops a conception of a human being's proper relationship to *tuche* that returns to and further articulates many of the insights of tragedy. His philosophical account of the good human life is . . . an appropriate continuation and an explicit description of those insights.

Plato's earlier conception of philosophy as a *techne* that can lift the individual above the level of normal humanity and so free him from the tyranny of luck Aristotle rejects in favor of a nonscientific mode of practical reasoning, which recognizes that some components of a good life are vulnerable to catastrophe. Turning his back on the philosophical tradition which held that appearances are deceptive and the opinions of the many false, Aristotle "insists that he will find his truth *inside* what we say, see, and believe, rather than 'far from the beaten path of human beings' (in Plato's words) 'out there.' "

Nussbaum's limitation of the scope of Aristotle's ethical inquiry to the common beliefs and conceptions of humanity depends on her interpretation of the word *phainomena*, literally "appearances," which occurs in Aristotle's discussion of his method at the beginning of Book 6 of the *Nicomachean Ethics.* The method consists of

> setting down the *phainomena*, dealing with the initial difficulties, and proceeding in this way to demonstrate the truth of all the common beliefs *(endoxa)* about these states of mind or, if that is impossible, the truth of the majority and the most important of them. For if the difficulties can be resolved and the beliefs *(endoxa)* still stand, the demonstration will have been adequate.

Shortly after this passage, Aristotle dismisses Socrates' claim that no one acts wrongly knowing that his action is wrong, but only in ignorance as "manifestly in contradiction with the *phainomena.*" Most interpreters and translators, some of them in one of these passages and some in both, have taken *phainomena* to mean "the facts," "the observed facts," "data of perception," "observations"—almost anything, as Nussbaum says, "but the literal 'appearances,' or the frequently interchangeable 'what we believe,' or 'what we say.' " The tendentious translations derive from a "long tradition in the interpretation of Aristotelian science," which sees Aristotle in Baconian terms: a scientist who gathers data through empirical observation and then searches for a theory that will explain the data. It is clear that in the texts quoted above such an interpretation of *phainomena* is not acceptable, since the *phainomena* are immediately identified with *endoxa,* "common conceptions or beliefs on the subject."

The correct interpretation of *phainomena* was established in what Nussbaum calls a "justly famous article" by G. E. L. Owen; according to her, however, he did not go far enough, since he understood the term in the Baconian sense in Aristotle's biological works and thus "forces us to charge Aristotle with equivocation concerning his method and several of its central terms." Finding this inadmissible, she devotes an important chapter, "Saving Aristotle's Appearances," to a "univocal general account" of *phainomena* in Aristotle's method of ethical inquiry.[5]

[5]"If we do not insist on introducing an anachronistic scientific conception," she says later, "the alleged two senses and two methods can be one. When

What is that method? The philosopher begins by "setting down" the relevant appearances, "the ordinary beliefs and sayings" and a "review of previous scientific or philosophical treatments of the problem, the views of 'the many and the wise.' " The next step is to sort out the confusions and contradictions such matter contains, to eliminate contradiction. But the process of bringing "the matter of life into perspicuous order" does not allow us to "follow a logical argument anywhere it leads." We must, in the end, show that the *phainomena*, or at any rate the greatest number and the most important of them, are true. "Theory must remain committed to the ways human beings live, act, see."

A more total rejection of Plato's fundamental precepts is hard to imagine, and Nussbaum quotes from, of all places, the *Posterior Analytics*, a "burst of exuberant malice that shows us aspects of Aristotle's temperament usually masked by a measured sobriety": "So goodbye to the Platonic Forms. They are *teretismata*"—the sort of sounds you make when you hum to yourself—"and have nothing to do with our speech."

Her next four chapters are devoted to an explanation and defense of Aristotle's articulation of "a conception of practical rationality that will make human beings self-sufficient in an appropriately human way." The chapter which she warns us "may seem rather technical for the nonspecialist reader" is a discussion of Aristotle's theories of animal motion and motivation which is relevant to ethical theory because it is part

---

Aristotle sits on the shore of Lesbos taking notes on shellfish . . . he will be describing the world *as it appears to*, as it is experienced by, observers who are members of our kind."

of Aristotle's ethical view that "our shared animal nature is the ground of our ethical development. It is our nature to be animal, the sort of animal that is rational."

This is followed by Nussbaum's discussion of "nonscientific deliberation"; it deals with Aristotle's claim that, contrary to Platonic doctrine, practical wisdom is not scientific wisdom. It deals also with Aristotle's emphasis on the anthropomorphism of the search for the good life, his attack on the Platonic commensurability of values and the Platonic demand for generality, and his affirmation of the role of nonintellectual elements in deliberation (a point on which he comes close to Plato's position in the *Phaedrus*). He has eliminated those elements in the Platonic "science" which conferred invulnerability to outside contingency. Rejecting both extreme positions—that luck is the sole decisive factor in the living of a good life and that good living is invulnerable to luck—Aristotle admits the possibility of "disruption of good activity" and even "damage to good states of character." For the ethical values that constitute good living cannot exist except in a context of human activity; though for animals and gods such concepts as justice, courage, generosity are irrelevant, these central human values "cannot be found in a life without shortage, risk, need, and limitation." This is true also of the values of friendship and political activity, the subject of Nussbaum's final chapter on Aristotle's ethical theory. This chapter ends with an eloquent assessment of the Aristotelian achievement.

> Aristotle has attempted . . . by setting our various beliefs before us, to show us that they contain a conception of human good living that makes it something relatively stable, but still vulnera-

ble, in its search for richness of value, to many sorts of accidents. We pursue and value both stability and the richness that opens us to risk. In a certain sense we value risk itself, as partially constitutive of some kinds of value. In our deliberations we must balance these competing claims. This balance will never be a tension-free harmony.

Good human deliberation is a "delicate balancing act . . . delicate, and never concluded, if the agent is determined, as long as he or she lives, to keep all the recognized human values in play." To those who find this picture of deliberation "mundane, messy, and lacking in elegance," Aristotle would reply "that we do well not to aim at a conception that is more elegant, or simpler, than human life is." This is one of several passages in the book which will seem to many readers to justify Nussbaum's belief "that Nietzsche was correct in thinking that a culture grappling with the widespread loss of Judaeo-Christian religious faith could gain insight into its own persisting intuitions about value by turning to the Greeks."

But this is not the end of her book. She began with tragedy and it is with tragedy that she ends. Plato rejected it as a corrupting influence, but Aristotle's ethical position clearly allows it a place, even an important place, in human life, since it "explores the gap between being good and living well." Under the heading "Luck and the Tragic Emotions" Nussbaum discusses Aristotle's treatise on tragedy and especially his remarks about pity and fear. "For Aristotle, pity and fear will be sources of illumination or clarification, as the agent, responding and attending to his or her responses, develops a richer self-understanding concerning the attachments and values that support the responses."

This interpretation of a much-disputed text depends on a new understanding of the key word *katharsis* in Aristotle's formula "through pity and fear to accomplish the *katharsis* of experiences of that kind." Developing an argument of Leon Golden, who pointed out that *katharsis* and related words, as used by Plato, have a strong connection with learning, occurring in connection with "the unimpeded or 'clear' rational state of the soul," Nussbaum looks at the history of these words and finds that their "primary, ongoing, central meaning is roughly one of 'clearing up' or 'clarification.'" The meaning "purgation," usually adduced in explanation of this passage in Aristotle, is a special medical application of this general sense.

In an epilogue Nussbaum presents an analysis of a play which Plato, though he does not mention it, must have regarded with indignation, for it shows us the complete deterioration of moral character under the pressure of calamity. It is the *Hecuba* of Euripides, a play rarely discussed in the voluminous literature on Greek tragedy, one which from the nineteenth century on into our own has often been censured as "episodic," "melodramatic," even, by one influential critic, "poor and uninteresting."

Nussbaum offers a convincing defense of its dramatic and thematic unity: the two main episodes, the sacrifice of Polyxena and Hecuba's atrocious revenge on the murderer of her son Polydorus, are seen as dramatic embodiments of contrasting views on the stability of good character under adverse conditions. The nobility of Polyxena, who refuses to plead

for her life and dies with dignity and courage, prompts
Hecuba to reflect that "among human beings . . . the noble [is
never] anything but noble, and is not corrupted in its nature
by contingency, but stays good straight through to the end."
But with the discovery of her son's body and the realization
that he has been murdered by the guest-friend Polymestor to
whom she has entrusted him for safekeeping, Hecuba's conception of a world governed by *nomos*, "deep human agreements concerning value," is shattered. In exchange she embraces a *nomos* of a different nature: revenge, the old law—an
eye for an eye and a tooth for a tooth. Using the same moral
convention of guest-friendship that Polymestor has betrayed,
and appealing to the greed which had prompted his murder
of her son, she lures him and his infant sons into the tents of
the captured Trojan women, where the children are killed
and Polymestor blinded. Later Polymestor prophesies that
she will fall from the yardarm of the ship on her way to
Greece and be transformed into a dog, a creature which, as
Nussbaum emphasizes, ranks, for the Greeks, "very low on
the scale of animal nobility." But she is already something less
than human. The destruction of the *nomos* of mutual trust can
produce, even in a stable character, "bestiality, the utter loss
of human relatedness and human language."

This is, as Nussbaum puts it, a "worst case," but Aristotle,
though he might insist on the rarity of such a combination of
disasters as that which overwhelms Hecuba, "cannot consistently close off the possibility of such events." He too, like
Hecuba, "bases human excellence on the social nature of the
human being" (*nomos*). He "stresses that all of excellence has
an other-related aspect" and that "personal love and political
association are not only important components of the good

human life but also necessary for the continued flourishing of good character generally." And he "mentions explicitly that trust is required to reap the benefits of these associations."

Euripides' play does show us, in the person of Polyxena, an example of uncorrupted nobility, but, as Nussbaum puts it, Polyxena has the "good luck" to die before life can bring disillusionment—"to live on is to make contact in some way at some time with the possibility of betrayal." The Platonic alternative, to "put the world in good order by sealing off certain risks, closing ourselves to certain happenings," and still retain a world "relatively rich in value, since it would still contain the beauty of the Platonic contemplative life" seems, when we look at the world of the *Hecuba*, an attractive one. And yet, as Aristotle, and for that matter the *Phaedrus* and the *Antigone*, have made clear, "there is in fact a loss in value whenever the risks involved in specifically human virtue are closed off. . . . Each salient Aristotelian virtue seems inseparable from a risk of harm"—courage, for example, exists only in a context of death or serious damage. "There are certain risks," Nussbaum concludes, "that we cannot close off without a loss in human value, suspended as we are between beast and god, with a kind of beauty available to neither."

This outline of Nussbaum's argument gives little idea of its originality, intellectual richness, and logical force, nor can quotations from her text convey more than a faint impression of the fluidity, grace, precision, and economy of her prose. In her opening pages she speaks of the problem facing a philosopher who chooses to deal with "competing conceptions of learning and writing, as embodied in poetic and philosophical texts": the decision whether to adopt "the hard 'philosophical' style" or "a mode of writing that lies closer to poetry and makes its appeal to more than one 'part' of the person," or else to "use different styles in different parts of the inquiry." Her choice is "to attempt to vary the way of writing so that it will be appropriate to the ethical conception to which it responds in each case; to try to show in my writing the full range of my responses to the texts and to evoke similar responses in the reader." She will "remain always committed to the critical faculties, to clarity and close argument" but will also "try to deal with tragic (and Platonic) images and dramatic situations in such a way that the reader will feel, as well as think, their force." Over the four hundred or so pages of text and the nearly one hundred pages of notes she succeeds handily in fulfilling these promises; this is a book which keeps a firm hold on the reader's attention, challenges the reader's intellectual capacity, and appeals, gravely and without fulsome rhetoric, to his or her deepest emotions.

It is also a book which, besides being required reading for anyone interested in Greek philosophy or literature, addresses a wider audience. It analyzes the attempts of poets and philosophers in the great creative age of Greek civilization to deal with problems that, as Nussbaum says in her opening chapter, are still problems for anyone who finds it hard to accept the Kantian view that the domain of moral value supersedes all other values and that it is altogether immune from the assaults of luck. "That much that I did not make goes towards making me whatever I shall be praised or blamed for being," she writes, that I must constantly choose among competing and apparently incommensurable goods and that circumstances may force me to a position in which I cannot help being false to something or doing some wrong; that an event that simply happens to me may, without my consent, alter my life; that it is equally problematic to entrust one's good to friends, lovers, or country and to try to have a good life without them—all these I take to be not just the material of tragedy, but everyday facts of lived practical reason.

Poet and *Polis*

In his pioneering sociological study of the ancient *polis*, or city-state, the French historian Fustel de Coulanges speaks of "the omnipotence and the absolute empire it exercised over its members. . . . The citizen was subordinate, in everything and without any reserve, to the city; he belonged to it body and soul. . . . It is a singular error, therefore . . . to believe that in the ancient cities men enjoyed liberty. They had not even the idea of it. They did not believe that there could exist any right as against the city and its gods."[1]

This is, of course, an exaggeration, but it contains more than a kernel of truth: the ancient Greek *polis* (by which of course we mean Athens, the only one on which we are relatively well informed) made de-

This essay originally appeared as the text of a lecture delivered for the Fondation Hardt in Geneva, Switzerland, and published in *Entretiens XXIV Sophocle.*

[1]*La cité antique* (Paris 1864). Quoted from the English translation (New York: Doubleday, 1956), pp. 219–20; 223.

mands on its male citizens which today would be considered unreasonable.[2] It expected and obtained military service (combat service, not chairborne) for its all too frequent wars on land and sea (from the battle of Plataea in 479 B.C. to Chaeronea in 338, Athens had not one interval of peace longer than ten years, and most of them were shorter). Men were liable for campaigns beyond the frontiers up to the age of fifty and might be called on to defend the city walls until the age of sixty. By its jealous restriction of citizenship the *polis* in effect limited its citizens' choice of wives; its wealthy citizens were liable to special income taxes as well as "liturgies"— public service which could range from the organization and financial responsibility for a dramatic performance to equipment (and command) of a warship. Participation in the meetings of the assembly and the jury sessions of the law courts was not, as far as we know, enforced, but it was certainly expected: "we alone," says Pericles, "regard the man who holds aloof from the city's affairs [*ta politika*] not as 'quiet' but as 'useless' "—*achreion*, a harsh word. It is Hesiod's term for the man who can neither think for himself nor take advice from others, and Herodotus' advocate for oligarchy in the Persian debate applies it to the common herd—"nothing more stupid or violent than a useless mob." The force of such public opinion (for this is clearly what Pericles expresses) should not be underestimated; in the modern megalopolis it is possible to live a completely private and anonymous life, but in the ancient Mediterranean city—crowded, walled and built for outdoor living—public disapproval, concentrated and op-

[2]Goethe had expressed similar sentiments in 1806. See Hugh Lloyd-Jones, *Blood for the Ghosts* (London: Duckworth, 1982), p. 57 and references there.

pressive, could not be ignored. There was no escape from daily contact with one's fellow citizens.[3] Even in peacetime communal cult and sacrifice could not be dispensed with, and in war the Athenian, side by side on the rowing bench of the galley or shield by shield in the hoplite phalanx, was an integral member of the body politic. The bonds which held the individual to the community were so strong that exile was considered a penalty on a level with death; the exile never ceased to intrigue, cajole, and plot for the day of his return to the *polis*, and his greatest fear was that his bones might not be buried in the soil where his ancestors lay. Themistocles, the hero of Salamis, was forbidden burial in Attic soil; he told his family to bring his body home, so Thucydides reports the tradition, and they did so secretly.

The city demanded a loyalty which overrode all others. Plato's Socrates puts its claims in the mouth of the city's laws, as they call on him to stand his ground and refuse to escape by leaving Athens:

> Is this your wisdom—to fail to see that your fatherland deserves your respect, awe, and reverence more than your mother, father, or all your ancestors? That it is considered more important both by the gods and by men of good sense? That when it is angry you ought to respect, obey and humor it more than you would an angry father; that you must either win its agreement or obey its orders, suffer in silence whatever suffering it assigns you—if

[3]The one Athenian we hear of who tried to withdraw completely from society, Timon, became proverbial. A fragment of the 5th century comic poet Phrynichus sums up the Athenian ideal of the unsocial man: "I live the life of Timon: no wife, no slaves, a quick temper; no visitors, no smile, no conversation—and my private point of view."

it orders you to be beaten, if it orders you to be bound, if it
leads you to war to be wounded or killed—its will be done.
. . . You must not give way, fall back, or leave the ranks but in
war and in the courts of law and everywhere you must do what
the city commands. . . . (*Crito* 51 b-c)

But the city demanded more than obedience and conform-
ity. In the great panegyric of Athenian imperial democracy
which Thucydides attributes to Pericles, it demands a fanat-
ical, irrational devotion, the devotion of a lover: the Athenians are to "fix their gaze daily on the power of the *polis* and
become its lovers." This is an extraordinary phrase, and its
significance has been generally undervalued; it is not to be
compared, as most translations suggest, with such bland
phrases as "love of country." The word *erastes* ("lovers") suggests an overwhelming romantic passion, an emotion usually
associated in Athenian society of this period with homosexual love, one which takes exclusive possession of the soul of
its victim, driving him to extreme demonstrations of devotion. Such love is characterized in Plato's *Symposium*, the *locus
classicus* for the subject, as "voluntary slavery"; the lover is
"willing to serve in slavish ways no real slave would put up
with." Pericles' phrase (and in view of the clear parody of it in
Aristophanes' *Knights* there can be little doubt that it is a genuine reminiscence of Pericles and not a Thucydidean invention) calls for a total dedication to the *polis*, a devotion inspired by contemplation of its power. That the call was
answered is plain from the extraordinary record of Athenian
activity in the years between 490 and 404 B.C. and the recognition on the part of Athens' enemies that they were facing no
ordinary adversary. "They use their bodies in the city's ser-

vice," say Thucydides' Corinthians, "as if they were not their own and their minds as very much their own, for action in the city's interest" (*Peloponnesian War* 1.70).

Sophocles' long life spanned almost the whole of the century which saw the creation, rise, and fall of the Athenian empire. As a youth he took part in the victory celebration for Salamis;[4] as a grown man he served the *polis* at the height of its power in military as well as civil offices. His last years were spent in the Athens of the Peloponnesian War, the protracted death agony of the *polis tyrannos*, but he died in 406, just before the ignominious end. Though he was by our standards a remarkably productive playwright (and we must not forget that he was also director of his own plays) his record of public service is impressive: he served as *stratégos* at least once (in the campaign against Samos, a dangerous crisis for the empire); he was treasurer of the Delian League (he may have been chairman of the board of ten, for his name appears first on the Tribute List inscription for the year 443–42); and it seems certain (though it has been doubted) that he was one of the *probouloi*, the committee of public safety appointed to emergency rule in Athens after the disaster in Sicily. This public career, combined with what must have been prodigious creation as a playwright-director (123 plays in sixty-two years), exemplifies Pericles' proud claim for the Athenian citi-

[4]This tradition is dismissed as one of those stories "meant as representations of the poet's heroic stature, not as statements of literal fact" by Mary R. Lefkowitz, *The Lives of the Greek Poets* (London, 1981), p. 77. It is not easy to see what such an anecdote about the poet's youth would have to do with "heroic stature," and, in view of Sophocles' birthdate, good family, and early musical training, there is nothing improbable in the choice of such a man for such an occasion.

zen: "Our citizens attend both to public and private duties and do not allow absorption in their own various affairs to interfere with their knowledge of the city's" (*Peloponnesian War* 2.40.2).

As a poet Sophocles inherited from his predecessor Aeschylus a dramatic medium which after some experiments with near-contemporary themes had narrowed its focus to stories of the heroes, kings, and dynasties of the splendid but violent age which ended with the first generation after the Trojan War. These stories reflected the rudimentary social organization of an unsettled age—hereditary kingship, dynastic feuds—and the violence, uninhibited by communal restraints, of the god-descended heroes. One of the achievements of Aeschylus was to impose on this primitive material the contemporary framework of the *polis*—still ruled by kings as in the saga but reminiscent in many suggestive details of the *polis* in which the audience lived. The king of Argos in *Suppliants* must consult his citizens before making a decision which will endanger the city, and in the *Oresteia* the murder of Agamemnon by his wife is the first act in a drama which culminates in the foundation of the Areopagos and a hymn of blessing for Athenian democracy and empire. The *Seven Against Thebes* opens with an eloquent plea from Eteocles, defender of a city under assault. He summons the Thebans to the walls: "Now is the time for all of you—you that fall short of maturity, you that are past the time of youth, fostering the full growth of your limbs, and you that are in manhood's prime—as is your duty, every one of you must protect the city and the altars of our native gods—let not their worship be abolished—protect, too, the children and the land, your mother and most tender nurse—she, who, welcoming all the travail of their upbringing, has reared them, young shoots on the kindly plain, to be makers of homes and bearers of shields."[5] This is a mythic hero speaking, but his voice is that of the man who fought at Marathon. Tragedy, as Sophocles inherited it from his rival, was a dramatic medium which could invest with broad contemporary significance the actions and sufferings of ancestral heroes, whose mythical remoteness, sustained by the dignity of the tragic style, ruled out facile identification with particular partisan issues or controversial figures of the day. It was only to be expected that Sophocles, given his record of participation in the highest offices of the *polis*, would follow the lead of his great predecessor.

When we speak of Sophoclean tragedy we often tend to forget that we have only a small fragment of a vast œuvre, seven complete plays out of 123. We can only hope that the seven are reasonably representative of the whole; in any case, it is on these seven that we must base our interpretation. And they do, in fact, show us a Sophocles who, like Aeschylus, poses the heroic figures of the ancient saga against the background of a half-mythical, half-contemporary *polis*, or, in the case of the Trojan War plays *Ajax* and *Philoctetes*, of the *polis* in arms, the *stratos*. There is only one exception: *Trachiniae*. This play deliberately emphasizes the primitive, even monstrous, features of the Heracles saga—the fight with the river in his bull shape, the centaur Nessos and his poisoned blood, the strident agony of Heracles' last hours and his bizarre end, whether it be death or apotheosis. The scene of the action is

---

[5]The emphasis on the city's role as nurse and mother of the citizen recurs in the Laws' address to Socrates (Plato, *Crito*, 50d, 51c and e).

not a *polis* at all; the family of Heracles are guests of a "foreigner" who is not even named and the *agora*, the meeting place of the people of Trachis, is a cow pasture. The only *polis* of any importance in the action is Oechalia, a city which Heracles has sacked and razed.[6] The characters of this play seem to be untrammeled by any sense that they are part of a community, and the young women of the chorus are given no words which will identify them, justify their presence, or attach them to a locality.

Electra, on the other hand, opens with the most precise location of the action in a city landscape to be found in extant Greek tragedy: Orestes' old tutor points out to him, from the vantage point of the Atridae's palace at Mycenae, the salient features of the city of Argos—the *agora* of Lycean Apollo and "on the left, the famous temple of Hera." Such a prologue seems the appropriate opening note for a drama which will emphasize the political aspect of Orestes' action: the overthrow of a tyranny, the restoration of freedom. But, in fact, nothing could be farther from the truth; Sophocles concentrates our attention almost exclusively on the violent hatreds and internecine violence of a doomed and cursed family. The dominant words in this text are not "city" and "citizen" (they occur only rarely) but "father," "mother," "sister," "brother," and "home"; they recur with obsessive frequency from beginning to end of the play. And the word "free," *eleutharos*, is used always of personal freedom: Chrysothemis' freedom to marry once Aegisthus is dead; Electra's freedom to speak now Orestes has come; freedom to rejoice and smile once success

---

[6]Cf. Charles Segal, *Tragedy and Civilization: An Interpretation of Sophocles* (Cambridge, Mass.: Harvard University Press, 1981), p. 62.

has been achieved. There is one passage, in fact, where the nonpolitical nature of this "freedom" is emphasized by a startling phrase which Sophocles puts in the mouth of Chrysothemis, the conformist and self-confessed coward. She admits that Electra has right on her side. "But if I am to live free," she says, "I must obey every word of those in power."

Even in the one passage where the language suggests a political theme, Electra's vision of the glory she and her sister will win if they murder Aegisthus—its striking use of the dual a reminiscence of the battle hymn of Athenian democracy, the Harmodios song—even here the achievement for which they will be celebrated is not the liberation of Argos but the salvation of the house of Atreus; to the words of the song—"The two of them made Athens a city of equality before the law"—corresponds, in Electra's speech: "Those two who saved the house of their father." And this restriction of the action to the domestic sphere is clearest of all in the final lines of the play, where "freedom" is mentioned again: "Seed of Atreus, after much suffering, you have through struggle won freedom at last"; it is the family, not the city, which has been freed. To appreciate the singularity of this treatment of the legend one has only to glance at Sophocles' model, the *Choephoroe* of Aeschylus. One of the motives which Orestes says would have urged him to action even if Apollo's oracle had not is the thought that "fellow citizens, most renowned among mortals, the men who sacked Troy with blazing courage, should be thus subject to a pair of women." And when the chorus of Trojan captives who see in the vengeance "good for the city" try to comfort Orestes and restrain him from going as a suppliant to Delphi, they tell him: "You have brought freedom to the whole city of the Argives."

The other Electra play, that of Euripides, reinforces the contrast, for it is just as political, though in a markedly different way, as that of Aeschylus. Though the setting is a remote country farm, the characters live and move and have their being in the charged atmosphere of the late-fifth-century *polis*. Orestes is all too easily recognizable as a political exile with a price on his head who has come home secretly, staying close to the frontier so that he can escape if recognized; he has returned to sound out the possibility of support for a coup. The vengeance itself—the treacherous assassination of Aegisthus, Electra's ghastly indictment of the tyrant's severed head—recalls, as has often been pointed out, Thucydides' account of civil war on Corcyra—"the ingenuity of their enterprises and the ferocity of their reprisals" (*Peloponnesian War* 3.82). And at the end of the play the Dioskouroi reset the action in its mythic frame: as in the *Eumenides*, Orestes is to be tried and acquitted in Athens. But Euripides takes the story farther still: he is to found a new *polis* in the West, one which will bear his name.

In his *Electra* Sophocles rejected the political element in the story of the Atridae, an element which, whether it was Aeschylean invention or traditional lore, was brilliantly exploited by Euripides in characteristically iconoclastic style. But in the remaining five of the extant Sophoclean plays we are securely placed in the world of the *polis*; in each play the *polis* or its wartime equivalent, the *stratos* ("citizen army"), provides the context for the heroic action; it has its own voice, the chorus, and its own spokesmen among the actors. In four of these plays the tragic tension stems from the incompatibility between the demands of the *polis* and the imperatives of the heroic will. In the fifth, *Oedipus the King*, a ruler who embodies the supreme virtues of the devoted citizen ends, through his own heroic persistence, as an outcast from the *polis*, like the heroes of the other four plays.

In two of them, the hero's defiance of the *polis* leads to death: both Ajax and Antigone die by their own hand. Death, but not total defeat: Creon gives way and admits that he was wrong; Ajax will have his hero's funeral in spite of the vindictive order of the generals. But though there are resemblances between Ajax and Antigone (since both share that stubborn irreconcilability Sophocles saw as the core of heroic character), there are some basic differences between the plays in which they appear. Antigone's action, for example, can be defended and is in the end vindicated, whereas Ajax's murderous intentions far outrun any justification his injuries might have afforded. But the most striking difference lies in the terms used to express the demand of the community, *stratos* or *polis*, for loyalty and obedience.

In the first part of the *Ajax* there is little discussion of the duty owed to the army, for attention is centered on the hero, his grievances, his failed revenge, and his resolve to die; not only does Ajax feel no loyalty to the army, he includes it in the curse he levels at the Atridae as he prepares to fall on his sword: "Go to it, swift and vengeful Erinyes, show no mercy, take your fill of the whole army, every last man." He had intended to kill the commanders only, but this all-inclusive curse gives some ground for the rhetorical exaggeration of the accusation leveled against him: that "his plot was against the Argives" (Odysseus); that he was a "plotter against the army" (the Argives); and finally that he "plotted the death of the entire army" (Menelaus). It is in the second half of the play, as the gigantic corpse of Ajax lies spitted on the sword of

Hector, that the *polis* announces its claims. In the mouth of
Menelaus, it does so in uncompromising terms. Ajax would
never listen to Menelaus, Teucer is told: "there's a worthless
man for you—a man of low degree who takes it upon himself
to ignore those set in authority over him." The words, as well
as the situation they denote, are utterly un-Homeric; this is
not the camp on the beachhead where rival chieftains grudg-
ingly accept (or violently throw off) the loose and temporary
authority of a preeminent king. The lines which follow make
this even clearer. "You cannot have laws working smoothly in
a city where fear does not have its established place, nor can
you have discipline in an army without the protective shield
of terror and respect." *Polis* and *stratos* are different sides of the
same coin; what goes for one goes for the other. When
Menelaus returns to the theme of discipline, he speaks of the
polis alone. "Where there is no curb on licence—all do what
they like—that's a city which may run now before a fair wind
but will one day go down to the bottom. No, let me have fear
installed, in due proportion. . . ." These sentiments are
echoed by Agamemnon. "Where such attitudes prevail"—(he
means Ajax's refusal to accept the award of the arms to Odysseus)—"there can be no establishment of law of any kind.
. . ." And Teucer's offense, his insistence on Ajax's right to be
buried, is characterized not only as intolerable insolence, but
also as "speaking freely."

These demands for discipline and submission, especially
the elaborate formulas put in the mouth of Menelaus, are
sometimes described as "Spartan"[7]; they are supposed to rep-

[7]For example, in R. C. Jebb, ed., *Sophocles: The Plays and Fragments, Part 7, The Ajax* (Cambridge, England: Cambridge University Press, 1907).

resent, for the Athenian audience, a point of view alien to the tolerant spirit of Athenian democracy. But there is actually little in those lines which would not have seemed acceptable, if perhaps harshly expressed, to most Athenian citizens. Aeschylus' chorus in the *Eumenides* had stressed that fear had its place in the *polis:* "there are times when terror is a blessing; it must have its permanent seat as watcher over the mind." And Athena herself echoes their claim: "Do not utterly expel terror from your city. . . ." Even the Funeral Speech, which so eloquently posed Athenian freedom of manners against the harsh Spartan discipline, reiterates the theme: "in our public life it is mainly through fear that we refrain from illegal action; we listen to those who are in office and to the laws. . . ."

Familiar as these pronouncements of Menelaus and Agamemnon may have sounded to the average Athenian in the audience, their dramatic content must have given him pause. They are being advanced in favor of a decision to expose the corpse—"throw it out on the sand as food for the shore birds"—of a man whom even his enemy Odysseus celebrates as the best man, after Achilles, of all those who came to Troy. The two kings who could not impose their will on Ajax living, as Menelaus admits, will have their way with him now that he is dead; Agamemnon even goes so far as to deny his preeminence in battle—"Where did he go or stand that I did not?"—a question which anyone familiar with the *Iliad* could answer at once. The two kings do not even claim that the horrifying penalty is meant to be exemplary; they simply exult vindictively in their power over the lifeless corpse of the hero whom they feared to cross when he was alive. The claims of the *polis* are advanced by unworthy spokesmen whose low and spiteful ranting enhances the dignity of that heroic corpse they wish to defile.

In the *Ajax* the voice of the *polis* is heard late in the play and it strikes a sour note. In the *Antigone*, on the other hand, it is given full and eloquent expression right at the start, in that speech of Creon which, as we know from the way Demosthenes later used it in the courtroom,[8] became a classic text of the Athenian patriotic spirit. And in this play, although the setting is the moment of victory in war and the ruler Creon is a *stratēgos* who issues commands by proclamations, the background is not the armed camp on the Trojan shore but a *polis*, one with pillared temples, battlemented walls and towers, gates, altars, hearths, and a council of elders. The *polis* is to be the scene of the execution by stoning, fixed as a penalty for disobedience to Creon's decree, which forbids the *polis* to bury Polynices. Ismene, who will reluctantly obey those in authority, identifies the will of Creon with that of the *polis* as a whole, for she professes herself unable to act "in defiance of the citizens." This judgment is confirmed by the conduct of the chorus, representatives of the *polis* summoned by Creon, who stand behind him and against Antigone until the last moment, when Tiresias makes it clear that Creon is wrong and also marked for punishment.

The emotional background for their support of Creon's harsh sentence is vividly presented in their opening song, which recalls the terrors of the enemy assault on the walls, the miracle by which the city has escaped collapse in a welter of blood and fire. The invaders were recruited and led by a fel-

[8] *Oration* 19 (*On the Embassy*), 247.

low citizen, the man whose corpse Creon has now consigned to the birds and dogs.

This lyric evocation of the dangers and terrors of the siege, the city's hairbreadth escape from destruction at the hands of one of its own citizens, prepares the audience for Creon's inaugural speech. "Gentlemen, as for the city . . . the gods who tossed our ship on a heavy swell have righted it again, it rides safely." The declaration of principles which follows, full of reminiscences (or anticipations) of Periclean rhetoric, states firmly the precedence of loyalty to the *polis* over all other loyalties, whether to friend or relative (both included in the one word *philos*). This is the same large demand which the laws of Athens make on Socrates in Plato's *Crito* and it is given some validity by Creon's implied claim that only in the framework of civilization made possible by the *polis* can friendship or any personal relationship exist. "This is the ship that brings us safe to harbor and we make our friends as we sail her and keep her upright." These, says Creon, are the laws through which he plans to make the city great. His first official act makes a distinction between patriot and traitor and asserts the right of the *polis* to honor the one and punish the other in life and in death.

Creon began by mentioning the gods, and he sincerely believes that the gods of the city approve of his decree. When the chorus tentatively suggests that the symbolic burial reported by the guard may be divine intervention, he turns on them in what is obviously sincere anger. "Intolerable," he calls their suggestion: how could the gods take any thought for one who came to burn their pillared temples and the treasures inside them? To an audience which probably believed, with

Herodotus, that the gods had punished at Salamis and Plataea the Persians who burned and sacked the temples on the Acropolis, Creon's religious beliefs, like his political principles, would have occasioned no surprise, still less objection.[9] In this play the case for the *polis* is made early and in impressive form, but, as in the *Ajax*, it is also a case for denial of burial to a corpse. And as the action develops, Creon, under the pressure of events, will abandon both his political and religious principles—will insist, in speeches which betray a temper both tyrannical and blasphemous, on his own will, no matter what the consequences. He no longer speaks for the *polis;* that role is assumed first by his son Haemon, who tells Creon that the people praise Antigone's action (though the chorus gives no sign that they share that opinion), and lastly by the spokesman for the gods, Tiresias, who tells Creon that communication with the gods has been cut off. The hearths and altars are polluted by dogs and birds who fed on the corpse. "And it is because of your will that this plague has come on the city."

Antigone never claims to speak for the *polis;* her loyalties lie elsewhere, to the ties of blood relationship, to the gods who, as she rightly insists, will disavow Creon's action. She acts and speaks for the most part as if the *polis* did not exist. In her farewell lament she mentions it only to turn away to other, more favorable, presences. "I am mocked," she replies to the chorus which has reprove her for comparing herself to Niobe. "By the gods of our fathers, why do you not wait for my

[9]This aspect of Creon's position is sympathetically explored and discussed in the context of Athenian religious beliefs in Borimir Jordan, *Servants of the Gods*, Hypomnemata 55 (Göttingen: Vandenhoek & Ruprecht, 1979), pp. 85–102.

death to insult me, but do it to my face? O *polis*, and its wealthy men!" this must be a phrase of indignant repudiation, for she goes on: "Hail, waters of Dirce, and grove of Thebes, city of chariots, you, at any rate, I have as witnesses to my sorrow, as I go unwept by friends . . . to the rockbound prison of an uncanny tomb." And in her defense of her action she makes a clear admission that the *polis* did not enter into the reckoning when she made up her mind: if it had been someone else than my brother, she says, a husband or a child, "I would not have taken up this burden, defying my fellow citizens"—(it is the same phrase Ismene used to excuse her inaction in the prologue).

Yet it was Antigone who knew what was best for the *polis*, knew that there were everlasting laws more valid than those made by man, for all his ingenuity and daring. And it was Creon, devoted champion of the *polis*, whose action aroused the anger of the gods and sowed the seed of future disaster for Thebes.

In both *Ajax* and *Antigone* the case for the *polis* was proclaimed by unworthy advocates and urged in defense of inhuman action; in the *Oedipus Tyrannos* the central figure is a model statesman, the savior of the *polis* in its hour of danger, a king whose every thought and action is dedicated to the welfare of his plague-stricken people. The protagonist this time is not a rebel against the authority of the *polis* but an embodiment of that authority itself, and in its noblest form. The voice of the *polis*, as we have heard it so far, expresses itself as a demand made on the citizens by the ruler; here the pressure is exerted on the ruler himself as the priests and citizens implore Oedipus to save them and as he suffers under his own sense of his obligation to the community. Nevertheless, this faithful servant of the *polis* will end, like Ajax and Antigone, as an outcast. The fault lies not in his attitude or conduct but in a dreadful pollution of which he is ignorant; the force which drives him on to discover it is, in the opening scenes, his devotion to the welfare of his fellow citizens.

Oedipus is not only the savior of the city to whom all men now turn for help; he is a compassionate and responsible ruler, tormented by his inability to save the citizens who have put their trust in him. "Your sorrow," he tells them, "comes on each one of you, each for himself, but my soul grieves for the city as well as for myself and you." He has already sent Creon to Delphi, and, after dismissing Creon's suggestion that the oracle's response be heard in private—it concerns the *polis* and so he proclaims: "Speak before all"—he accepts the god's command and begins the search for the murderer of Laius. The solemn curse which makes the murderer an outcast from the *polis* is pronounced, and Tiresias arrives, sent for by Oedipus. His stubborn refusal to speak is rebuked as "unfriendly to the city," and his even more categorical refusal after phrases which hint that he knows something vital is interpreted as treason: ". . . you intend to betray me and destroy the city?" His veiled accusations of Oedipus are an "insult to the city." But when he hints darkly that Oedipus' successful encounter with the Sphinx was his destruction, the answer is a proud defiance: "But if I saved this city, I don't care." Later when Creon, at the height of their altercation, returns Oedipus' characterization of him as "bad" with a charge that he is a bad ruler, he appeals indignantly to that *polis* which it has been his life's work to protect and preserve.

In the next scene Jocasta's attempt to comfort him plunges him into an agony of fear that he may have been the man who killed Laius where the three roads meet. And from this point on, though his unrelenting search for the truth is still the action of a ruler intent on the rescue of his people from the plague, it is also the convulsive effort of a frightened man to establish his own identity. At its end he stands revealed as the source of the pollution which afflicts the city and as an outcast doomed to death or exile by the terms of his own solemn curse. As he explains and defends his self-blinding he counts among the sights he could no longer bear to look on the physical features—town, tower, holy statues of the gods—of that *polis* from which he has expelled himself. He had accused Creon of conspiracy to expel him, but his future as a blind beggar in exile is the product of his own strange destiny and the zeal with which he fulfilled his function as protector and preserver of the *polis*.

In all three of these plays—*Ajax, Antigone,* and *Oedipus Tyrannos*—the action of the protagonist brings about exclusion from the society of the *polis*, in two cases through defiance of its representatives, in the other through devotion to its welfare. But in the remaining two plays, this motion is reversed: the hero begins as an outcast and ends reestablished, Oedipus in a *polis*, and Philoctetes in the *stratos* which cannot take Troy without him.[10]

Philoctetes is the most abused of all the heroes: he has been left to fend for himself for ten years, a sick man on a desert island, not because of any misconduct on his part but simply because he has been afflicted with a painful and offensive disease. The army has now learned that it cannot win

[10]On these two plays see K. Matthiessen, "Philoktet oder die Resozialisierung," in *Würzburger Jahrbücher,* N.F. 7 (1981), pp. 11ff.

without him; the man it despised and rejected must now be courted and brought back into the ranks. It will not be an easy task; in fact, since the army has given the assignment to Odysseus, whom Philoctetes is ready to shoot on sight, it can only succeed through elaborate deception. Odysseus' chosen instrument for this is the young son of Achilles, Neoptolemos.

As in the *Ajax*, the spokesman for the *polis* does it no credit. When he urges Neoptolemos to play the liar in his plot to capture Philoctetes, the argument we expect to hear, that without Philoctetes' cooperation the army cannot return home victorious, appears only as a veiled suggestion: "If you don't do this, you will inflict pain on all the Argives." The main thrust of Odysseus' argument is the advantage Neoptolemos will win for himself—his share in the glory of Troy's fall; to this he adds the prospect that if successful, Neoptolemos will be called *sophos* (clever, like Odysseus) as well as *agathos* (brave, like his father, Achilles). It is only when Neoptolemos decides to make amends for his deceit by giving back the bow that Odysseus invokes the army's name; he does so in a series of threats which begin as a challenge to arms but end ignominiously in a hurried exit: "I will go and tell this to the whole army—*they* will punish you." At the climactic moment, as Neoptolemos hands the bow back to its owner, Odysseus, in a surprise entrance which is perhaps the most abrupt in extant tragedy,[11] forbids the action "on behalf of the sons of Atreus and the army as a whole." If it had not been for Neoptolemos' intervention, he would have paid for this gesture

[11]See O. Taplin, *Greek Tragedy in Action* (Berkeley, Calif.: University of California Press, 1978), p. 32.

with his life; Philoctetes is in no mood to listen to the commands of the army. And when Neoptolemos now tries to persuade him to come to Troy he does not mention the common good of the army at all; his arguments are based on what would be best for Philoctetes. Whatever right there may have been in the community's case has been thoroughly compromised by Odyssean deceit; Philoctetes cannot be expected to trust appeals to his generosity and sense of duty after what has happened. Neoptolemos bears down hard on the fact that Philoctetes' only hope of cure from his painful sickness is to come to Troy, where the sons of Asklepios will restore him to health, so that, together, the two of them can take Troy. All this, he tells him, is fated to happen, and furthermore it is to happen this very summer. So Philoctetes should comply willingly with what must happen anyway; he will regain his health and also, by taking Troy, win the highest glory. This plea moves the outcast at first, but the memory of his wrongs comes flooding back in and he rejects it bitterly. Furthermore, he demands passage home, as promised, and Neoptolemos is in honor bound, now, to fulfil that promise, lie though it was. And Troy will not fall this summer, after all.

It does, of course; this time Philoctetes' patron and exemplar, the divine Heracles, appears to bring him into line. But not even now do we hear the argument from duty to the *polis*. Heracles makes known the will of Zeus; it is that Philoctetes, using the bow and arrows of Heracles, shall take Troy, killing Paris, the cause of all the suffering. Philoctetes is to dedicate part of the spoils at the place where he lit Heracles' funeral pyre, near his home in Oeta. And Philoctetes will be healed; Neoptolemos had promised a cure by the sons of Asklepios, but Heracles will send Asklepios himself. To these divine commands Philoctetes makes no resistance, but there is no enthusiasm in his acquiescence. There is more than a hint of regret in his farewell to the island, and his closing words are mere acceptance, no more. "Send me off with a fair wind and no complaints to where great Destiny conveys me, the wisdom of friends and the all-victorious divinity who made this decree." What he accepts is the will of Zeus, not the right of the community, in war as in peace, to demand compliance.

The Oedipus of the last play is just as much an outcast as Philoctetes; he is not a sick man, but he is old, blind, ragged, and filthy—a wandering beggar—and he has no such resource as the unerring bow and arrows of Heracles. The Greeks remembered Philoctetes only when the Trojan seer Helenos told them Troy could not be taken without him; the Thebans, on both sides, seek possession of Oedipus only when the Delphic oracle tells them his burial site will bring victory in battle to the land in which it lies. As against Philoctetes, lies, force, and persuasion are all deployed, but to no effect. But in this play no god appears to bring about the reintegration of Oedipus in the *polis*. He does become a citizen *empolin* but a citizen of Athens, not Thebes; and his citizenship begins and ends with his mysterious death, a death which, we learn from the messenger's account, is the will of the gods.

When Oedipus is challenged by the chorus to name his fatherland, he calls himself *apoptolis*—a word which can mean simply "absent from the city" but also, as it must mean here, "exile." Exiles, in Greece, had little thought for anything but their return; "the true lover of his city," says Alcibiades at Sparta, "is not the man who, unjustly deprived of her, fails to take the offensive, but the one who because of his desire for her, will go to any length to regain her" (*Peloponnesian War* 6.92.4). This is, of course, exactly the program of Polynices in *Oedipus at Colonos*. But Oedipus is no ordinary exile; he has no wish to return to Thebes. As soon as he heard that the grove which sheltered him was sacred to the Eumenides, he announced his immovable decision to stay; the gift of victory which his body brings with it is to be offered not to Thebes but to Athens.

Toward his own *polis* Oedipus is bitterly hostile; the hatred of Philoctetes for the Atridae and Odysseus was nothing compared to his for Thebes and everyone in it. His destructive hatred for his native *polis* is implicit in his recognition of the holy ground on which he stands as the place prescribed in the prophecy where he was to find rest and bring profit to those who received him and "destruction to those who drove me out and sent me here." For this "destruction," as we learn later, will not be confined to the individuals he blames for his present condition but will fall on a Theban army fighting on the ground where he lies buried. For his expulsion from Thebes he blames not only Creon and his own sons but the *polis*; he can even speak of the *polis* driving him out with violence. His rage against the *polis* of Thebes has even deeper (and darker) sources: he lays on the *polis* the responsibility for the marriage which has made his name a byword. "The city," he tells the chorus, "bound me, all unsuspecting, in a marriage with destruction, a bed of evil." It was a gift, he says later, a return for services rendered, which he wishes he had never received from Thebes. The Thebans will repay him with their blood. "This is the place," he tells Theseus, "in which I shall have victory over those who threw me out." Creon is speaking truth, for once, when he tells the old man: "You want victory over your own fatherland and your friends."

The city's claim on Oedipus' loyalty is put in the mouth of Creon, who comes, he says, "not sent by one man, but under orders from the whole citizen body." This spokesman for the *polis* is even more suspect than the older Creon of *Antigone* or the Atridae of *Ajax*, for, like Odysseus, he deals in lies. His invitation to come home pulls out all the stops of duty and affection: "Come of your own free will to the town and the home of your fathers, bidding a kind farewell to this city (Athens), for she deserves it. But your home city, as is only just, has a stronger claim on your devotion for it was she who nursed you long ago."[12] Not only does he intend, as Ismene has already told her father, to deny Oedipus burial in Theban soil; he has already seized Ismene as a hostage. He fully deserves the fury of Oedipus' rejection; the case for the *polis* could hardly have had a more contemptible spokesman.

There is another, of course, later in the play. Polynices implores Oedipus to come with him to Thebes and invokes "the springs and the gods of our people"; he promises to settle the old man in his house and settle himself there too. But he is calling for his father's help in an assault on his native city to be launched by foreign troops under his command. And his appeal is rejected with even more terrible imprecations than that of Creon.

Oedipus has a new *polis*, Athens; Theseus declares him a citizen (*empolin*) as he announces that he will settle him in the

---

[12]This customary appeal for loyalty (cf. note 5 above) happens to be falsely based: Oedipus did not grow up in Thebes—his "nurse" was Corinth.

land. But that status has not been easy to win. Though he knows, as soon as the name of the Eumenides is pronounced, that Athens is the land foretold in the prophecy as the recipient of his gift, he still has to convince the inhabitants and the king that his unsightly body and polluted name should be received into the Athenian community. He concludes his prayer to the goddesses of the grove with an appeal to Athens—"most honored city of all"—for pity: "pity this wretched ghost of Oedipus the man—this is not the body he possessed once long ago."

Pity is not what he gets from the outraged chorus of old men from Colonos. He is ordered off holy ground with a promise of protection that is broken when they know his name; they want to be rid of him. "Out! Be off! Leave this land!" Only his eloquent appeal to the reputation of Athens, protector of the weak and suppliant, saves him from expulsion; they will await the decision of the king. He has proclaimed himself to the chorus as a "savior" for Athens; with Theseus he explains the meaning of this large claim. Theseus, when he learns that the Thebans want him back, reproaches him for refusing; it is the natural reaction of any Greek. But he is admonished in his turn and accepts not only Oedipus' explanation of his gift of himself to Athenian soil but also his sermon on the instability of all things human—Thebes may be friendly now but "the same wind does not blow forever between man and man, city and city."

Oedipus is a citizen of Athens now, and when under Creon's assault he calls for help, it is Athens he is calling on for help against Thebes. The help comes in time, and Oedipus, his daughters restored to him, prepares to make good his promise. Once he hears the thunder he knows the time is short; he wants, he says to Theseus, "to die without failing to keep the promises I made to you and the city." With Theseus alone present he makes his way to where the gods impatiently summon him, and the promise is fulfilled: Theseus will hand on to his son and he to his the secret of Oedipus' last resting place and "thus," as he told the king, "the city you live in will never be sacked by the men born of the dragon's teeth." Someday, he had prophesied to Theseus, the Thebans will invade Attica; "on some small pretext they will shatter with the spear the pledged agreements which now hold. And then my sleeping, hidden corpse, cold though it be, will drink their warm blood. . . ."

These two final plays, as has often been pointed out, deal with the same situation: a community's attempt to reassert, by lies and force, control over a man it has rejected utterly and now finds essential to its welfare. This formulation is, as far as I can see, an exact description of what has been referred to in recent criticism as "an outcast's reintegration into society" or "*Resozialisierung*." It is, of course, true that Philoctetes returns to take his place in the army for the final assault on Troy and that Oedipus becomes a citizen of no mean city— welcomed by a Theseus who is the living embodiment of that Athenian civilization praised by the chorus in its famous ode. But the solution of the dilemma posed by Philoctetes' stubborn insistence on going home leaves, as Matthiessen rightly says, a "bitter aftertaste"; Hercles' warning against offending the gods when Troy falls could not fail to remind the audience that Neoptolemos would kill Priam on the altar of Zeus. Oedipus, on the other hand, turns against his own *polis* with malevolent hatred; there is a fierce exultation in his language as he dwells on the Theban blood which will be shed over his grave. Ajax prayed for destruction to fall not just on the Achaean princes who had injured him but on the whole host of the army; Oedipus knows that in his grave he will have his revenge not just on Creon and his sons but on the whole Theban host. The joyful theme of his adoption by Athens is of course dominant in the play, but the dark side of his action, the injury to his mother city, should not be forgotten.[13] It is hard to think of a mythical parallel, but a historical parallel springs immediately to mind. It is, of course, Alcibiades, who cold-bloodedly gave the Spartans advice which, followed with alacrity, led to the defeat of his native city.

Matthiessen sees, in the ambivalent attitude to the *polis* which characterizes the last two plays, Sophocles' reaction to the sordid, desperate politics of the last phase of the war. There is some warrant for this claim but it does not take into account the fact that the early plays, *Ajax* and *Antigone,* also raise questions about the right of the *polis* to demand obedience in all things—"in matters small and just, and their opposites," to quote Creon's cynical euphemism in *Antigone.* And in the *Oedipus Tyrannos* the hero's devotion to the welfare of the *polis* is the instrument of his downfall. In fact, all five of the plays which explore the relation of the tragic hero to his *polis* end by suggesting that the *polis* is not the be-all and end-all of human life, that there are powers and laws which transcend its authority. The *polis,* as Sophocles had his chorus sing

---

[13]It is given what may be deliberate emphasis by the contrast with the attitude of Theseus, who specifically exempts Thebes from blame for Creon's conduct.

in *Antigone*, is a human invention, perhaps man's greatest creation, but it is no more than that. Such an attitude would not be out of place in a poet who has been called "the last great exponent of the archaic world view," but it is a little unexpected in a man whose life was such an exemplary record of full participation in the highest councils of the city's feverish activity. And yet that very fact may explain the paradox. Without that involvement in the politics and wars of the *polis* which in its brief imperial career justified the Corinthians' claim that it "was born never to rest itself and to prevent the rest of the world from doing so," he might not have become so keenly aware of the dangers inherent in the Periclean ideal. The word *theos* does not appear in the Funeral Speech (nor, for that matter, in any of the speeches Thucydides puts in the mouth of Athens' leading statesmen);[14] there is more than a hint that this *dynamis* of Athens, which its citizens are to contemplate till they become its lovers, is the real object of Periclean religious feeling.

Jean-Pierre Vernant in the first chapter of his *Mythe et Tragédie en Grèce ancienne* summed up, in a characteristically stimulating formula, the new vision which tragedy, with its chorus representing the community, imposed on the epic heroes it put on stage. ". . . ils sont en quelque sorte mis en question devant le public. . . . Dans le cadre nouveau du jeu tragique, le héros a donc cessé d'être un modèle: il est devenu, pour lui-même et pour les autres, un problème" ("They are, in a way, under examination before the public. . . . In the new

---

[14]In the summary of Pericles' financial report to the Athenians (*Peloponnesian War* 2.13) the word occurs, but Pericles is talking about using the gold on the statue of Athena in case of emergency.

framework of tragic interplay, then, the hero has ceased to be a model. He has become, both for himself and for others, a problem").[15] For Sophocles, one is tempted to add, the *polis* also, has become a problem.

[15]Jean-Pierre Vernant and Pierre Vidal-Naquet, *Myth and Tragedy in Ancient Greece*, translated by Janet Lloyd (New York: Zone Books, 1988).

And in Better Condition

B ernard Williams's brilliant, demanding, and disturbing book[1] is the fifty-seventh volume of the Sather
Classical Lectures, which are delivered annually at
Berkeley on a classical subject. Its title calls to mind
the work of a predecessor in the series, E. R. Dodds,
who called the second chapter in his book *The Greeks
and the Irrational*[2] "From Shame-culture to Guilt-culture." The echo is deliberate; Williams's preface
makes admiring reference to Dodds, under whom he
studied Greek at Oxford, as the author of "one of
the most helpful and enduring books in the series,
and . . . one of the closest in subject matter to the
concerns of this study."

It is true that in his first two chapters Dodds is

[1]Bernard Williams, *Shame and Necessity* (Berkeley, Calif.: University
of California Press, 1993).
[2]University of California Press, 1951.

concerned, as Williams is, with "ideas of responsible action, justice, and the motivations that lead people to do things that are admired and respected." But Dodds, working with anthropological constructs such as "shame and guilt cultures," saw the ideas of the archaic Greeks on these matters as very different from ours. A shame culture, such as Dodds believed existed in Homeric times, puts high emphasis on preserving honor and on not being publicly disgraced; it relies on "external sanctions for good behavior." The allegedly more evolved guilt culture emphasizes personal responsibility and relies on "an internalized conviction of sin."[3] Others have seen the ideas of the archaic Greeks as not just different, but inferior, or rather, as Williams puts it, "primitive ideas" which "have been replaced by a more complex and refined set of conceptions that define a more mature form of ethical experience." There are, of course, real differences between our outlook and that of the archaic Greeks, but Williams rejects firmly the now fashionable picture of Greek ethical ideas and their relation to our own, which is "developmental, evolutionary, and—in an ugly word that I have found no way of avoiding—progressivist." He proposes to "stress some unacknowledged similarities between Greek conceptions and our own," unacknowledged because "it is an effect of our ethical situation, and of our relations to the ancient Greeks that we should be blind to some of the ways in which we resemble them." For in studying them we are not like cultural anthropologists who observe other societies to learn about

[3]The quotations are from Ruth Benedict, *The Chrysanthemum and the Sword* (Boston: Houghton Mifflin, 1946) where the terms shame- and guilt-culture were first used.

"human diversity, other social or cultural achievements, or, again, what has been spoiled or set aside by the history of European domination." The Greeks "are among our cultural ancestors" and to learn about them is "part of self-under-standing" and "will continue to be so," for the "Greek past is specially the past of modernity . . . the modern world was a European creation presided over by the Greek past."

Yet this is not, in itself, reason enough to study the ethical ideas of the ancient Greeks; "it is too late to assume that the Greek past must be interesting just because it is 'ours.' " Such study would have importance (and here Williams is quoting Nietzsche) only if it is "untimely," so that what it does is "to act against the age, and by so doing, to have an effect on the age, and, let us hope, to the benefit of a future age."

Such untimeliness can indeed, Williams asserts, be claimed for an attempt "to understand how our ideas are related to the Greeks', because, if we do so, this can specially help us to see ways in which our ideas may be wrong." And he goes on to make a challenging claim. "In some ways . . . the basic ethical ideas possessed by the Greeks were different from ours, and also in better condition. In some other respects, it is rather that we rely on much the same conceptions as the Greeks, but we do not acknowledge the extent to which we do so."

"[A]nd also in better condition." This surprising phrase seems to go beyond a mere rejection of the progressivist view, to substitute for it what might be described, in an equally ugly but apparently nonexistent word, as "regressivist." Coming from a professor of Greek it might well be dismissed as one more inflated paean to the glory that was Greece, but Williams is White's Professor of Moral Philosophy at Oxford and Monroe Deutsch Professor of Philosophy at Berkeley as well as the author of two books, *Moral Luck*[4] and *Ethics and the Limits of Philosophy*,[5] that explore, with brilliant insight and cogent argument, the moral dilemmas and ethical thought of our own distracted time.

He is not, of course, advocating a simple return to the ancient Greek "ideas of human agency, responsibility, regret, and necessity." Their embodiment in literature, especially in tragedy, where the supernatural plays a part that is alien to our conceptions of divinity or necessity, demands "that we should look for analogies in our experience and our sense of the world to the necessities they express." This, as he goes on to say, "would be a large task, both historical and philosophical," one which in this book he hopes "to situate . . . and to help us, perhaps, to reach an understanding of our relations to the Greeks that will make clearer what the task means." He has no illusions, either, about Greek society, as his fifth chapter, which deals with slavery and the subjection of women, makes amply clear. Nor does he think that there was no development, no evolution of ethical ideas in the centuries that separate us from the archaic Greeks. It is just that he does not think that the developments deserve to be characterized as "progress."

Williams's devastating case against the progressivist view begins with a discussion of Homeric man, or rather, as he is careful to point out, the fictional characters of the Homeric epics,

[4]Cambridge University Press, 1981.
[5]Harvard University Press, 1985.

whose thoughts and actions are described in the heroic style created by many generations of oral bards, a style rich in formulaic phrases shaped by the stringent metrical demands of the epic hexameter. Bruno Snell's still influential vision of Homeric man as one who "does not yet regard himself as the source of his own decisions" is one of Williams's targets here. It is a vision, he says, in which, "by an analogy to individual moral development, Homer's characters are seen, in effect, as childish." Critiques of Snell's theories, from many different angles, have not been lacking in the years since the publication of his *Discovery of the Mind*,[6] but none of them can claim the authority of a moral philosopher who sets out "to show . . . that many of the most basic materials of our ethical outlook are present in Homer and that what the critics find lacking are not so much the benefits of moral maturity as the accretions of misleading philosophy."

His analysis of Snell's vision of the "Homeric Greeks" as men who had no conception of the body as a unit or of the mind as anything other than "components" defined by the analogy of physical organs exposes the ideas that lie at its base: a distinction between body and soul and "the assumption that, not only in later Greek thought, but truly, a distinction between soul and body describes what we are." However, as he remarks, "We do not, *pace* Plato, Descartes, Christianity, and Snell, all agree that we each have a soul."

And the phrase "what we are" is a significant echo of some similar words he used earlier, in his devastating critique of

---

[6]It has often been attacked before, from different perspectives. The most thorough assault is that of Sir Hugh Lloyd-Jones, *The Justice of Zeus* 1971 (University of California Press). The second edition (1983) contains a characteristically vigorous reply to criticisms of the first.

Snell's denial that Homeric man thought of the body as a unity. He there cited the passage in *Iliad* XXIV where Priam asks Hermes "whether my son still lies / beside the ships, or whether by now he has been hewn / limb from limb and thrown before the dogs by Achilles." He receives the answer that Hector is still intact and uncorrupted—"the blessed immortals care for your son, / though he is nothing but a corpse." Both of them clearly "grasp the body as a unit" as opposed to the separate limbs; their words clearly imply an idea of the body as a person, as a whole. Snell, he says, has

> overlooked what is in front of everyone's eyes; and in the case of Homer and others of the Greeks, this oversight is quite specially destructive of their sensibility, which was basically formed by the thought that this thing that will die, which unless it is properly buried will be eaten by dogs and birds, is exactly the thing that one is.

This use of Homer's text to confute Snell's theories is typical of Williams's handling of the issues: it is evident again, for example, in his dismissal of the idea that "Homer does not know genuine personal decisions; even when a hero is shown pondering two alternatives the intervention of the gods plays the key role." This is, as he says, simply not true; every reader of Homer will recall passages in which a hero deliberates and decides on action independently of divine admonition or advice. But even when a god does intervene, it is not, as he wittily puts it, a case of "simply making people do things—winding them up, so to speak, and pointing them in a certain direction." The god gives reasons for one or the other of the courses the hero is weighing, or urges a course of action the hero has not considered, "but whatever kind of reason the god gives an agent, the question that the god helps to answer is a question asked by an agent deciding for reasons—and when the agent decides for those reasons and acts on them, he acts on his own reasons."

Normally Williams's attack on the progressivist case takes the form of close philosophical analysis, but he can also bring to bear a mordant wit. Snell at one point refers to a passage in the *Iliad* in which Glaukos, wounded in the arm and in great pain, can no longer fight. He prays to Apollo—"make well this strong wound; / and put the pains to sleep, give me strength"—and Apollo "made the pains stop . . . and put strength into his spirit." For Snell this is one more example of a missing element in the archaic conception of the personality. "We believe," Snell writes, "that a man advances from an earlier situation by an act of his own will, through his own power. If Homer, on the other hand, wants to explain the source of an increase in strength he has no course but to say that the responsibility lies with a god." Williams points out that Apollo eased Glaukos' pain, healed his wound, and made him able to do what he very much wanted to do—rescue the corpse of his friend Sarpedon, who had just been killed by Patroclus. "If Snell really thought," he goes on, "that these services would be replaced in the modern world by an effort of will, I am glad he was not in charge of a hospital."

Sometimes Williams's criticism of the progressivist view takes the form neither of philosophical analysis nor of scathing wit but of what can best be described as the revelatory radiance of plain common sense. As, for example, his second reason why "we cannot conclude from the role of the gods that Homer has no concept of deciding for oneself." It is, he says, "embarrassingly simple." It is that "the Homeric gods

themselves deliberate and come to conclusions": they do so in
the same formulas of doubt and decision used by mortals
when no god intervenes; and even if they always intervened in
human decisions, "it would still not show that Homer lacked
the concept of a deciding for oneself. He could not apply to
the gods a concept of decision he did not have."

If the reason is "embarrassingly simple," the people who
should feel embarrassed are literary scholars of the Homeric
epics like myself, who should not have had to wait for a
moral philosopher to produce from the text so clear and obvious an objection to Snell's picture of Homeric man as innocent of the concepts of choice and decision. In his preface
Williams warns the reader that he is "not primarily a classical
scholar" but "someone who received what used to be called a
classical education, became a philosopher, and has kept in
touch with Greek studies primarily through work in ancient
philosophy." But in this book, though he does discuss Greek
philosophy (Plato and Aristotle in particular), most of his exemplary texts are drawn not from philosophers but from
poets, whom he tries to discuss "as poets, not as providing
rhythmic examples for philosophy."

He is aware that his book "does not stay within the limits
that this experience might advise"; he can even refer light-
heartedly to his classical expertise as his *violon d'Ingres*. He is
overmodest. Time and again the professional classicist will
find in these pages arguments drawn from Greek poetic texts
and interpretations of passages in those texts that will command his respectful admiration—witness, to take one example, Williams's masterly discussion of the puzzling distinction Phaedra, in Euripides' *Hippolytus*, makes between the two
kinds of *aidos* ("shame").

Williams's main purpose in these chapters is to expose the fallacies inherent in the claim that the Homeric mind, because Homer had no equivalents for such words as "intention" and "will," functioned on a more primitive level than ours. "Beneath the terms that mark differences between Homer and ourselves lies a complex net of concepts in terms of which particular actions are explained, and this net was the same for Homer as it is for us." He goes on to cite the passage in Book V of the *Odyssey* in which the hero, shipwrecked naked on the Phaeacian shore, considers in detail the alternatives open to him: to sleep where he is, by the river mouth, and risk death from cold and exhaustion, or to go inland to find shelter and risk death as prey to some wild animal. He finally decides to go inland. "Granted," Williams asks, "that Homer has so much, what is it that he is supposed not to have? What is this concept of the will that . . . the early Greeks lacked, and perhaps no Greeks ever fully developed?" Homer does indeed have

> no word that means, simply, "decide." But he has the notion.
> . . . All that Homer seems to have left out is the idea of another mental action that is supposed necessarily to lie between coming to a conclusion and acting on it: and he did well in leaving it out, since there is no such action, and the idea of it is the invention of bad philosophy.

In the two chapters that follow, he deals with the concepts of intention, responsibility, shame, and guilt with the same enlightening combination of careful philosophical analysis and thoughtful readings of Greek texts that distinguished his critique of Snell. An example of such reading is his discussion of "intention" in the lines of the *Odyssey* (XXII, 154–56) in which Telemachus confesses to his father that he had left the door of the armory open, thus allowing his mother's suitors access to the weapons with which they are now preparing to defend themselves. He obviously did not intend to do so; it was an oversight. "We cannot," Williams comments,

> . . . say that Homer has a certain concept simply because he presents us with an incident that we would describe in terms of that concept. It is reasonable, however, to say that there is a certain concept in Homer when he and his characters make distinctions that can be understood only in terms of that concept. This is certainly true of intention, with regard to what Telemachus says.

And there are other similar passages that strengthen the case, and "might well be enough to let us say that Homer had a concept of intention even if he had no word that was related to the general notion at all."

Thus far we have the logic and the careful distinctions of the moral philosopher. However, the case is then buttressed by the keen observation of the literary and philological reader. "But, in fact, he has such a word, *hekon*, which very often means 'intentionally' or 'deliberately' and in the *Iliad* rarely means anything else." So, in Book X of the *Iliad*, Diomedes throws a spear at Dolon and misses him, *hekon*, deliberately. The spear goes close enough to him to frighten him and stop him in his tracks; he is taken alive, so that Diomedes and Odysseus can extract vital information from him before they kill him. "It is a very significant fact about this word," Williams points out, "that it occurs in the *Iliad* and the *Odyssey* only in the nominative singular: it works like an adverb, attached to verbs of action. This in itself focuses its sense on intention."

In the long and detailed discussion that follows, centered first on the concept of responsibility and then on shame and guilt, Williams still moves from texts, tragic as well as Homeric, to analysis of their underlying assumptions and comparison with our own conceptions, or, as he rather acidly puts it at one point, "what we think we think." There is no point in trying to summarize his treatment of these difficult problems. He is a writer who never uses an unnecessary word and his skillfully constructed argument must be read in its entirety for full comprehension and appreciation. But his conclusion, on the subject of responsibility, echoes his basic claim that though in many of these matters our ideas are different from those of the Greeks, they are not necessarily clearer or better. In an analysis of two passages in the *Iliad*, for example, in one of which responsibility is admitted and in the other partly denied, he finds the concepts of cause, intention, state, and response. "These," he says, "are the basic elements of any conception of responsibility." These four elements, however, can be adjusted to each other in many ways and "there is not, and there never could be, just one appropriate way" of doing so—"just one correct conception of responsibility." Not only are these elements not always related to one another in the same way; they can themselves be interpreted in many different ways. One has only to think of a murder trial in which it has been established that the defendant is guilty, definitely established as the cause. But intention, state (of mind at the time), and response are all debatable and interrelated matters.

Some of the ways that the Greeks had of interpreting and arranging these materials . . . are different from any that we now have or would want to have. Other ways they had are the same as some of ours, while yet others speak to concerns that we might do better to acknowledge. Above all, what we must not suppose is that we have evolved a definitely just and appropriate way of combining these materials—a way, for instance, called the concept of moral responsibility. We have not.

In his fourth chapter, "Shame and Autonomy," in which many of his examples are drawn from Greek tragedy, Williams rejects the idea, "which is associated particularly with the work of A. H. Adkins, that in the Homeric shame culture individuals were overwhelmingly concerned with their own success at the expense of other people" and also the idea that "the shame system . . . supposedly pins the individual's sense of what should be done merely onto expectations of what others will think of him or her." In a demanding and convincing argument he confutes these two theories with examples drawn from tragedy (*Ajax, Philoctetes,* and *Hippolytus*) as well as from Homer; they show that the archaic conception of shame is much more subtle and complex than critics have been able to see or willing to admit, that the word *aidos* "cannot merely mean 'shame,' but must cover something like guilt as well." Which does not mean that "Homeric society was not, after all, a shame culture," for

what people's ethical emotions are depends significantly on what they take them to be. The truth about Greek societies,

and in particular the Homeric, is not that they failed to recognize any of the reactions that we associate with guilt, but
that they did not make of those reactions the special thing
that they became when they are separately recognized as
guilt.

This difficult chapter, with its important endnote, "Mechanisms of Shame and Guilt," is the most professionally philosophical in the book, but it is also, in its sensitive discussion
of the texts and its illuminating footnotes, the most rewarding for the literary and philological reader, for it exposes the
inadequacy of most of the terms, such as "shame" and "necessity," in which matters vital for an understanding of the epic
and tragic texts have so far been discussed.

The "mechanisms of shame," Williams writes, impose on
the individual "a necessity to act in certain ways," a necessity
"grounded in the *ethos*, the projects, the individual nature of
the agent [i.e., the acting person], and in the way he conceives
the relation of his life to other people's." But there is also a
form of external necessity, one "at the other end of the universe, as one might say," a divine necessity like the plan of
Zeus that caused the deaths of so many heroes at Troy. What
happens to an individual may indeed be the result of a divine
decision or purpose, a necessity, *anangke*, but it may seem to
him or her to be simply the effect of luck, *tuche*. Both words
are combined in a striking phrase Sophocles puts in the
mouth of Tecmessa in the *Ajax*. Warned that Ajax, who has
gone off alone to the seashore, may never return, subject as he
is to the wrath of Athena for the rest of the day, she implores
the chorus to help her shield him from this "necessary luck,"
anangkaias tuches—an expression that, as Williams puts it, "un-

nervingly combines most of the thoughts available about supernatural necessity."

But earlier in the play she has used the same phrase to describe her own fate; "necessary luck" or "chance" has made her the slave, the possession of Ajax. This, she says, "was decided somehow by the gods, but most of all by your hand." To be enslaved may be the result of a divine decision, or it may be just the play of chance, but for the victim it is the imposition of necessity, of force. In the ancient world there was no more dreaded, no more spectacular example of bad luck than to be enslaved, to be one moment free and the next moment the possession of another. It is with the prevalence of slavery, a radical difference between the Greek world and our own, that Williams's fifth chapter, "Necessary Identities," is mainly concerned, though he also discusses the subordinate position of women.

Slavery was so basic an institution that though occasional doubts about its justness were voiced, no free Greek could imagine that civilized life was possible without it. One feature of it that helped mask the ugliness of the relation between master and slave was the fact that, in Athens at least, the slaves were mostly foreigners, barbaroi, a word that simply means people whose native language was not Greek. In modern Athens, in the Epigraphical Museum and the museum of the Agora, visitors can study the broken remnants of an inscription that recorded, in 414 B.C., the prices paid for the confiscated property of the men who had been denounced as responsible for the mutilation of the Hermae on the eve of the departure of the great expedition to Sicily. (The men concerned had either been executed or exiled, or, like Alcibiades, had avoided arrest by going or staying abroad.)

Among the goods auctioned off were forty-five slaves, and in thirty-five cases their origin is recorded. They were Thracians (the largest group), Carians, Scythians, Illyrians, Syrians, and a small group (three) of house-bred slaves. Colchis, Lydia, Macedonia, Phrygia, Messenia, and Cappadocia each contributed one to the total. But it could happen to Greeks too, especially in time of war; the Athenians in the Peloponnesian War, first at Scione and then at Melos, put the male population to the sword and sold the women and children. It may even have happened to Plato, and in peacetime; some writers report that Dionysius, the tyrant of Syracuse, offended by Plato's freedom of speech, had him sold into slavery, from which he was rescued by the generosity of friends. The sources for this story are late, confused, and contradictory,[7] but even if it is not true, the fact that it was widely disseminated and evidently believed suggests that no one in the ancient world could discount the possibility of such "a contingent and uniquely brutal disaster."

Williams's main concern in this chapter is with Aristotle's attempt, in the first book of the *Politics*, to define slavery as "natural." Such a view, Aristotle informs us, is opposed to the opinion of "some people" who hold that it is "against nature (for it is by convention that one man is a slave and another is free, and in nature there is no difference); therefore it is not just, either; since it is imposed by force." Williams analyzes, as political philosophy, Aristotle's tortuous and in the end contradictory arguments about slavery, and the analysis does indeed serve to demonstrate, as Williams announced that it would, "the truth that if there is something worse than ac-

[7]See Alice Riginos Swift, *Platonica* (Leiden: Brill, 1976), pp. 86–92.

cepting slavery, it consists in defending it." The ancient Greeks did not try to defend it; the opponents of Aristotle's view, those he described as "some people," were in fact a large majority of his fellow Greeks. They recognized that slavery was based on the use of force against human beings who were unlucky enough to have been reduced to a servile condition. But they could imagine no alternative; the life of the citizens in the *polis*, the only form of civilized organization they knew or could imagine, would have been impossible without that leisure they prized so highly, leisure to haunt the gymnasium, the roofed porches where men congregated for conversation and dispute, the theater, the assembly, the courts, and all the varied, time-consuming duties and pleasures of the free male citizen.

Slaves in Athens worked not only as domestic servants and farmhands but also in industry. Cephalus, for example, the wealthy old man whose house Plato chose as the setting of the *Republic*, owned a shield factory that employed 120 slaves. And the Athenian state treasury, the source of those silver coins—"Attic owls"—that became the most prized currency of the Greek world, depended on slave labor for the exploitation of the silver mines at Laurion. Individual slave owners leased their property to the state for a fixed period and made a handsome profit. Nicias, the wealthy statesman whom Thucydides, commenting on his execution by the Syracusans, characterized as a man who "of all the Greeks of my time least deserved such a fate, since the whole course of his life had been regulated with strict attention to virtue," owned a thousand slaves who worked in the mines at Laurion.[8]

[8]Xenophon, *Vect.*, iv.14.

The silver mines there, long since worked out, are still in good condition and can be visited. The mine shafts, two meters by 1.30, go down as far as 130 meters; the miners climbed down on ladders and carried the ore up in baskets. The galleries along which they had to crawl to get to the work face are one meter high and from .6 to .9 meters wide. I once crawled into one of these galleries—not, needless to say, one that ran off a shaft. It was at ground level, cut into a rock face. In five minutes or so I was round a sharp bend and in total darkness. By this time my hands and knees were badly scraped by the scarred surface of the rock floor; to get out I had to crawl backward. I got stuck in the bend and for a few moments wondered if I would ever get out, but finally did, with badly scratched knees and hands and frayed shirt and trousers. How anyone could work in such conditions, with the crude oil lamps that were all the ancient world could provide, I cannot imagine. But the Laurion miners worked ten hours on and ten hours off.

When, in 413 B.C., the Spartans, following the advice of Alcibiades, established a permanent fort on Attic territory at Decelea, twenty thousand Athenian slaves made their way there in the following years, and there can be no doubt that many of them, perhaps most of them, were runaways from Laurion. In fact Thucydides pictures Alcibiades assuring the Spartans that one result of fortifying Decelea would be the Athenian loss of the revenues from the silver mines.[9]

Slavery was unjustifiable, and nobody but Aristotle seems to have tried to defend it since "considerations of justice and injustice were immobilised by the demands of what was seen

[9]VI. 91, 7.

as social and economic necessity." But Williams allows us scant grounds for complacency. "We have social practices," he writes,

> in relation to which we are in a situation much like that of the Greeks with slavery. We recognise arbitrary and brutal ways in which people are handled by society, ways that are conditioned, often, by no more than exposure to luck. We have the intellectual resources to regard the situation of these people, and the systems that allow these things, as unjust, but are uncertain whether to do so, partly because we have seen the corruption and collapse of supposedly alternative systems, partly because we have no settled opinion on the question about which Aristotle tried to contrive a settled opinion, how far the existence of a worthwhile life for some people involves the imposition of suffering on others.

It is a point made in vivid and personal terms by Sir Kenneth Dover in his short but intriguing book *The Greeks*,[10] where he discusses the injustice of Greek slavery. But Dover continues:

> What are we to say of conditions which are very different from slavery in the eye of the jurist or the economic historian, but not all that different at the receiving end? I think, for example, of my great-grandfather, orphaned in 1848 and going to work in a factory at the age of eleven, where he was lashed across the back by the foreman if he grew dozy at the end of a long day.

"Slave" and "free" were one pair of "necessary identities"; the other was "man" and "woman." Aristotle had to work

[10]University of Texas Press, 1980, p. 28. The book is based on his participation in a BBC television series of the same name. It is a lively and stimulating introduction to Greek civilization.

very hard to try to prove that the first pair were "natural" identities; the second presented no problem since it was "received opinion" and "the conventional view" that men and women had different social roles to play. A respectable woman's place was in the home, the *oikos*, where she raised the children, trained and supervised the domestic slaves, managed the storage and distribution of grain, oil, and wine, and helped to spin the wool and weave it to make the family's clothes. A woman at the loom, in fact, was an artistic cliché of the vase-painters and a literary cliché of the poets; in the *Odyssey* not only does Penelope weave her never-to-be-finished web but even the goddess Circe, when first seen by Eurylochus, was "singing while she went to and fro on her great loom."

For most Greeks the biological identities were also social identities. "There was by nature a position to be filled, and there were people who by nature occupied it. In trying to show that being a slave was a necessary identity, Aristotle was, up to a point, suggesting that if slavery were properly conducted, slaves would become what women actually were." But, again, Williams does not allow us to congratulate ourselves too loudly.

> Quite apart from the fact that prejudice based on traditional religious conceptions flourishes in the contemporary world, the idea that gender roles are imposed by nature is alive in "modern," scientistic forms. In particular, the more crassly unreflective contributions of sociobiology to this subject represent little more than continuations of Aristotelian anthropology by other means.

The final chapter, "Possibility, Freedom, and Power," though it too bases its argument on detailed and enlightening discussion of Greek literary texts, is, at least for those who, like the reviewer, are not initiates in the analytic school of moral philosophy, the most difficult. It is also the most rewarding, for in it the themes of earlier chapters—"necessity imposed on some human beings by others" and "the necessity encountered when an agent concludes that he must act in a certain way" are linked to a different and more mysterious necessity: what was "meant when an ancient Greek said that something was brought about by a god." This is a necessity that is "not part of our world."

It is, however, a necessity by which many Greek tragedies, as Williams says, are "shaped" and his discussion begins with an examination of two passages that have given rise to much scholarly controversy, both of them from tragedies of Aeschylus: Agamemnon's decision to sacrifice his daughter at Aulis, and Eteocles' decision to fight against his brother at Thebes. Agamemnon's decision (and Williams points out that he does not, as some have translated the phrase, "submit to the harness of necessity," but puts it on "as someone puts on armour") is a choice between two evils, a choice imposed by the goddess Artemis.

For reasons not explained in the play, Artemis decrees that only the sacrifice of his daughter would enable his stalled fleet to sail. In the case of Eteocles the necessity is not suddenly imposed; it has been in the background for some time. Eteocles decides to fight his brother, and answers the attempts of the chorus to dissuade him by sounding the themes of justice, shame, and honor. But at the same time he realizes that he is fulfilling the curse of his father, Oedipus, and that what he is doing has been decreed by the gods. Neither of these situations, Williams claims, involves "immediate fatalism or anything like it." Necessity here "presents itself to the agent as having produced the circumstances in which he must act, and he decides in the light of those circumstances." But it may also shape events without presenting itself at all; it may be recognized only after the event, or announced beforehand but only in riddling, ambiguous terms, through omens or oracles.

In such cases the agent may, like Laius and Jocasta when they exposed their child on the mountain, or Oedipus, when he turned his back on Corinth and walked towards Thebes, take steps designed to avoid fulfillment of the prophecy that nonetheless have the effect of bringing it about. For those involved, the "necessity . . . applied to human actions was purposive or at least had the shape of the purposive." And this notion "introduces . . . the idea of being in someone's power." In the archaic and tragic vision of the world the purpose was not seen as benevolent; it belonged "to an order of things" that had "the shape and the discouraging effect of a hostile plan, a plan that remains incurably hidden from us."

Williams sees Euripides as a dissenter from this view, but hardly along optimistic lines; he abandons "these expressions of a shaping necessity" and subjects "his audience as much as his characters to the uncertainties of an unnerving chance." Unlike Tecmessa he sees no connection between necessity and chance; for him *tuche* (luck) is not *anangkaia* (necessity). Between these two views of the universe as shaped by external necessity and subject to blind chance there stands, "revealingly," says Williams, a more optimistic one, "associated with Protagoras"—that we may hope to control the political and practical world by empirical, rational, planning. It is a view implicit in the first of the speeches put in the mouth of Pericles by Thucydides in his history of the Peloponnesian War, though he himself had "a powerful sense of the limitations of foresight, and of the uncontrollable impact of chance."

Sophocles, in whom Dodds saw "the last great exponent of the archaic world-view," and Thucydides, in whose book the gods play no part and who had nothing but contempt for oracles and prophecies, may seem at first sight to have little or nothing in common. But Williams sees them as similar in their refusal to believe, as Plato, Aristotle, Kant, and Hegel did, that "the universe of history or the structure of human reason can, when properly understood, yield a pattern that makes sense of human life and human aspirations." Different though they are in so many other respects, they stand, together with Homer and other archaic poets and thinkers, apart from

> all those who have thought that somehow or other, in this life or the next, morally if not materially, as individuals or as an historical collective, we shall be safe; or, if not safe, at least reassured that at some level of the world's constitution there is something to be discovered that makes ultimate sense of our concerns.

Though we can join Thucydides in his acceptance of the possibility that "the actual turn of events may proceed on just as stupid a course as the plans of human beings," the Sophoclean necessity, with its gods and prophecies, is not "part of our world." This sort of necessity "is like the operation of an effective agent, but this agent, unlike the Homeric gods with their individual schemes, has no characteristics except purpose and power . . . he has, so to speak, no style." So, in our world, "social reality can act to crush a worthwhile, significant, character or project without displaying either the lively individual purposes of a pagan god or the world-historical significance of a Judaic, a Christian, or a Marxist teleology."

The last pages of *Shame and Necessity* spell out what Williams meant by his initial claim that the ethical ideas possessed by the Greeks "were different from ours and also in better condition." The justification of that startling phrase turns out to be that most of what are commonly regarded as improvements on the ethical ideas of the archaic Greeks, that "complex and refined set of conceptions that define a more mature form of ethical experience," are illusions or "myths," conceptions that do not stand up to philosophical examination. In the centuries since Homer, Sophocles, and Thucydides, we have acquired a lot of intellectual baggage that we would be better off without. "The Greeks," Williams quotes Nietzsche's brilliant paradox, "were superficial out of profundity."

"We are in an ethical condition," he sums up,

that lies not only beyond Christianity, but beyond its Kantian and its Hegelian legacies. . . . We know that the world was not made for us, or we for the world, that our history tells no purposive story, and that there is no position outside the world or outside history from which we might hope to authenticate our activities. We have to acknowledge the hideous costs of many human achievements that we value, including this reflective sense itself, and recognize that there is no redemptive Hegelian history or universal Leibnizian cost-benefit analysis to show that it will come out well enough in the end. In important ways, we are, in our ethical situation, more like human beings in antiquity than any Western people have been in the meantime. More particularly, we are like those who, from the fifth century and earlier, have left us traces of a consciousness that had not yet been touched by Plato's and Aristotle's attempts to make our ethical relations to the world fully intelligible.

Our world is of course very different from the world of Sophocles, and Williams is not countenancing nostalgic fantasies. But if, as he says, "we find things of a special power and beauty in what has survived from that world, it is encouraging to think that we might move beyond marvelling at them, to putting them, or bits of them, to modern uses." And he closes the long argument by quoting, in his own elegant translation, an apposite image from Pindar:

> If someone with a sharp axe
> hacks off the boughs of a great oak tree,
> and spoils its handsome shape;
> although its fruit has failed, yet it can give an account of
> itself
> if it comes later to a winter fire
> or if it rests on the pillars of some palace
> and does a sad task among foreign walls,
> when there is nothing left in the place it came from.[11]

[11]Pythian, iv. 264–69.

Philosopher and *Polis*

I first met I. F. Stone in the early seventies, when I was the director of Harvard's Center for Hellenic Studies, in Washington. He had already, for health reasons, closed down the remarkable *I. F. Stone's Weekly,* a classic of investigative reporting whose issues were awaited with eager anticipation by most of its subscribers but with nervous apprehension by the White House staff or at the Pentagon. In his retirement he had gone back to the study of ancient Greek, which he had started years before, in college. Greek, he had discovered, was an indispensable tool for his major project, a history of free speech. This was a concept that had first seen the light in the context of Athenian democracy in the fifth century B.C., and Stone had found that "one could not make vital political or philosophical inferences from translations, not because the translators were incompetent but because the Greek terms were not fully congruent . . . with their English equivalents." One chapter

This essay first appeared in *The Atlantic,* January 1988.

in *The Trial of Socrates*,[1] in fact, is devoted to a study of the four ancient Greek words for "free speech." But his studies in Greek literature brought him squarely up against the problem of the trial and execution of Socrates, who was convicted not of offenses against the law but on vague charges that barely masked an intolerance of his opinions and teaching.

I saw much of Stone in the ensuing years, as he studied in the library of the Center. We often discussed Greek texts (he was reading the *Oresteia* and Plato as well), and I heard him lecture on the problem of Socrates' execution as he tried out his ideas before scholarly audiences. When the book was ready for the press, I was called in as a technical adviser on such small but worrisome matters as the transliteration of Greek names. So, though I cannot claim to have been present at the conception, I was there, so to speak, for the gestation and the birth, and have been invited to report on the well-being of the offspring, *The Trial of Socrates*.

As any reader of *I. F. Stone's Weekly* could have predicted, it is a lively specimen, a challenging investigative probe of the evidence. Stone has read the texts the way he did the *Pentagon Papers*—with an eye for the significant detail and the latent connection. His book is an attempt to reconstruct the "missing case for the prosecution." Our picture of the event is based exclusively on accounts written by admiring disciples of the defendant: the gossipy memoirs of Xenophon and the portrait of Socrates, in debate and in the courtroom, drawn by a philosopher pupil who was also a literary genius—Plato, son of Ariston.

Plato's unforgettable re-creation of Socrates' life and death

[1] I. F. Stone, *The Trial of Socrates* (Boston: Little, Brown, 1988).

presents us with a puzzle: How could the fifth-century Athenians, of all people, put to death the wise, witty, and noble figure we see at intellectual work and play in the dialogues? The trial, Stone says in his preface, "was a black mark for Athens and the freedom it symbolized. . . . How could Athens have been so untrue to itself?" He set out to discover "how it could have happened" and to uncover the real, unspoken charges that Socrates was facing.

He finds the grounds for Athenian hostility to Socrates in "three basic philosophical questions" on which Socrates "differed . . . profoundly" from his fellow citizens "and, indeed, from the ancient Greeks generally." The first and most serious disagreement was over the nature of the human community. For most ancient Greeks it was a *polis*, a city-state ruled by its citizens; for Socrates it was a "herd," which had to be ruled by a "shepherd," or, as he often puts it in Plato's dialogues, "by one who knows"—government by an expert. The second disagreement stemmed from Socrates' conviction that virtue is knowledge. But since—as his search for definitions by cross-examination so often and so brilliantly revealed—true knowledge is almost impossible to attain, this position reinforced the first, denying the fundamental democratic principle that all citizens possessed the modicum of understanding needed to run their common affairs. "If few of us are originators," Pericles said in his Funeral Speech, "we are all sound judges of a policy." Lastly, Socrates "preached and practiced withdrawal from the political life of the city," a far cry from the ideal of citizen participation proclaimed in the Funeral Speech: "If a man takes no interest in public affairs we . . . do not commend him as quiet but consider him useless."

Socrates' distaste for democracy was not merely theoretical

but was accompanied by a snobbish contempt for the men who constituted the bulk of the democratic assembly. "Dunces and weaklings," Socrates called them, according to Xenophon, "fullers, cobblers, builders, smiths, farmers, merchants or traders."

In the *Memorabilia*, Xenophon, who knew Socrates but was absent from Athens at the time of his trial and death, defends his memory against an attack made on it by a writer he does not name, but who was almost certainly a rhetorician named Polycrates. In his pamphlet (which has not survived), Polycrates stated that Socrates "often recited" the lines from Book 2 of Homer's *Iliad* which tell how Odysseus restores order when the Achaean troops react in disconcerting fashion to Agamemnon's rash decision to test their morale by suggesting that they give up the siege of Troy and go home. Instead of indignantly rejecting the proposal and reaffirming their unshakable determination to fight on to victory, they rush for their ships in a wild melee. Odysseus, at the suggestion of the goddess Athena, takes Agamemnon's royal scepter in hand and proceeds to restore order in the ranks:

> Whenever Odysseus met some man of rank, a king,
> he'd halt and hold him back with winning words:
> "My friend—it's wrong to threaten you like a coward,
> but you stand fast, you keep your men in check."
>
> . . .
>
> When he caught some common soldier shouting out,
> he'd beat him with the scepter, dress him down:
> "You *fool*, sit still! Obey the commands of others,
> your superiors—you, you deserter, rank coward.[2]

[2]Translated by Robert Fagles (New York: Viking Penguin, 1990).

Socrates, according to his accuser, interpreted this passage as Homer's approval of the practice of beating commoners and poor people. Xenophon denies that Socrates ever said anything of the kind; his reading of Odysseus' speech to the common soldiers is that "those who perform no service either in word or action, who are incapable of helping the army or the city in time of need, especially if they are insolent into the bargain, should be stopped, even if they happen to be very rich." So far, so good (though in the Homeric context Socrates' interpretation of the passage is not easy to accept), but Xenophon, as Stone points out, is not playing fair. For Odysseus' speech goes on beyond the point at which he cuts it off, and the last lines of the speech are such pure gold for Polycrates' portrait of an antidemocratic Socrates that he must surely have cited them.

> How can all Achaeans be masters here in Troy?
> Too many kings can ruin an army—mob rule!
> Let there be one commander, one master only . . .

"Here," as Stone points out, "democracy is directly attacked . . . an antidemocrat could find no better text in Homer."

Socrates' distrust of the common man was combined with an admiration for the regimented way of life of Athens' opponent, Sparta. But these sentiments were not unique with Socrates. They were the age-old prejudices of Athenian aristocrats, the clichés of oligarchic conspirators. And two of Socrates' young associates, Charmides and Critias, were prominent members of the so-called Thirty Tyrants, who, with a Spartan garrison in support, imposed a reign of terror on a defeated Athens at the end of the Peloponnesian War.

Another young associate of Socrates', Alcibiades, deserted to the Spartans when political enemies made capital of his licentious way of life to bring charges of impiety against him. The advice he gave the Spartans resulted in tremendous damage to Athenian interests.

But when Socrates was arraigned, in 399 B.C., his unpopular views had been common knowledge for years. Aristophanes' *Clouds* (423 B.C.) was neither the first nor the last comic travesty of his personality and teaching. Socrates was seventy years old. The Athenians had submitted to his infuriating questioning for decades. Why did they suddenly decide to prosecute him? Why not wait for this eccentric figure to give their ears a rest by dying a natural death?

Stone attributes the decision to what he calls the "Three Earthquakes": the temporary overthrow of the democracy by oligarchic conspirators, in 411; the ascendance of the Spartan-backed regime of the Thirty Tyrants, in 404; and, in 401, just two years before the trial, the unsuccessful attempt by members of the Thirty to renew the civil war. The generous terms of the amnesty proclaimed when the democracy had been restored in 403 had ruled out the possibility of referring in court to Socrates' political opinions and his close association with oligarchic leaders. But the revolutionary upheavals of the closing years of the century had eroded the Athenians' tolerance for Socrates' radical critiques of their cherished democratic institutions. It was no accident that among the three citizens who indicted Socrates (there was no public prosecutor in Athens) the most prominent, Anytus, had gone into exile when the Thirty took over, had had his property confiscated, and had been a leader in the armed resistance that restored the democracy in 403.

It is clear, however, that by no means all Athenians believed that Socrates deserved punishment, and it seems likely that fewer still imagined that he would be put to death. Even though he made a defiant speech in court, provoking an uproar in the audience on more than one occasion, the verdict against him was carried by an astonishingly small majority: if thirty of the five hundred jurors had voted the other way, he would have been acquitted—as he might well have been had he made a less recalcitrant speech in his defense. (According to Xenophon, he was advised to do so but refused.) The penalty was to be decided by the jury's choice between proposals made by the two parties to the case; the prosecutors asked for death. The figures for and against acquittal suggest strongly that the jury would have accepted a reasonable alternative—a fine, for example. But Socrates proposed that he be awarded free meals in the Prytaneum, the committee room of the city's representatives; this was a privilege reserved for foreign ambassadors, Olympic victors, and heroes of the democracy. He withdrew this astonishing proposal and offered to pay a fine, but the damage was done. The jury voted for death, 360 to 140. "Socrates himself," Stone writes, "seems to put the hemlock to his lips."

Stone makes an eloquent and forceful plea for a measure of sympathy with the Athenians, a better understanding of the hostility that Socrates' subversive dialectic aroused in a city that had twice suffered under an oligarchic reign of terror. But this is not an apologia for the trial. "I could not defend the verdict when I started," he writes, "and I cannot defend it now. . . ." What he offers is a corrective to the one-sided picture of Socrates drawn by his disciples.

Stone's adversary is, of course, Plato. If we had only Xenophon's uninspired *Memorabilia* to go by, Socrates would never have become the awesome figure we know so well: philosophy's first martyr, the secular saint whom Erasmus was tempted to include among the recipients of his prayers (*"Sancte Socrates, ora pro nobis"*). This Socrates, philosophy's tragic hero, is the creation of Plato, who invented a new literary form, the philosophical prose drama, which in his hands marshaled the deepest notes of Attic tragedy and the brilliant wit of Attic comedy to impose on succeeding ages a vision of his beloved teacher which is almost irresistible. Stone, who is as charmed by Plato's poetry as he is appalled by his principles, has tried "to find out what Plato does not tell us, to give the Athenian side of the story, to mitigate the city's crime and thereby remove some of the stigma the trial left on democracy and on Athens."

Even Plato's most loyal admirers will have to concede that Stone has to some extent succeeded. But Plato will probably have the last word. *His* Socrates, a combination of fact and fiction in proportions that have always been a mystery, will retain his hold on our imaginations. Pindar said it long ago: "The charm of poetry, which creates all delights for mankind, confers authority on what is unbelievable, and makes it believed."

Two Emperors

François Mitterrand's description of Margaret Thatcher's face—"the eyes of Caligula and the mouth of Marilyn Monroe"—must have left most of his audience wondering what Caligula's eyes looked like. (Suetonius says that they were "sunken" and Pliny that they were "staring.") As for Mrs. Thatcher, whatever may have been her reaction to the second item, she was almost certainly taken aback by the comparison to Caligula, even though his favorite quotation from an early Latin poet—*"Oderint dum metuant,"* "Let them hate, provided that they fear"—might well have served as her political motto. But Caligula is the classic boogeyman of the Western historical tradition: a lustful, incestuous, murderous, sadistic, insane tyrant, who, not content to wait for the posthumous deification that had been decreed by the Senate for his predecessors Augustus and Tiberius, announced to his terrified subjects that he was a living god. Suetonius, our principal an-

This essay first appeared in *The Atlantic*, April 1990.

cient source, starts his *Life of Caligula* with an account of the man's political career and then proceeds, "So much for the emperor; now I have to tell the story of the monster." In 1945 Albert Camus put him on stage as a sort of existentialist hero, convinced by the death of his beloved sister Drusilla that life is a cruel, meaningless farce and determined to demonstrate the fact to his unfortunate fellow citizens. Robert Graves's portrait of him in *I, Claudius* (1934) was later re-created in a television serial that had huge audiences on both sides of the Atlantic eagerly awaiting the next installment.

Caligula has had a bad press. Tacitus and Suetonius, the two historical writers nearest to him in time (but both born after his death, in A.D. 41), are representatives of an aristocratic, senatorial tradition bitterly hostile to the Julio-Claudians, the first five emperors. The part of Tacitus' *Annals* that dealt with Caligula's four years in power has not survived, but it is clear from remarks in the extant portion that the historian's judgment must have been severe; he quotes a contemporary's comment on Caligula's slavish subservience to his predecessor Tiberius—"there was never a better slave or a worse master." As it is, the only full account of Caligula's life and principate is that of Suetonius, a writer uncritical of his sources and, as Anthony Barrett puts it in *Caligula: The Corruption of Power*, one whose "main failing is not, apparently, that he fabricates material, but rather that he has a tendency to believe, or at least to record, the worst, and is unable to resist colorful anecdotes, especially if they reflect badly on his subject."[1] Barrett's book was "undertaken without *parti pris* and

[1]Anthony A. Barrett, *Caligula: The Corruption of Power* (New Haven, Conn.: Yale University Press, 1990).

without preconceptions"; it "does not attempt to rehabilitate Caligula." Barrett offers "a reconstruction of events" but warns that the opportunities "to look beyond the events themselves and to identify significant trends" are limited; the reconstruction of events is itself, given the contradictions and omissions of the sources, often "hypothetical."

The traditional image of Caligula as an insane monster has its weak points. As Barrett demonstrates in impressive detail, the provinces of the vast empire seem to have been the beneficiaries of orderly, stable government under Caligula, and he left the imperial finances in such good shape that his successor Claudius could abolish some taxes and launch expensive building programs. On the empire's disputed frontiers, where the legions faced Germans across the Rhine and Parthians in the East, the status quo was maintained. Certainly Caligula savagely punished people he thought were conspiring against him (and most of them probably were), but the total of named victims was not a large one, and the popular reaction in Rome to his assassination was anger. Barrett suggests that the systematic blackening of Caligula's name was a political necessity for his successor. For Claudius, who owed his position to the murder of his predecessor, it was "important . . . to promote the notion that Caligula had died, not because the imperial system was inherently evil, but because Caligula was an inherently evil emperor."

The "imperial system," developed by Augustus, had a built-in defect—the problem of succession. Augustus had engineered a situation in which, through control of the legions and his prestige as the restorer of peace after generations of civil war, he had a firm enough grip on power to share some of it with the senatorial aristocracy and maintain a fiction that he was merely *princeps*, first citizen, in a republic. Though he could designate a successor, it had to be a man experienced in office and adept in politics if the power base he had created was to be preserved. When he died, in A.D. 14, he had been in control of the Roman world for some forty years, but the members of his family who had been appointed to high office so that they could take his place had died before him one by one. For the last ten years of his life his stepson Tiberius had been associated with him in office, and just before Augustus died he made him coregent, with instructions to designate as his successor his nephew Germanicus, the popular commander of the Rhine legions, who was also the father of Caligula. But Germanicus died five years after Augustus, and Tiberius, though a capable military officer and administrator, lacked the political skills that had enabled Augustus to keep the Roman aristocracy acquiescent in his supremacy. He left Rome for the island of Capri, where he spent the last ten years of his life, communicating with the Senate by letter— and suspecting, probably with good reason, conspiracies against him right and left. He abandoned the direction of affairs at Rome to his confidant Sejanus, the commander of the Praetorian Guard, who proceeded to build a power base of his own.

The Praetorian Guard, an elite company established by Augustus for the protection of his person in Italy, were better paid than the men of the legions at the frontiers and were fiercely loyal to their master; they were to play the role of kingmaker in the years to come. Sejanus concentrated the guard's units in barracks just outside Rome; he also filled military commands at the frontiers with his own nominees. He was clearly planning to establish himself as Tiberius' successor, perhaps to supplant him. But Tiberius struck first. He instructed one of the officers of the guard, Sutorius Macro, to assume command and win the loyalty of the troops by offering a bounty; he then sent the Senate a long letter (*"verbosa et grandis epistula,"* Juvenal called it) that kept everyone, especially Sejanus, in suspense until in the final paragraphs it denounced him as a traitor. Sejanus was executed, and Tiberius named as his successors Caligula, son of Germanicus, and Gemellus, his own grandson.

When Tiberius died, on Capri, in A.D. 37, Macro, now Caligula's man, submitted his master's name to the Senate, which granted him full powers amid general rejoicing. Caligula began his career in office as an almost universal favorite in Rome, as he had been as a boy among his father's soldiers on the Rhine. ("Caligula" is an affectionate nickname—"Bootsie"; the Roman equivalent of the GI boot was called *caliga*, and the general's young son wore a diminutive pair of them specially made for him.) But the initial enthusiasm did not last long. Six months after he assumed power, he fell ill; after his recovery he seemed to be a different man, suspicious of conspiracy on all sides. The executions of the young Gemellus, his associate in power, and of Macro, who had paved the way for his accession, were the first of many. It now became clear that the Augustan accommodation was a thing of the past; the emperor was an autocrat, not *princeps*. A series of conspiracies, real or suspected, were punished with ever-increasing severity until, in A.D. 41, Cassius Chaerea, an officer of the Praetorian Guard, killed Caligula as he made his way from a performance in the theater to lunch in the palace.

The consuls called a meeting of the Senate, which proceeded to act as if it were about to restore the republic. But the Praetorian Guard had decided otherwise. They took Caligula's uncle Claudius to their barracks and saluted him as emperor. The Senate soon came to its senses and accepted what it had not the power to oppose.

On the details of Caligula's assassination our sources present a very confusing picture; both Barrett and Barbara Levick, in her book on Claudius,[2] attempt to make sense of it. Both dismiss the account given by Suetonius and the much later Greek historian Dio Cassius that in the chaos following Caligula's death—his German bodyguard ran amok and began killing indiscriminately—Claudius hid in a closet in the palace, where he was discovered by a Praetorian Guardsman who had the bright idea of taking him off to the barracks and proclaiming him emperor. Claudius came to power, Suetonius says, *"mirabili casu,"* "by an astonishing accident." Barrett comments on Claudius' assumption of power within twenty-four hours of Caligula's death: it was "an operation . . . so remarkably smooth that it provokes questions about the possible role of Claudius himself, or at least of those around him." He comes to the cautious conclusion that Caligula's death was the outcome of a conspiracy that involved many individuals acting from different motives and that "Claudius may or may not have been a party to such a plot from the outset." Levick has a more positive and sophisticated interpretation. Claudius' "precise role cannot be determined," she writes. "Very likely it was kept indeterminate, his agents having to interpret or anticipate his wishes." This

---

[2]Barbara Levick, *Claudius* (New Haven, Conn.: Yale University Press, 1990).

was, as she says, a "technique, disreputable, essentially infan-
tile, but useful . . . that of allowing others to act or engineer-
ing them into it, while the principal continues 'ignorant' of
what is going on." The technique has been "adopted," as she
says, "by others, among them Henry II of England"—the
murder of Thomas à Becket—"and Elizabeth the First"—
the execution of Mary Queen of Scots—"and by Reagan in
the U.S.A. against Iran and Nicaragua."

Claudius was an unlikely candidate for supreme power; he
was "the ugly duckling of Augustus' family." He had some
kind of physical defect—the symptoms have been described
as the result of poliomyelitis or, more recently, as "cerebral
palsy involving some degree of spasticity." However,
Claudius showed no sign of the epilepsy and mental retarda-
tion that in some cases may accompany cerebral palsy. Under
Tiberius and Caligula he may have slyly exaggerated his apparent unfitness for high office; as a possible successor he
would have been an object of suspicion and a focus for intrigue. Indeed, later, when he was emperor, he claimed that he
had saved his life under Caligula by pretending to be stupid.
His formula for survival was to be "an attendant lord . . . Full
of high sentence, but a bit obtuse;/At times, indeed, almost
ridiculous—/Almost, at times, the Fool."

He was none of these things. He was the most learned and
intellectual of the Julio-Claudians. His early exclusion from
active political life (Augustus feared that his mannerisms and
physical awkwardness might bring discredit on the imperial
family) left him leisure for literary pursuits. He wrote in
Greek an Etruscan history in twenty volumes and a Car-
thaginian history in eight. In Latin he wrote a history of
Rome that, according to Suetonius, began with the assassina-

tion of Julius Caesar and then skipped to the end of the civil wars and the establishment of the principate of Augustus, thus discreetly omitting such matters as the alliance of Octavian (not yet Augustus) with Mark Antony and their proscription of 43 B.C., in which more than two thousand prominent Romans were murdered, the orator Cicero among them.

These were the pursuits of his years of isolation and neglect (though he continued to work on the Roman history when he became emperor); his interest in these studies was genuine, but they were also part of his strategy for survival in the dangerous atmosphere of the imperial court, where superior capability or wide popularity might arouse the suspicions of Tiberius or, worse still, of Caligula. Claudius might have replied, if asked, like Sieyès, what he had done during the Terror, *"J'ai vécu."* It was no mean achievement.

Levick quotes a statement by one of her teachers, C. E. Stevens, that "Claudius was the first Roman emperor." Perhaps Caligula has a better claim to that title, for it was to him that the Senate, overjoyed to welcome the son of Germanicus as successor to his grim and suspicious uncle, voted en bloc the powers that Augustus had so carefully disguised as legitimate—"a bundle of powers collected at different times, cemented by the authority of success, and reinforced by the ultimate sanction of force," to quote Levick's apt formulation. Barrett, in fact, blames the Senate for what happened:

> To make an inexperienced and almost unknown young man, brought up under a series of aged and repressive guardians, master of the world, almost literally overnight, on the sole

recommendation that his father had been a thoroughly decent fellow, was to court disaster in a quite irresponsible fashion. The Romans may have resented the subsequent burden of autocracy, but it was an autocracy largely of their own making.

The Senate granted Caligula absolute power in a burst of enthusiasm, but conceded it to Claudius with reluctant acceptance of superior force. Unlike his predecessor, however, Claudius held power long enough (A.D. 41–54) to consolidate and make use of it; his reign is distinguished by a number of impressive achievements. Not least among them is the conquest of Britain, in 43. Ever since Julius Caesar's two incursions almost a hundred years earlier, Roman policy had been to maintain fictional dominion over and trade relations with the tribes on the British coasts opposite Gaul which had surrendered to Caesar. The powerful tribe of the Catuvellauni, farther inland, had of recent years, under its King Cunobelin (Shakespeare's Cymbeline), cultivated friendly relations with Rome. But when Cunobelin died, sometime after 39, his sons Caratacus and Togodumnus moved against the coastal tribes, a direct challenge to the Roman requirement that the coasts of Gaul should be free of contact with independent peoples hostile to Rome. In 43, southern Britain was subdued in a short campaign for which Claudius arrived in person, with reinforcements and war elephants, to take part in the final advance and the occupation of Camulodunum (Colchester), the capital of the Catuvellauni. The conquest of the Midlands, the North, and Wales was to take many more years, but Britain was now part of the empire, and, as the archaeology of recent years has amply demonstrated, under several centuries of Roman rule it became a remarkably prosperous and civilized province.

This does not seem like the work of the clumsy stutterer portrayed in the biographical sources. The success of the campaign is of course due to the general in the field, but it was Claudius who appointed him and mobilized the resources of the empire in support. Though the Greek historian Appian, writing in the next century, claimed (in Levick's words) that "Britain continued to be a drain on manpower beyond anything it could contribute in taxation or materials," the conquest, to quote Levick (who tends to agree with those who think it was a mistake), was for Claudius "the greatest event of the reign, and one of his prime claims to rule."

Claudius was also one of the great builders of Rome. He developed on a grand scale the port of Ostia, the destination of the ships that brought the grain of Egypt to feed the population of Rome. He repaired old aqueducts, including the one that brings water to the Fontana di Trevi, where tourists throw their coins, and built new ones, like the "Claudian aqueduct" that still, in its ruined state, towers over the Campagna beside the Via Appia Antica. Claudius also began the draining of the Fucine Lake, to provide rich arable land close to home, a project not completed until the nineteenth century.

His misfortunes stemmed from his private rather than his public life. He was, to use a Roman term of strong disapproval, *uxorius*—too fond of his wife, or, rather, since he had two in succession while he was emperor, of his wives.

The first wife, Messalina, has become proverbial. But, though we can doubt the truth of Juvenal's brilliant picture of her hurrying off, as soon as Claudius was asleep, to a down-town brothel where she took on all comers until closing time, there is no doubt that she did, while still married to Claudius, go through a form of marriage with a prominent member of the senatorial aristocracy, one Gaius Silius. This was proba-bly part of a conspiracy that threatened Claudius' power and perhaps his life, but Claudius could bring himself to deal with it, by executing both partners, only at the very last mo-ment and at the stern insistence of his advisers.

Claudius' second wife, Agrippina, was later to secure the succession for Nero, her son by a previous marriage, by en-listing the support of the commander of the Praetorian Guard. Claudius' son by Messalina, Britannicus, who had an equal if not a better claim, did not long outlive his father, who died in 54. Agrippina may well, as our sources assert, have hastened the day of Nero's accession by poisoning Claudius with a dish of his favorite mushrooms.

In these two authoritative but highly readable books the de-fects and achievements of the two emperors are assessed criti-cally and with full exploitation of the nonliterary sources— epigraphical, archaeological, and, especially important, numismatic—that often throw light on or raise doubts about the evidence provided by the ancient writers. The result is a sober, balanced estimate.

And yet the lurid, half-legendary figures of the Julio-Claudian emperors as we see them through the eyes of Suetonius and Tacitus haunt our imagination still; they are powerful images of what can happen when absolute power over vast regions is concentrated in the hands of one person.

Faced with the most extravagant of the biographer's tales—for example, that Caligula believed he was a god on earth, or that he built a bridge of boats, more than four kilometers long, over part of the Bay of Naples and then charged across it in a chariot, for no other reason than that Tiberius' astrologer had said Caligula had no more chance of becoming emperor than he had of riding over the Bay of Naples—we suspend belief.

Perhaps we do so too readily. For similar examples of megalomania and self-delusion in the minds of absolute rulers we have only to look at recent events in a country that was once a Roman province and still bears the Roman name. We have only to look at Nicolae Ceauşescu, who destroyed the historic center of Bucharest to build himself a huge palace, complete with tunnels for the rapid deployment of his Praetorian Guard, the Securitate; and at his wife, a high school dropout, who rebuked the tribunal that condemned her and her husband to death because it failed to treat her with the respect due to the president of the Academy of Sciences.

Los Olvidados

One of the most popular tourist attractions of eighteenth-century Venice was the all-girl orchestra and
choir of the Ospedale della Pietà, for which Antonio
Vivaldi, appointed director in 1714, wrote music in
such prodigious quantity that much of it lies still
unpublished in the National Library in Torino. The
girls were foundlings. Abandoned by their families,
brought up in the charitable institutions of the
Catholic Church and trained as musicians, they were
eventually married off with a dowry provided by the
Serenissima, or assigned to a convent. The large
audiences at the concerts saw the girls only from a
distance, through convent gratings, but Jean-Jacques
Rousseau, secretary to the French ambassador in
Venice in 1743, managed to get a closer view. A
friend who was one of the governors of the Ospedale invited him to a meal with the musicians.

This essay originally appeared in *The New York Review of Books*, June
29, 1989. Reprinted with permission of *The New York Review of Books*.
Copyright © 1989 Nyrev, Inc.

Jean-Jacques went there full of anticipation, feeling an "amorous trembling" but was cruelly disappointed when he saw the "angels of beauty" close up. "Sophie was hideous. . . . Cattina . . . had only one eye. . . . Bettina . . . was disfigured by smallpox. Scarcely one of them was without some notable defect."[1] It was all too clear why their parents had abandoned such unmarriageable girls to the care of the Church.

Jean-Jacques was not unacquainted with the phenomenon of abandoned children. During his tour of duty in Venice he joined with his friend from the Spanish embassy, Carrio, in the purchase of a "little girl of eleven or twelve" to be raised as their shared mistress. Carrio, he tells us, was tired of "going to women who belonged to others and took it into his head to have one of his own." Jean-Jacques himself had to leave Venice before the girl was, to use his word, "mature," and in any case his feelings toward her had by that time become paternal. What happened to her after his departure we do not know, though he thought he detected similar feelings in Carrio.[2]

By the time he came to write his *Confessions* (1765–70) he had himself made a considerable contribution to the foundling population of the period. "My third child," he tells us,

> was thus deposited in a foundling home just like the first two, and I did the same with the two following: I had five in all. This arrangement seemed to me so good, so sensible, so appropriate, that if I did not boast of it publicly it was solely out of regard for their mother. . . . In a word, I made no secret of my action

[1]Jean-Jacques Rousseau, *The Confessions*, translated by J. M. Cohen (Harmondsworth, England: Penguin, 1953), pp. 295–96.
[2]Ibid., pp. 302–8.

... because in fact I saw no wrong in it. All things considered, I chose what was best for my children, or what I thought was best.[3]

This extraordinary statement is the epigraph for the introductory chapter of John Boswell's account of the abandonment of children over a long stretch of Western history—from the classical age, through the Middle Ages, to the eighteenth century.[4]

Until well into the nineteenth century of our era, most of the population of Europe lived at the sheer edge of the subsistence level. Family limitation was a grim necessity for the poor, but it was an imperative also for the upper and middle classes if they were to avoid a ruinous division of property among their children. Contraceptive methods were crude and unreliable; married couples who wished to limit the number of their children often had recourse to nonreproductive forms of intercourse. Herodotus tells the story of the Athenian tyrant Pisistratus, who married the daughter of a powerful political opponent as a condition of his support, but since for dynastic reasons he did not want to have children by her he "cohabited with her in an unnatural way." He got away with it until the bride innocently, or, as Herodotus slyly suggests, under questioning by her mother, revealed the truth, whereupon the political alliance came to an abrupt end and Pisistratus was forced to go into exile (*Histories* 1.61). Almost a thousand years later St. Augustine roundly con-

---

[3]To do him justice, Rousseau later regretted his action; he even tried, unsuccessfully, to trace one of his sons.
[4]John Boswell, *The Kindness of Strangers: The Abandonment of Children in Western Europe from Late Antiquity to the Renaissance* (New York: Pantheon, 1989).

demned "embraces in which conception is avoided"; the practice was evidently widespread.

Abortion, of course, whether tolerated by society or frowned on, legal or illegal, has always been an option open to the unwed mother, the rape victim, or the overburdened family. It may well have been, over the centuries, as common a recourse as abandonment, but it is only for recent years that statistics are available, and those who resorted to it or made it their profession in the times when it was illegal have naturally left us no evidence. In ancient Greece, it is widely believed, doctors were specifically forbidden by the famous Hippocratic oath to perform it. But we know neither the date nor the provenance of this text and have no reason to think it was generally administered. In fact it contains one provision—an undertaking not to perform surgery in cases of the kidney stone—which was certainly not binding on most Greek physicians, who regularly used the knife. One medical writer, the author of the Hippocratic treatise *The Nature of the Child*, gives a detailed description of a six-day-old embryo and explains how he came to see it. A kinswoman of his owned a slave girl, a valuable *danseuse* who was employed as a prostitute, and who would have lost her value if she became pregnant. She was worried because, after intercourse with a customer, "the seed had not come out of the womb." The doctor advised her "to jump up and down, touching her buttocks with her heels at each leap." After she had done this seven times, the embryo fell out. It seems unlikely that the doctor had sworn the Hippocratic oath.[5]

[5]G. E. R. Lloyd, ed., *Hippocratic Writings* (New York: Viking Penguin, 1982), pp. 325–26.

In the Roman Empire, official disapproval of abortion (for example, under the Augustan program of laws designed to promote larger families among the governing class) and, later, legislation with harsh penalties (under the Severan emperors) seem to have had little effect; Juvenal, in his long invective against women, mentions abortion casually and without comment—some women, he says, prefer a eunuch as their sexual partner ("no need for an abortion")—and Ovid, with the Augustan moral program in full career, includes in his racy *Amores* ("warning to Puritans: *This volume is not for you*"[6]) a prayer for his mistress Corinna, who has tried an abortion and is lying between life and death. The triumph of Christianity put an end to permissiveness on this front, but Tertullian's denunciation of the practice in the early years of the third century bears witness to the fact that it was still widespread in pagan society before the Church established its full ecumenical authority, and abortion was driven underground until its legalization in the civilized countries of the twentieth century.

But from antiquity through the Middle Ages and on to the eighteenth century the safest and most favored method of family limitation was abandonment. In pre-Christian ages this took the form of exposure: the child was left in a public place in the hope that someone would take it up to raise it as a foster child, a servant, or a slave. Or the child, especially if it was a girl, might be sold, usually to be raised as a prostitute.

[6]Ovid, *The Erotic Poems*, translated by Peter Green (New York: Viking Penguin, 1982), p. III.

In later ages the child would be consigned to the care of the Church, by exposure at the church doors or by delivery to religious institutions for foundlings. Sales of children, however, went on in the Christian Middle Ages (Boswell quotes thirteenth-century German and Spanish legal documents that attempt to regulate the process) and, as is clear from the case of Rousseau and his friend Carrio, they were not uncommon in eighteenth-century Italy.

In his highly original, learned, and skillfully written book Boswell charts the course of this phenomenon from ancient to modern times. He is a medievalist, author of a prize-winning and revolutionary study, *Christianity, Social Tolerance, and Homosexuality*, and in this new book he again presents a bold and controversial thesis. It is supported by his mastery of an astonishing range of recondite sources in languages that include Greek, Latin, Hebrew, Arabic, Syriac, and Old Norse as well as modern and medieval French, German, Spanish, and Italian. The footnotes, in fact, which constitute a good third of the book, are a mine of fascinating and surprising information about every aspect of the history of family limitation in ancient, medieval, and Renaissance Europe.

Abandonment, Boswell claims, has not been given its due attention by ancient historians, who often identify it with infanticide. In the regimented society of archaic and classical Sparta, where children judged unlikely to grow up fit for arduous military service were abandoned in a mountain ravine, this was in fact the case. But abandonment of children in a city, especially when the child was left in a much-frequented public place, was more likely to result in its appropriation by others, to be reared as a foster child (the original meaning of the word *alumnus*), as a household slave or for later sale as an industrial slave (in the mines, for example), or as a prostitute. Greece and Rome, Boswell reminds us, were slave societies "in which the major source of energy was human labor." Abandoned children could be a valuable investment.

Evidence for the practice is relatively spotty for ancient Greece and early Rome but swells to an impressive volume for the centuries of Roman imperial rule. From such diverse materials as the hypothetical (and melodramatic) law cases of the elder Seneca, the correspondence between the younger Pliny, governor of Bithynia, and the emperor Trajan on the "problem of persons born free and abandoned, then picked up by someone and brought up in slavery" (a problem, Trajan says, which "has often been discussed"), from the writings of the Roman jurists and the edicts of Constantine, from Roman mythology, Greek novels, Roman comedy and satire, Boswell makes a convincing case for the abandonment of children as a practice accepted by law, though decried by moral philosophers—a practice affecting "every type of extant record, from inscriptions to novels, from laws to plays, from moral advice to imperial chronicles."

The triumph of Christianity made surprisingly little difference; Christians abandoned children just as their pagan predecessors had done. The early Fathers of the Church, Tertullian for example, roundly denounced those who abandoned children "to the kindness of strangers," but later authorities, such as St. Basil of Caesarea in the East and St. Ambrose of Milan in the West, recognized that though the rich exposed children for selfish reasons, to avoid division of the family property when they died, the poor had no alternative. Ambrose, in Boswell's words, "exemplified, if he did not effect, the transition . . . from early disapproval of abandonment to the resignation that would characterize Christian writings for the next millennium." Children were now left at church doors, but since most Christian churches were converted Roman public buildings (a basilica was a columned hall used for official proceedings or commercial exchange before it became a place of Christian worship) little had changed except that attempts to regulate the process took the form of ecclesiastical canons instead of imperial decrees.

Yet the spirit behind the regulation had changed:

> Christians saw themselves as God's *alumni*, and, directly or by implication, Christian literature was filled with positive and idealized images of adoption and of transference from natal families to happier and more loving adopted kin groups, including such influential metaphors as the "adoption" of the Gentiles, adoption into a monastic "family," or baptism itself, the foundation of Christian experience.

In a controversial chapter Boswell claims as part of his province a medieval institution that has been much discussed in terms other than his, especially in its religious implications. This is the procedure known as oblation. The Latin word *oblatio* means "offering"; oblation was the gift of a child to a monastery to be a lifelong servant of God. Boswell is, he admits, the first modern author to consider oblation as a form of abandonment, but his argument is impressive. The Rule of St. Benedict, dating from the first half of the sixth century, contains instructions for the donation of a child "to God in the monastery" and though it does not specify that the child, once grown, could not leave the monastic life, such a prohibition was firmly fixed in ecclesiastical canons by the early years of the seventh century.

There were, of course, cases of oblates who on reaching manhood tried to return to secular life. Gottschalk of Orbais, in the ninth century, asked permission to leave the monastery of Fulda, to which he had been offered as a child. It was refused by his abbot, the celebrated churchman Rabanus Maurus (himself an oblate); Gottschalk appealed to higher authority and the Council of Mainz freed him in A.D. 829. Rabanus appealed to the Carolingian emperor, who ruled against Gottschalk. Back in the monastery, he wrote theological treatises, but Rabanus condemned them as heretical; he was finally imprisoned in the monastery of Hautvilliers, where he died, insane, twenty years later. His case, however, was unusual; Boswell's verdict on the institution of oblation is positive. Employed as a means of family limitation it "placed a major form of abandonment not merely under public scrutiny, but under the control of the most admired, conscientious, orderly and public-spirited institution of the Middle Ages, an entity . . . more likely than almost any other social body to discharge its responsibilities in good faith."

The eleventh and twelfth centuries were a period of economic expansion and population explosion in Europe. By the year 1000 the population had surpassed the level achieved under the Roman empire; in the next two centuries the figures more than doubled. During these two centuries of comparative prosperity abandonment declined to a low point. Yet these were the centuries that saw, to quote Boswell's title for his chapter dealing with the phenomenon, "Oblation at Its Zenith." Those responsible seem to have been not the poor but the well-to-do, who wished to avoid partition of the family estate and for whom "oblation may have become . . . a convenient way of divesting the family of supernumerary or awkward children."

Boswell marshals figures that, inadequate though they may be as statistics, "strongly suggest that oblation accounted for a high proportion of monks from the tenth through the end of the eleventh century and only began to decline in the twelfth." And there are constant complaints in monastic literature about the quality of the oblates. Ulrich of Cluny, for example, in the second half of the eleventh century, laments that "this holy institution has been corrupted by the greed of parents, who, for the benefit of the [rest of the] family, commit to monasteries any hump-backed, deformed, dull or unpromising children they have."

Meanwhile pressure increased for release from monastic life for those children who found it unbearable and who had been committed to it long before they reached the "age of reason" (around fourteen for males and twelve for females, according to Aquinas). A series of ecclesiastical rulings made a repetition of the sad fate of Gottschalk of Orbais unlikely if not impossible. Partly as a result of these rulings, perhaps (the monasteries were increasingly reluctant to accept oblates under such conditions), oblation declined between the twelfth and fourteenth centuries—declined, that is, for males. As a method of disposing of unwanted daughters it "remained an important demographic factor in prosperous houses throughout the Middle Ages."

In the thirteenth century, economic development, for reasons that are not fully understood, slowed, and with it the population expansion; after the Black Death of the mid-fourteenth century the population of Europe fell to a low from which it would not recover for centuries. And it is in the thirteenth century, to judge from the wealth of documentary evidence submitted by Boswell, that abandonment of children, by the old method of leaving them at the church doors, resumed on a large scale. "Parents at the close of the thirteenth century," Boswell concludes, "were, in the end, probably in much the same situation as parents during the previous thirteen hundred years."

But in the course of the next two centuries a new solution to the problem posed by unwanted children had been developed in many large French, German, and Italian cities: the foundation of institutions specifically designed for the reception and care of abandoned children. In Florence the foundling hospital of Santa Maria da San Gallo opened its doors at the end of the thirteenth century; Santa Maria della Scala was opened in 1316; and the best known of them all, Santa Maria degl'Innocenti, its portico on the Piazza della Santissima Annunziata designed by Brunelleschi, began receiving foundlings in 1445. Within fifty years it was accepting nine hundred children a year. And all over Europe similar institutions were soon offering a more convenient, and, for the parents, more reassuring way to dispose of children they could not support than the age-old practice of exposure to the kindness of strangers.

Unfortunately the concentration of newborn children in foundling homes, in an age that knew little of hygiene or of scientific medicine, resulted in an appalling death rate, mostly due, in all probability, to communicable disease. At San Gallo, for example, in the late fourteenth century, 20 percent of the arrivals died within a month, another 30 percent within a year; only 32 percent reached the age of five. The outside world was unaware of these grim statistics; the problem of unwanted children had been removed from the streets and the view of ordinary citizens; society could, and did, forget them. "Society's efforts to minimize the possibly tragic consequences of anonymous abandonment produced, with bitter irony, a system that guaranteed the deaths of a majority of exposed children by magnifying their communal vulnerability to ordinary disease."

The main problem faced by the author of this magisterial survey is of course that of his sources. One particularly admirable feature of his book is the careful discrimination he displays as he elicits support for his thesis from a polyglot accumulation of disparate, often ambiguous, and sometimes enigmatic material. For an investigation of family limitation in the modern world the historian turns at once to official records and statistics, but for antiquity no such information is available. Even for Periclean Athens and Augustan Rome, the two best-known periods of ancient history, estimates of the population are conjectural and controversial. As for later centuries, by Boswell's own account,

> from all of Europe during the whole of the Middle Ages, at most a half dozen reliable bits of demographic data survive, and they are so widely scattered in time and place that it is nearly impossible to know whether they are typical or peculiar, indicative of continuity or change, meticulously reliable or grossly misleading.

Abandonment of children is not an action parents are likely to leave records of (Rousseau's confession is a rare item). The evidence consists mainly of legal documents (late Roman and medieval) dealing with the problems involved, moral and ethical texts (Christian diatribes against the practice, for example), and, richest but most difficult to evaluate, fiction.

The legal texts, Boswell is frank to admit, "can be misleading. The fact that statutes are enacted . . . does not mean that they are enforced, or even taken seriously." Yet the huge corpus of imperial Roman law contains, besides edicts and rulings, "summaries of actual cases, legal opinions citing custom and practice," and also "observations about legal and social structures introduced as incidental factual premises rather than arguments," which "are revealing for precisely this reason." The ethical treatises—pagan philosophers deprecating the practice or Christian theologians inveighing against it—attest to its prevalence but yield little in the way of detailed information. The last, and most controversial, category, fiction, forms a large part of Boswell's source material; chapter two is entitled "Rome: Literary Flesh and Blood," and his discussion of the High Middle Ages includes a chapter headed "Literary Witnesses." This is of course a very rich vein. Abandonment of a child and its eventual recognition is a standard plot device of tragedy, melodrama, and comedy all the way from Oedipus, left in the wilds of Mount Cithaeron, through the comedies of Menander, Plautus, and Terence, and the child Perdita exposed "in some remote and desert place," left "to its own protection and favor of the climate," through the Figaro of Beaumarchais and Mozart to Oscar Wilde's Ernest deposited in a black leather handbag "in the cloak-room at Victoria Station—the Brighton Line."

Fictional abandonment may be a rich vein, but it is not historical evidence of the same weight as demographic data, legal decisions, and moral or religious writings that deal directly with the problem or illuminate it tangentially. Boswell has to defend his method on this point, and he does so with skill and telling effect. He is fully aware that fictional abandonment of children, given its rich payoff in terms of plot, may be what he calls a "quicksand problem." We have all frequently read about, and seen on the screen, characters engulfed in quicksand (there is a striking example in the reconstituted *Lawrence of Arabia*). We even know, from reading fiction and watching movies, what one should or should not do in an attempt to rescue such an unfortunate. But few of us have ever seen quicksand or known anyone who has. "This is not to say," Boswell points out, "that quicksand does not exist, or is never a problem for humans: simply that its role in fiction is not a realistic reflection of its importance."

He presents some illuminating analogies from the relation of modern fiction to real life. One of the mainsprings of the novel is adultery; it is hard to imagine the modern novel without it. As is clear from Kinsey's figures alone, fiction is not presenting its readers with quicksand here; in real life the incidence of adultery leaves fiction far behind. Abortion, on the other hand, a not unfamiliar feature of modern life, is rare in fiction; the obvious reason is that it is the end of something rather than a beginning, not a useful device for forwarding a plot. Boswell cites murder as an event that is more likely to happen in fiction than in real life, but this may be a reflection of the fact that he lives in New Haven, Connecticut (he is professor of history at Yale), rather than New York or Washington, where statistics suggest that the prospect of one's life ending prematurely has to be seriously considered by the ordinary citizen.

In addition to his defense of fiction as a mirror of real life
he is able to buttress his case by citing real statistics when at
last they become available—in the late eighteenth century. It
was, as he says, the first century with extensive records and it
was also "the last before advances in industrial and agricultural technology could support a much larger population—
and before techniques of contraception rendered abandonment less necessary than it had been." The figures are
startling. In the late eighteenth century at Toulouse "one
child in every four was *known* to have been abandoned" (Boswell's italics). In poorer quarters the rate reached 39.9 percent.
In Lyons between 1750 and 1789 the number of children abandoned was approximately one-third of the number of births.
In Florence in the early nineteenth century 43 percent of all
baptized babies were abandoned. Seen against these figures
the revelation in Beaumarchais's *Marriage of Figaro* that Figaro
is actually the son of Marcelline, the older woman he once
promised to marry if she would lend him money and who
now demands her due, would not have seemed as wildly improbable to the play's original audience as it does to us.[7] "It is
a curious turn of history," Boswell sums up, "that the difficulties of conjugal life and childbearing have been so profoundly eased during the twentieth century that the dark
backdrop they provided for audiences of previous ages has
come to seem comic fancy to viewers in more fortunate circumstances."[8]

[7]Corinna's abortion may be more than freewheeling imagination if, as Peter
Green suggests in the introduction to his brilliant translation (cf. footnote 6),
"Corinna was based, at least in part, on Ovid's mysterious first wife" (p. 23).
[8]Beaumarchais was very well aware of the "dark backdrop." Simon Schama, in
his *Citizens: A Chronicle of the French Revolution* (New York: Knopf, 1989), de-

Los Olvidados

Boswell's inquiry extends no farther than the early years of the nineteenth century: abandonment of children condoned or even regulated by society is not a feature of civilized modern life. But we have no reason to congratulate ourselves. In many parts of the world children are still sold into prostitution; a recent report from Thailand (*New York Times*, March 30, 1984) describes the sale of daughters by their parents for the thriving "sex industry" of Bangkok. And no one who saw Luis Buñuel's 1950 film *Los Olvidados* will ever forget the faces of the rejected and mindless sadistic criminals. The scene of Buñuel's tragic story is Mexico City. "Concealed behind the imposing structures of our great modern cities," runs the opening voiceover, "are pits of misery, hiding unwanted, hungry, dirty and uneducated children." But the image on the screen that accompanies these words is that of New York harbor and the island of Manhattan.

<hr>

scribes Beaumarchais's proposal to devote the proceeds of the phenomenal success of his play to the establishment of an Institute of Maternal Welfare "that would provide subsidies to mothers who would otherwise have to send their infants out to village wet nurses in order to be able to work." They used the services of "an official bureau and its traveling agents—the *meneurs*—to find village wet nurses in the countryside. . . . For every one in two babies sent away in this manner, village wet nursing was a death warrant. . . . Desperate for the pittance that they received for nursing, the woman sometimes deceived the *meneur* about their lactating ability and fed the infant animal milk or a *bouillie*-pap, made of water and boiled (and often moldy) bread. Sometimes their mouths would be crammed with rotting rags. Infants sat in human and animal filth, were suspended on a hook in unchanged swaddling bands or were slung from the rafters in an improvised hammock. Dysenteric fevers put them out of their misery by the tens of thousands."

III

Renewals

Odysseus of Arabia

In 1928, T. E. Lawrence, then serving under an assumed name in the ranks of the Royal Air Force, was known to the world as the Lawrence of Arabia who had inspired and led the Arab irregulars in a guerrilla war against the Turks. His talent as a writer, however, was known only to those few subscribers who had seen his masterpiece, *Seven Pillars of Wisdom*, Lawrence's full account of his involvement in the desert war. This work, which was originally published in a limited edition of some two hundred copies, would not be made available to the general public until 1935, the year of his death. When, in 1928, Bruce Rogers, a famous book designer, was commissioned to produce a fine edition of a classic text and decided on the *Odyssey*, he could find no translation that satisfied him; they were all, he said,

This essay originally appeared as the introduction to *The Odyssey of Homer; Newly Translated into English Prose* by T. E. Lawrence (New York: Oxford University Press, 1991). Copyright © 1991 by Oxford University Press, Inc. Reprinted by permission.

"lacking in speed." A friend passed on to him the proofs of *Seven Pillars.* "It suddenly came to me," he wrote to Lawrence much later, "that if the swing and go of your English in the *Seven Pillars,* which held me to it when I was not specially interested in some of your expeditions, could be applied to the *Odyssey,* we would get a version that would out-distance any existing translations."[1]

Rogers could not have known, when he first made his proposal to Lawrence, how welcome it would be. Since boyhood Lawrence had been an assiduous reader of the *Odyssey.* Of their time together at an Officer Training Corps camp, a fellow student at Oxford wrote: "If I remember rightly, it was a copy of the *Odyssey* carried inside his tunic pocket that was his constant companion."[2] Lawrence's record in Greek at school had been far from brilliant—a score of 186 against a possible 353 in an examination taken at age sixteen—but he read Homer in the original. He made no claim to scholarly expertise: "I read it only for pleasure," he wrote to the friend who had passed Rogers's proposal on to him, "and have to keep a dictionary within reach." Nonetheless, he went on to write, "it goes with me always, to every camp, for I love it."[3] He expected that the job would take him two years, but because of the pressure of his duties in the RAF, the book did not appear until 1932.

Homer was not the only Greek author Lawrence read in the original. During his years as an undergraduate at Oxford

---

[1]Quoted from Jeremy Wilson, *Lawrence of Arabia: The Authorized Biography of T. E. Lawrence,* (New York: Macmillan, 1989), p. 813.
[2]E. F. Hall in *T.E. Lawrence by His Friends,* edited by A. W. Lawrence (London, 1937; reprint New York, 1963), p. 41.
[3]Wilson, p. 814.

and later as an archaeologist in Syria, Lawrence acquired a remarkable knowledge of Greek literature and philosophy. Robert Graves remembered him at Oxford after the war talking to the Regius Professor of Divinity about the influence of the Syrian Greek philosophers on early Christianity. "He went on to speak about Meleager and the other Syrian-Greek contributors to the Greek Anthology, and of their poems in Syrian . . . which were as good [as] (or better than) their poems in Greek."[4] In the famous thirty-third chapter of *Seven Pillars of Wisdom*, in which Lawrence tells how, sick with fever in a tent, he worked out the theory and practice of guerrilla war in the desert, he uses Plato's words *epistēmē* and *doxa*, which appear in his text in Greek characters. The first, *epistēmē*, he assigns to the scientific, "mathematical" element—calculation of troops and resources; the second, *doxa*, to the intuitive understanding of the great commander—his "feel" for the situation and the enemy's intention. In searching for a name for the psychological element, in this case the winning of the Arab's hearts and minds for the cause, "I went," he writes, "to Xenophon and stole . . . his word *diathetics*, which had been the art of Cyrus before he struck."[5] The word *diathetikos* does not occur in the text of Xenophon (in fact, it first appears in an author of the first century after Christ known only as Anonymous Londiniensis); Lawrence must have been thinking of a passage in Xenophon's *Anabasis* (1.1.5). There the verb *diatithenai*, from which Lawrence formed his technical term, is used to describe Cyrus's policy of winning the friendship and

[4]*T. E. Lawrence by His Friends*, p. 272.
[5]T. E. Lawrence, *Seven Pillars of Wisdom* (New York: Doubleday, 1935), pp. 193–95.

devotion of visiting officials from the court of the Great King, his brother, whom he was secretly preparing to attack. This is not the only passage in *Seven Pillars* where Lawrence relies on ancient Greek to carry his meaning. In the fascinating third chapter of the book, where he attempts to define the desert Bedouin's conception of God, he quotes—again in the original Greek—Plato's description of "truly existing being": it is *achromatos, aschēmatistos, anaphes*—colorless, formless, intangible (*Phaedrus* 247c).[6]

Just before he received the proposal for a translation of the *Odyssey*, he had written from an RAF base in India to Charlotte Shaw, who had asked what he was reading. "My Greek books? Certainly. I have never forgotten it: so I began with Xenophon's *Anabasis*. . . . Till now I've only read forty or fifty pages. After Xenophon, who will last me for many weeks, I'll tackle Herodotus, and then the *Odyssey*, spending only a little time daily on them, using a dictionary for the doubtful words. Greek literature is so good that it is almost the best second language for a reader."[7] It was from Herodotus that he chose the words of the Greek inscription he carved on the lintel of the cottage in Dorset he planned to inhabit after his retirement from the RAF: *Ou phrontis*, literally, "No care." Hippoclides, son of Tisander, Herodotus tells us, was the favorite among the many rich and powerful suitors for the hand of the daughter of Clisthenes, the despotic ruler of Sicyon. During the feast at which Clisthenes was to announce his decision, Hippoclides, who had perhaps taken a little too much wine, began to dance. He was so pleased with his dancing that

[6] *Seven Pillars*, p. 40.
[7] Wilson, p. 1137.

he called for a table and began to dance on that, a performance that would not be out of place in a bouzouki joint in
modern Greece. He ended up standing on his hands with his
feet in the air. This was too much for his host, who burst out
in a rage: "Son of Tisander, you have danced your marriage
away." Still dancing, Hippoclides replied: *"Ou phrontis Hippok-
leidei,"* "Hippoclides doesn't care." Lawrence evidently hoped
that his cottage would be a place where he could spend care-
free years in the company of his friends and his books. It was
not to be. He was killed in a motorcycle accident less than
three months after his discharge.

A competence in Greek and a love for the poem were not
the only qualifications Lawrence could claim as a translator
of the *Odyssey*. In a letter to Rogers he listed some of the others. "For years we were digging up a city of roughly the Odysseus period." (This was Carchemish, a Hittite city in Syria,
where Lawrence had worked for several seasons under the
Oxford archaeologist Hogarth.) "I have handled the weapons, armour, utensils of those times, explored their homes,
planned their cities. I have hunted wild boars and watched
wild lions, sailed the Aegean (and sailed ships), bent bows,
lived with pastoral peoples, woven textiles, built boats and
killed many men. So I have odd knowledges that qualify me
to understand the *Odyssey*, and odd experiences that interpret
it to me. . . ."

Lawrence's experience in Arab countries, in peace and in war,
had indeed given him a basis for understanding Homer's fictional world that was unrivaled among translators of his time.
But he did not know as much as we now know, or perhaps

think we know, about Homer. We do know enough to discount Lawrence's picture of the author of the *Odyssey* as "a bookworm . . . very bookish, this house-bred man. His work smells of the literary coterie, of a writing tradition. His notebooks were stocked with purple passages. . . ." Whether or not Homer could write, and if he could, what part writing played in the composition of the epics, are questions that have been discussed at great length ever since Milman Parry convincingly demonstrated that Homer, composing his poems probably in the eighth century B.C., was heir to a centuries-old oral tradition. His predecessors and contemporaries were illiterate bards, who improvised their versions of well-known tales with the aid of a huge stock of typical scenes and formulaic phrases expressly shaped for the demanding dactylic meter in which the tales were told. Examples of Greek alphabetic writing (on fragments of pottery) have been found all over the Greek world on sites dating from the eighth and early seventh centuries B.C. The letters, adapted from a Phoenician consonantal system with the crucial Greek addition of signs for the vowels, are crudely and laboriously formed; they suggest that Greek writing at this period was in its infancy. It seems possible (and to some scholars probable) that Homer used this nascent script as a helpmate in the creation of epic poems that in their length and complexity defied the limits imposed on oral performance by the attention span of the audience and the stamina of the bard. What does not seem possible is that anyone at such an early stage of Greek literacy could have been a bookworm, a member of a literary coterie, or an inheritor of a literary tradition.

In one of his judgments, however, Lawrence now seems

more perceptive than most of the Greek scholars of his day, men who were engaged in the endless task of disassembling the poem into what were believed to have been separate tales composed at different times by different bards and clamped together, often clumsily, by later editors. Lawrence had no doubts about the poem's unity. "However scholars may question the text in detail," he writes, "writers (and even would-be writers) cannot but see in the *Odyssey* a single, authentic, unedited work of art, integrally preserved." Yet like many readers, he thought it a lesser work than the *Iliad.* "The shattered *Iliad* yet makes a masterpiece; while the *Odyssey,* by its ease and interest, remains the oldest book worth reading for its story and the first novel of Europe."

In the Oxford edition, this remark appears at the head of the text, in what is there called the "Translator's Note." It should be remembered, however, that Lawrence did not originally write it for publication in this form; it was part of a letter to the printer, answering a request for material that might prove useful in a prospectus. Lawrence sent him his "notes on translating the *Odyssey,* copied from the back of the book over the fly-leaves of which I scribbled my comments as I worked on it."[8] The printer thought highly of this material, and after some expansion and polishing it was printed, at Lawrence's request, after the translation. Lawrence had written his letter very late in the process of making the translation—he was working on Book 21 at the time—and, to judge from some of his comments, had by then become somewhat disenchanted with the poem.

Although he honors the poem as "the first novel of

[8]Wilson, p. 882.

Europe," at the same time he denies its author what many
would consider an essential element of the novelist's art—the
creation of character. "Obviously," he writes, "the tale was
the thing; and that explains (without excusing it to our ingrown minds) his thin and accidental characterization." The
examples he cites—the princess Nausicaa and the swineherd
Eumaeus—do little to support his case. "Nausicaa," he says,
"enters dramatically, and shapes, for a few lines, like a
woman—then she fades unused." Since marriage to Nausicaa
is one of a series of temptations Odysseus has to resist if he is
to find his way home, her presence in the narrative cannot be
prolonged; it is an episode, like the appearance of Calypso
and Circe. But I find it hard to believe that any other reader of
Book 6—Homer's account of Nausicaa's dream, her excur-
sion with her maids and the laundry to the seashore, her confrontation with the naked Odysseus, and her subtly veiled
proposal of marriage hinted at in her instructions for his entrance to the city—could feel that she "fades unused." She is
one of the most intelligent young women, and certainly the
most charming, in all of Greek literature. And she is only one
of a whole company of minor characters who have caught and
held the attention of many generations of readers: Menelaus
and Helen at Sparta, fencing adroitly with their pointed anecdotes about old times at Troy; Calypso grumbling to Hermes
about the resentment of the Olympian gods when a goddess,
even a minor one, falls in love with a mortal; Ajax, as unfor-
giving in the land of the dead as he was in the land of the
living . . . even the monster Polyphemus, giant and cannibal
though he is, stands out as a complete personality, not least
when, blinded and baffled, he talks to his beloved ram. As for
the principals—Odysseus, Penelope, and Telemachus—even

Lawrence, who ended by despising them, has to admit that
they are fully formed characters, "consistently and pitilessly
drawn."

Even more surprising than Lawrence's judgment about
Homer's skill at characterization is his complaint that the
poet displays an "infuriating male condescension to inglorious woman." In fact, the *Odyssey* is sharply distinguished from
most of the other great works of Greek literature by the repeated emergence of women, not as subordinate presences or
passive victims but as effective, even decisive, agents. Nausicaa, Calypso, and Circe all play crucial roles, first trying to
keep Odysseus for themselves and then helping him on his
way. At home, Penelope, through the long years of waiting
and mounting despair, holds off her unruly young suitors
with a combination of stubbornness, duplicity, and charm
until her husband at last returns. Indeed, her announcement
of a contest to see who can string Odysseus' bow precipitates
his revenge and their reunion. Even in secondary scenes
women stand out. At Sparta, it is Helen who recognizes
Telemachus as Odysseus' son, and well before her less quick-
witted husband does; the nurse Eurycleia is the first to recognize Odysseus in the house; his mother, Anticleia, is the first
person Odysseus allows to drink the blood in the land of the
dead. Later he sees and questions a long line of the strength-
less souls of famous and infamous women: Tyro, Antiope,
Epicaste (Homer's name for Jocasta), Chloris, Leda, Phaedra,
Procris, Ariadne, Eriphyle, and many another: "so many
wives of heroes, so many daughters. . . ."

There is no condescension here, and no inglorious woman
either. Coming from Lawrence, the complaint rings false; he
held no brief for the independence or importance of women

and did not seek their company; in fact, he seems to have spent most of his life avoiding contact with them. In the desert with the Bedouin he was in an exclusively male world, of which he writes in lyrical terms in the opening chapter of *Seven Pillars*. He spent much of the rest of his life far from female society, in the coarse, masculine environment brilliantly portrayed in all its harsh vulgarity in his book *The Mint*. His attitude to women is characterized by a woman friend, Celandine Kennington, the wife of the artist who drew most of the striking portraits that crowd the pages of *Seven Pillars*. She was devoted to Lawrence because he had talked her out of a deep depression caused by a miscarriage; he had, in her own words, saved her life. "Was he a woman hater?" she wrote. "It is so often asked. I don't think he was at all, but he had not the usual interest in them from the sexual point of view, and he deeply disapproved of what many women do, that is, they hamper a man in fulfilling his destiny; they tend to make him non-adventurous; they hold him back to attend their comfort. This he fought steadily and relentlessly."[9] Since Calypso, Circe, and Nausicaa all try at first to hamper Odysseus from fulfilling his destiny, one might expect that Lawrence would approve of Homer's characterization. Perhaps he mistakenly thought he saw in Homer a mirror image of his own bourgeois romantic prejudice and reacted against its exposure. But neither did he have a good word for Penelope, who held the fort at home for ten years; "the sly, cattish wife," he calls her. Not that the rest of the family fares any better: "that cold-blooded egotist Odysseus and the priggish son. . . ." It looks as if the long, drawn-out labor on the trans-

[9] *T. E. Lawrence by His Friends*, pp. 260–61.

lation, much of it accomplished after a full day's work on his service assignments, had ended by filling him with a distaste for the whole enterprise. "I am so bored," he wrote at one point, "with the resourceful Odysseus."[10] Happily, these feelings do not surface in the translation. In fact, if he had not written his "Translator's Note" they could not have been detected. His version preserves, as well as prose can hope to do it, much of the force, charm, and dignity of the original poem.

Prose, however, has its limitations. Homer is not just a storyteller, although he is one of the most accomplished storytellers of his or any age; he is also a poet, and a very great one. From the vast stock of convenient formulas and type scenes bequeathed him by the oral tradition he fashioned, by invention, variation, and subtle modulation, a poetic diction that avoids monotony and adapts itself to changing voices and situations with the utmost versatility and grace. It is a language far removed from common speech, a language that has a vigor, directness, and nobility all its own. It needs the formality of verse to do it full measure of justice in translation. What is more, a verse translator has an advantage in that the medium itself suggests, if not demands, an appropriate formality. The prose translator is hampered by the medium.

In searching for a style that will give the reader an impression of Homer's unique combination of high formality and narrative vigor, the translator has to walk a line between the pitfalls of an archaism that may verge on the ridiculous and

[10]Wilson, p. 861.

an idiomatic realism that may lapse into vulgarity. Archaism might seem not only suitable but even desirable, since Homer's language is an amalgam of words and grammatical forms stemming from different dialects and even different centuries. But of course this strategy can be carried to excessive lengths, as it was in the nineteenth century and even later. Writing in 1947, Dudley Fitts commented acidly on a twentieth-century verse translation of Euripides' *Medea*, citing the exchange in which Aegeus announces to Medea that he is childless. Medea asks him if he is married and Aegeus replies that he is. "No human being in any age of the world's history," Fitts wrote, "has seriously remarked, 'Nay, not unyoked to wedlock's bed am I,' even if a lady *has* just asked him, 'This, with a wife, or knowing not the couch?' It is done only in the standard translations."[11]

This was in what passed for verse, but Butcher and Lang's prose version of the *Odyssey* (1879) was no better. They followed the Greek word order and syntax as closely as they could and took for their stylistic model the magnificent English of the Authorized Version of the Bible, a book more widely and deeply read by their generation than by ours. But their slavish imitation of the syntax and idiom of the Greek brought their prose more than once to the very border of intelligibility: "Oh, that the fellow may get wherewith to profit withal, just in such measure as he shall ever prevail to bend the bow."[12] And their language never approached the poetry

[11]*Greek Plays in Modern Translations*, edited by Dudley Fitts (New York: Dial Press, 1947), p. xvi.
[12]Cited by E. V. Rieu, *Homer: The Odyssey* (Harmondsworth, England: Penguin, 1946), p. xvi.

of their model at its best: "Ere ever the silver bow be loosed, or the golden bowl be broken. . . ." Or its directness: "And he said, 'Throw her down.' So they threw her down: and some of her blood was sprinkled on the wall, and on the horses. . . ."

Samuel Butler, a rebel against Victorian primness, made a prose version that he claimed was plain English but that ended up with the worst of both alternatives. Not only is his prose still mottled with fancy archaisms and inversions, his tone can range from indecorous to downright vulgar. He even manages to make an elegant Homeric meal in the palace sound like a cheap meal in a London chophouse. Lawrence was determined to avoid this error. "I would have a version of Homer mannered, certainly," he wrote to Charlotte Shaw as he began work on the translation.[13] "Butler has missed, I find, all the picturesque side . . . and most of the poetry has evaporated with Homer's queer, archaic dignity."[14]

He worked very hard on his version. "Book II is harder than Book I," he wrote, again to Charlotte Shaw. "I have done three hundred lines this month: only three lines per hour! and those aren't finished. . . ."[15] And later: "The fair copy represents the fourth writing, and is the fourteenth revision: by and large I do five lines an hour. . . ." And he often went through a painful process familiar to all conscientious translators. "I have spent five hundred hours over these fourteen hundred words [Books 1–3] and have reached a sort of finality—arriving at that negation of improvement, when

[13]Wilson, p. 838.
[14]Ibid., p. 829.
[15]Ibid., p. 837.

after a cycle of alternatives one returns to the original word. . . ."[16]

His difficulties stemmed from his decision to avoid a pedestrian style, to aim at a prose that would suggest performance, a heightened decorum for a formal, public occasion. Perhaps the best way to appreciate what he was trying to do is to compare a passage from his *Odyssey* with that of a famous later translation, that of E. V. Rieu (1947), who, like Lawrence, saw in the *Odyssey* "the true ancestor of the long line of novels that have followed it." Rieu, however, accepted the logical consequence of that insight and adopted a plain, low-key style that avoided Butler's inelegancies but had no other aim than to tell the story in the simplest and most direct way possible in idiomatic English. It was, of course, a great success, a prodigious best-seller in fact, but over the years its plain style has lost much of its original appeal as poetic versions, those of Lattimore and Fitzgerald prominent among them, have restored to Homer some of his poetic brilliance.

Here is Rieu's version of *Odyssey* 15. 325–50. Odysseus, still unrecognized, has told his host, the swineherd Eumaeus, that he intends to make his way to the palace and try to earn his keep by doing manual work for the suitors.

> But the swineherd was most indignant. "My good sir," he exclaimed, "what on earth put such a scheme into your head? You will simply be courting sudden death if you insist on attaching yourself to a set of men whose profligacy and violence have outraged heaven itself. *Their* servants are not at all your kind, but smartly dressed young fellows, who always grease their hair and keep their pretty faces clean. That is the kind that wait on

[16]Wilson, p. 842.

them—at polished tables, groaning under their load of bread and meat and wine. No, sir, stay with me, where nobody finds you a nuisance. I certainly don't, nor does any of my mates here. And when Odysseus' son arrives, he'll fit you out in a cloak and tunic and send you on wherever you would like to go."

"Eumaeus," replied the good and gallant Odysseus, "may Father Zeus look on you as kindly as I do for putting a term to my wandering and hopeless want. Surely a tramp's life is the worst thing that anyone can come to. Yet exile, misfortune, and sorrow often force a man to put up with its miseries for his wretched stomach's sake. However, since you press me to stay and await the prince's arrival, perhaps you'll be so good as to give me the news about King Odysseus' mother, and his father, whom he left on the threshold of old age when he went abroad. Are they still in the land of the living? Or are they dead by now and in the Halls of Hades?"

Here is Lawrence's version of the same passage:

Ah, then, Eumaeus, how your heart sank while you answered him.

"Alas, my guest, that this notion should have come to your mind. You must thirst for your own destruction if you would push among that mob of suitors whose rank cruelty affronts the steely sky. Their lackeys are not men like you, but young rufflers in gay cloaks and robes, sleek-headed and blooming-cheeked. Already their tables groan with bread and meat and wine. So stay with us. No man here, not myself nor any of these my fellows, grudges your tarrying: and when Odysseus' good son returns he will clothe you newly and forward you whither your spirit bids."

To this Odysseus said: "May Father Zeus love you, Eumaeus, as I do for your sparing me further distressful vagabondage, that saddest of human fates. For their loathly belly's sake do men incur these pains and griefs of vagrancy. But now, if I am to settle here till the son returns, tell me about the mother of Odysseus and the father whom his going left behind stricken in years. Are they yet living in the eye of day, or dead in Hades' mansions?"

Lawrence, unlike Rieu, has preserved Homer's direct address to Eumaeus, who is distinguished in this fashion fourteen times in the *Odyssey* and is the only character so treated; this is a significant detail, but not the one that suits the novelistic prose style. Lawrence's word *steely* exactly renders a vivid adjective in the Greek that Rieu omits; his *thirst for* is much closer to the Greek than *courting*, so is *push among* than *attach yourself to* and *mob* than *set*—and all three are more vigorous. Rieu's *grease their hair* is a Butlerian touch that is badly off-key here; the Greek refers to the custom of smoothing down the hair with perfumed olive oil—a mark of elegance and wealth. Lawrence's Shakespearean reminiscence *sleek-headed* is much better. So with the closing sentence of the extract: *in the eye of day* is closer to the Greek and fresher than *in the land of the living*, and *mansions*, with its perhaps ironical echo of the Gospel of John, a more striking word than *halls*.

Rieu expressed the hope that he would not "fall into the most heinous crime a translator can commit, which is to interpose the veil of his own personality between his original and the reader." But this is of course what no translator can escape, whether what is interposed is the translator's own personality or the literary convention of the time, or, most likely, a combination of both, for the translator is engaged in the often thankless task of remolding the original in terms intelligible and acceptable to the translator's idea of the appropriate literary style. Rieu saw the *Odyssey* as the work of Homer the novelist and toned his English down to fit that vision of his author. Lawrence, although he too mentions the novel, is always conscious of the oral, one might even say the rhetorical, basis of the text. "The tale is very dignified," he wrote to Charlotte Shaw, "told for chiefs, and masters of households, to pass dark evenings."[17]

Some thirty years after Rieu, in 1980, Walter Shewring published a new prose translation that follows Lawrence rather than Rieu. His version, he writes, is to be "prose . . . but not the language of careless day-to-day talk and writing; a certain formality seems needful if the reader is to have some inkling of Homer's own much greater formality." As so often in the parade of literary fashions, the wheel has come full circle. But even though it will someday turn again, Lawrence's translation of the *Odyssey* will always have its admirers. It is the work of a writer with a vigorous individual style, a writer who had lived and fought for two strenuous years by the side of men who, in their devotion to war and plunder, their passionate self-esteem and prickly sense of personal honor, in their code of hospitality for the stranger as well as in their cunning and unpredictability, were not unlike the heroes of the world Homer created in his two great epic poems.

[17]Wilson, p. 837.

On Two Fronts

The title for this essay is yet another example of my penchant for military metaphors. It is drawn from the experience of the great German nation, which, finding itself surrounded by other countries, felt cramped. "Germany," so ran the first sentence of a school geography book in use under the Weimar Republic, "has nine neighbors and that is Germany's biggest problem." It turned out, of course, that it was the neighbors who had the problem, as, twice in this century, the rulers of Germany tried to reach a happy state in which they would have no neighbors at all. They were repeatedly warned by their military experts not to go too fast, above all not to fight on two fronts, east and west, at the same time. They disregarded this advice both times, with the result that Germany was for a long time divided like Caesar's Gaul into three parts. We philologists have

This essay originally appeared, in a slightly different form, as the text of an address to the American Philological Association, New Orleans, 1980.

been fighting on two fronts for some time now; but we had no choice. We have also, even without losing the battle, been divided into three parts.

When the American Philological Association was first formed, in 1869, everyone knew what a philologist was. And they were all interested in the same thing. As witness the contents of Volume 1 of *Transactions and Proceedings of the American Philological Association*, 1869–70:

> On the nature and theory of the Greek accent
> On the nature and designation of the accent in Sanskrit
> On the aorist subjunctive and future indicative with *hopos me* and *ou me*
> On the best method of studying the North American languages
> On the German vernacular of Pennsylvania
> On the present condition of the question as to the origin of languages
> On certain forms of the English verb which were used in the 16th and 17th centuries
> On some mistaken notions of Algonkin Grammar
> Contributions to Creole grammar

A look at the contents of the most recent volume of *Transactions and Proceedings of the American Philological Association* conjures up a vision of the Muse of Philology with a Virginia Slims cigarette over the caption "You've come a long way, baby."

The founders of the American Philological Association were interested in language, the Greek and Roman languages primarily but—as is clear from the contents of Volume 1—in *any* language, for, to quote the presidential address (the first) by William D. Whitney, of Yale College: "The scientific study of languages has opened innumerable new points of view and multiplied the value of all linguistic material." It was not long, however, before the philologists interested in mistaken notions of Algonkin grammar branched off and became linguists and very soon the bulk of our membership consisted of teachers of Latin and Greek. But as the years went by, fewer and fewer of them were interested primarily in such topics as the future indicative with *hopos me* and *ou me*. They had caught up with the Germans, who, adopting the name coined by Friedrich August Wolf, *Altertumswissenschaft*, and the program worked out with German thoroughness by August Böckh, were pursuing highly specialized topics in an approach to classical studies that embraced all aspects of the ancient world. And this process led inevitably to a division of the body philological into three main parts. Though philologists are all, by the mere chronological facts, historians in some sense or other, some of us became more historically minded than others and began to think and speak of themselves as historians; they are now, for the most part, to be found as often in the department of history as in the department of classics. Though we all have to know something about philosophy, some of us took to Plato and Aristotle not just as texts illustrative of Greek thought and attitudes but as philosophical texts, posing real philosophical problems; these scholars began to think of themselves as teachers of philosophy rather than of "classics" or *Altertumswissenschaft* or even philology, and are now to be found, for the most part, not in the department of classics but in the department of philosophy. Even those of us whose main concern continues to be the literary texts have tended to become literary historians and critics rather than philologists in the original sense of the word. The pure philologists among us are rare and, I may say, precious birds.

But these divergencies of interest produced gaps between us which were more than departmental. The Böckhian vision of the specialist whose work in his restricted field is illuminated by an acquaintance with all aspects of the ancient world dimmed in the face of professional necessities. The ancient historian found it essential to his understanding, and, if he was in a history department, for his teaching, to know medieval and modern history as well as ancient. Though he remained a devoted student of Herodotus and Thucydides, of Tacitus and Ammianus, in the original, and though he might still read Homer and Virgil, the tragic poets and Horace, he found himself devoting more time to, for example, von Ranke, Pirenne, and Salvemini, not to mention the classics of anthropology and sociology, than to Callimachus, Pindar, Ovid, and Catullus. The philosopher, too, though deep in Plato, Aristotle, and perhaps Heraclitus, might try to maintain familiarity with nonphilosophical ancient texts, but found himself assigning a higher priority to Wittgenstein, Kant, and Hegel than to the Greek Anthology and Juvenal. Even those of us devoted primarily to literature had to find time away from the Greek and Latin authors to acquaint ourselves with modern literary criticism, to read Derrida instead of Demosthenes (but not for long), to have at least a nodding acquaintance with Brecht on drama, Propp on folktale, and the increasingly complicated field of "oral" literature. With all these diverse directions philologists pursue, is there any sense at all in which we have the right to call ourselves philologists?

Of course there is. We are all *philologoi*—lovers of *logos*, of discourse, of the words in which discourse is expressed. Words are the basis of our discipline, the tools of our trade, as well as the object of our study. The historian deals with words on stone and papyrus as well as on the printed page, and without words his evidence is hardly ever conclusively located—if only, for example, there had been an inscription in that tomb at Vergina![1] The philosopher too, though the words themselves present him with some of his most tantalizing philosophical problems, cannot do without them—unless he falls back on the mathematical symbols of formal logic. Of those of us who deal with literature, there is no need to speak; and even our colleagues the archaeologists, who are fond of telling us that one picture is worth a thousand words, seem to need many thousands of words to explain one picture. Like Eliot's Sweeney, we are all servants of the word: "I gotta use words when I talk to you."

The word unites us, makes of our three divisions an army, and we are engaged in a struggle on two fronts. On one, in the academy itself, the world of scholarship and research, we fight to maintain the value and establish the necessity of our disci-

---

[1]In 1977 the Greek archaeologist Manolis Andronikos excavated a tomb at Vergina, in northern Greece, which was clearly a royal tomb and may well have been that of Philip II, father of Alexander. An inscription would probably have confirmed or ruled out the identification.

pline for the humanities, which are themselves under pressure and losing territory rapidly. On the other, we compete in the marketplace for undergraduate students, for the numbers which will establish our credentials with the university administration. On both fronts we bear the brunt of a general assault on and loss of interest in the humanities as an academic pursuit.

It is only logical that in such a situation our discipline should take heavy punishment. Our texts *are* the humanities, the original humanities, the humanities in their most concentrated and genuine form. Without the two languages and literatures which are our province the humanities are hardly conceivable—without the Latin which preserved the heritage of civilization through the Dark Ages and beyond, without the Greek which came west to fuel the driving forces of the Renaissance and Reformation. And it is only to be expected that in this age of cultural dilution, of plastic substitutes, of mindless television shows, not to mention television dinners and instant coffee, the genuine article is no longer valued. It is too expensive; too much work has gone to produce it. To the general public we are an unknown entity; when identified, we are regarded as a freak. I remember telling a man on a plane once (he asked what I did) that I was a philologist and after a few seconds a look of bewilderment was replaced by one of deep respect and he said: "That's some kind of far-out shrink, isn't it?" The reaction to the information that one is a professor of Greek is no more encouraging. At fashionable Washington dinner parties (where I am sometimes invited for reasons I have never been able to fathom) when the lady next to me turns dutifully and inquires, "What do you do?" if I reply that I am a professor of ancient Greek she turns away in stunned silence as if she were the man in Lewis Carroll's poem who

> thought he saw a rattlesnake
> that questioned him in Greek.
> He looked again and saw it was
> the middle of next week.

If my neighbor is a man, he is just as appalled but makes a quick recovery. "I'll tell you one thing," he says, slapping me on the shoulder, "it's Greek to me." There is nothing to do but join in his boisterous laughter, though of course what one would like to do is to point out that the joke was already very old when Shakespeare fed it to the actor playing Casca in his *Julius Caesar*, produced in 1599.

No wonder boards of trustees, university regents, and budget efficiency experts look with moistening lips at departments which attract few students and whose members are engaged in research which, unlike the equally arcane investigations carried on by economists, social scientists, and physicists, can boast no special relevance. When a harassed university president wakes up in euphoric mood, with a delicious but unaccountable impression that he has cut half a million off next year's budget, he has been dreaming about *us*.

But you cannot blame him; we have not done all that we could to defend our position. On this front, the standing of our discipline in the academic world, we have, on the whole, fallen short of what the crisis demands. Heirs to centuries of privilege and place, even to a tradition of otherworldliness tolerated with amused affection in more spacious days, we have tended to carry on our esoteric dances as if nothing had changed since the Reverend Thomas Gaisford's Christmas Day sermon, delivered in Christ Church Oxford sometime in the first half of the nineteenth century. It ended with the memorable words: "Nor can I do better, in conclusion, than impress upon you the study of Greek literature, which not only elevates above the vulgar herd, but leads not infrequently to positions of considerable emolument."

We often tend, in a kind of perverse pride, to emphasize the inaccessibility of our work to outsiders, even educated outsiders, colleagues in the humanities in fact. We are justly proud of our familiarity with languages, not only ancient but modern also, the German, French, and Italian which are almost as much tools of our trade as Greek and Latin. But we yield too often to the temptation to quote our sources in the original, sure, of course, that our classical colleagues can understand them and unwilling to relinquish the melody of the Italian, the rhetorical neatness of the French, the sturdiness of the German. We also, at times, especially in footnotes, write in a sort of shorthand which certainly saves space and is usually (but not, alas, always) clear as day to our fellow professionals but which gives the outsider unmistakable warning that he is off limits. Even in the body of the text we tend to take it for granted that cryptic allusions to nineteenth-century scholarly controversies, to Byzantine scholiasts and nameless lexicographers, will present no problem to the reader.

It all depends, of course, on who we think we are addressing; there are certain subjects on which we are talking exclusively to each other (the future indicative with *hopos me*, for example, or problems in stemmatics). A great deal of what we read and write is of no interest to anyone except ourselves. The words Pope put in the mouth of Aristarchus–Bentley for his address to the goddess Dullness still ring true:

> For thee we dim the eyes, and stuff the head
> With all such reading as was never read . . .

And again

> What Gellius or Stobaeus hashed before
> Or chewed by blind old Scholiasts o'er and o'er.

In such areas of learning we are sometimes writing not even for each other but only for the one or two people still alive who have read the same arcane documents. But when we deal with less recondite matter we should try, if possible, to write in a way that does not exclude fellow humanists whose specialties are not ours. Ideally, the text of what we write should be intelligible (we should also try to make it interesting) to colleagues in English, history, and philosophy departments, who have not been obliged—as we have in order to function at all—to absorb foreign languages like a sponge. Where it is really necessary to cite the original, it should, of course, be done, but we should be wary of leaving anything in the text of our article or book untranslated. The notes are another matter, and there are also special cases. If you are reviewing a book written in German, for example, there is no need to translate the quotations, since anyone who can't read German is not going to read the book in the first place. What I am suggesting is simply that whenever we write on a subject which might conceivably interest the uninitiated, we should take pains not to bar them at the threshold. Let us try to write, when we are not settling *Hoti*'s business and the doctrine of the enclitic *de*, to write so that all men and women of culture, intelligence, and goodwill can, if they so desire, understand what we say.

We should make our learned discourse accessible to our fellow humanists, but we should beware of abandoning our own cant phrases only to adopt theirs. Our understanding of our subject matter has been continuously enriched by the application to it of new insights and methods drawn from modern disciplines—from anthropology and psychology, to name only two. But the enrichment comes only when these approaches to our material have been thoroughly absorbed, critically assessed, and selectively adapted—as, for example, in Walter Burkert's use of modern anthropology and psychology in his studies of Greek religion. Unfortunately the process is sometimes rushed; the resulting production is more remarkable for its strange terminology than for the light it throws on the matter at hand. There may be something to be gained by discussing tragic characters along Freudian analytical lines (though I personally have never seen any firm evidence of such gain), but a prose bristling with terms such as "cathexis," "parapraxis," "castration," and *"vagina dentata"* will repel everyone but the steadily diminishing number of Freudian true believers. There may be things we can learn about Greek myth from the structural gymnastics of Levi-Strauss (though most professional anthropologists have long since washed their hands of him), but interest fades before the prospect of mysterious mediations and diagrams which demonstrate relations between opposites (not all of which have a base in this text) so complicated that the only way to understand the diagram is to try to write out what you think it means. Perhaps semiotics and deconstruction can improve our understanding of the texts of which they deny the existence (or at any rate the kind of existence which we can understand), but first their champions will have to write intelligible English, a standard so far reached by few of them and only intermittently by those few. And let us all remember that these fashions pass, more quickly in fact with every year; the bright new terms of today may well be the neglected curiosities of tomorrow.

Ingrown learned obscurity, however, and a fascination with pseudoscientific terminology are not the only vices to which we philologists are prone; we have another besetting sin. We write too much. Not only do we often use up more space than the subject really demands or deserves; we also are quite capable of worrying a scholarly bone to near disintegration and then digging it up again later to have another go at it. Once again Pope is right on target, as Bentley continues his recital of the scholar's services to the goddess Dullness:

> For thee explain a thing till all men doubt it.
> And write about it, Goddess, and about it.

We should ask ourselves as we look over our manuscript: Is this article really necessary? And if so, does it really need this footnote, this paragraph, this page? Even if excision means the loss of a polished phrase, a treasured witticism, a pungent critique, a self-satisfying display of arcane bibliographical knowledge, we should cut to the bone; we should try to live up in our own humble work to the spare classic line we admire in our great models. In the matter of persuasion (and we write to persuade), we should bear in mind Hesiod's phrase (though this is not the sense in which he meant it): "Fools! They do not know how much more than half is than the whole." We should think with affection and respect of the Athenian statesman Phocion, who, when asked what he was thinking about as he paced uneasily up and down before the meeting of the Assembly, replied: "I am thinking about how to shorten my speech to the Athenian people." For a motto we might adopt the famous phrase of Thucydides, adapting it with a change of mood and a few syllables: "*philologomen met' euteleias,*" "Let us practice philology—with economy."

This call for fewer words may appeal more to those philologists whose position is assured than to the younger ones, who are striving desperately for promotion, for tenure, or just to hold on to their jobs; for in the present highly competitive situation, evaluation committees raise their standards and look for solid evidence of scholarly achievement. Things in this country are not as bad as they used to be in Italy, where, so an Italian friend once explained it to me, the inordinate length and abundance of scholarly articles were due to the existence (or belief in the existence) of a large machine in the basement of the Ministero de la Pubblica Istruzione on which the offerings of candidates for the *libera docenza* were weighed by government officials. But it must be admitted that even here, colleagues are apt to be impressed by sheer bulk. I have the distinct impression, however, that they are not so impressed by it as they once were. And since in many institutions promotion is no longer a matter of a department recommendation which the chairman must negotiate with the dean, but rather a decision made by a dean's committee which includes extradepartmental members, the quality and above all the accessibility of the writing may be a vital factor. If the historians, philosophers, modern language scholars, and history of art scholars on such committees can read with interest and pleasure the offprints submitted to them, instead of having to take the department's word (or not take it) that this almost impenetrable mass of arcane matter is truly creative scholarship, they are more likely to react favorably to the department's proposal.

As philologists, young or old, we should dedicate ourselves to the task of winning, through the quality of our writing, the respect of our colleagues in the humanities, of commanding recognition not only as the legitimate but also as the most effective interpreters and expositors of the classical tradition in all its aspects. We should so write and teach that no English department would any longer dare, for shame, to teach Homer, tragedy, and Virgil in translation. (I remember an English department colleague at Yale who told me: "Homer is too important to be left to the classics department." Unfortunately, at that time, with the department buried in the ruins of Dura-Europos, he was right.) We should so write and teach that history departments, if they have no properly trained ancient historian, should turn to us for their survey courses, that philosophy departments will not dare think of teaching Plato and Aristotle without our people aboard, and that political scientists will turn to us when they have to deal with the *Republic* and the *Politics*. We should aim to be known not just as specialists and experts who are guardians of a great cultural heritage but also as the best and most eloquent conveyors of that heritage from one generation to the next. Few of us can hope to be as admired a spokesman for the classics as Gildersleeve, Shorey, and Murray were in their day, but we can all strive to be forceful and eloquent voices, speaking not just to each other but also to the whole cultural community at large. Like the torch racers in the Republic, to whom we often compare ourselves, we hand on the flame; let us hand it over not guttering and smoky but steady and bright.

But we are fighting also on another front, the struggle to win students, to recruit, if I may use the World War II soldier's cynical term for reinforcements, "warm bodies." We need students, not so much graduate students (though there will always be some devoted souls who will go that road no matter how dire the prospects), not just undergraduate students in the languages (though we would never pass up a chance to hook one); what we need most of all is a large student audience for the general courses we offer in translation. Without this we could win the respect of our colleagues in the humanities and still fall victim to the budgeteers. And here the problem we face is very different. On this front it is not a matter of lost ground to be regained; it is a case of virgin territory to be claimed and exploited. We face here not adversaries who know the value of our inheritance and, in their heart of hearts, would like to declare us incompetent and take it over but an increasingly semiliterate mass which has hardly any idea of what we stand for. If on the one front we must deal with colleagues and potential rivals who though of a different sect and persuasion are yet members of the same religion, on the other we have to become apostles to the gentiles, we have to bring the word to the barbarians, the heathen.

On this front, the danger we face is not that we shall shut ourselves off from our audience by esoteric language and a failure of clarity, for here we shall have no audience at all unless we go out and win it over in the first place. On this front the danger is that we may make the mistake of stooping to crass vulgarization, to gimmickry, to the fabrication of courses designed to attract by their titles but devoid by their very nature of the vital content which will sustain them for the long haul. We certainly have to design imaginative and attractive-sounding courses, but we should remember one of our own maxims: *Maxima debetur puero reverentia,* "We owe the greatest respect to the young." The current generation of students may be, by our standards, close to illiteracy, but they are not stupid.

If it is true that we must avoid the merely fashionable in our scholarly writing, the same holds true with even greater force for our undergraduate courses. Even where the approaches used have established themselves as more than just fashionable, they should not become the main content of the course. Many an introductory course on mythology has left students with a general idea of Freudian, Lévi-Straussian, and Dumézilian approaches to myth but without a firm grasp of the principal myths of the ancient world; the objective should, however, be to bring the students to the great poetic literature in which those myths are preserved for us—the modern analyses only a means to an end. For our task, to repeat, is a missionary one: to bring as many students as possible into contact with the great writers of the ancient world to whom later in life they may return, even if they do not broaden their acquaintance with them while still at school. I do not want to underestimate the great progress which has been made in this direction by many teachers, especially the young, at many institutions, especially the smaller ones; I wish only to call for more and continuing effort, and for general recognition that such activity is not to be lightly dismissed as mere popularization nor to be esteemed as less honorable than scholarship, as that word is usually understood. Gilbert Murray would have made no distinction between his formidable scholarship and his immensely successful popularization of Greek literature; the one activity fed the other, and both found expression in beautifully readable prose (some of it in what was, in its own time, regarded as beautifully speakable verse). Often, in fact, the problem posed by teaching, in translation, whole works in a limited time may demand from the scholar a deeper understanding of the work than classes in the language; it is easier for a philologist to explain to a Latin class the subtleties of the word order *saevae memorem Iunonis ob iram* than it is for him to tell a class of young people in fifty minutes what the *Aeneid* is really about and why it has been, ever since it was written, one of the basic texts on which Western civilization has been built. I have not done any regular teaching for many years now, but when I did, three-quarters of my time was spent teaching the classics in translation. What my own scholarly work may be worth I leave to others to judge, but I am not ashamed to say that all of it, from the first article on Virgil to the most recent review in *The New York Review of Books*, has its roots in these translation courses—in the necessity imposed by such courses to understand at some communicable level the works as artistic wholes and in their historical context, or in the questions asked by the student, whose innocent eye so often penetrates to the basic fault in a confused presentation.

That eye is also quick to recognize intellectual condescension, to diagnose unerringly the boredom and contempt expressed by too easy assignments, by lectures made entertaining by topical reference but devoid of real content. Students may take advantage of such an offering, but they will despise it and eventually despise themselves for doing so. We are in a competitive market and must present our wares in attractive shape and settings, but we must promise no spoon-feeding; our courses, it should be made clear, have immense riches to offer but only to those who work. *Philologomen*, if I may travesty the other half of the Thucydidean phrase, *aneu malakias*, without flabbiness.

Students will respond with work to an instructor who is working hard for them; and anyone who has had to design and teach courses of this kind knows what demanding work they can be. I remember vividly the achievement of Tony Raubitschek, a young professor teaching at Yale in the mid-forties, an Austrian refugee, who offered a course in ancient political theory. Within two years the enrollment was over a hundred; the course was eventually declared a prerequisite for its majors by the political science department. This was not done by handing out easy assignments—in fact, the reading list was formidable; but there was also a mimeographed booklet (this was before the age of Xerox) containing specimens of political thought from Homer through Plato, Aristotle, Cicero, Augustine, Aquinas, Macchiavelli, and Hobbes all the way to Jefferson, Hegel, Marx, Lenin, and Adolf Hitler which was an education in itself. The sequence and juxtaposi-

tion of these texts provoked at sight an intellectual excite-
ment which guaranteed active and rewarding class meetings.
The teacher who wrought this pedagogical miracle was
known in the scholarly world as a skilled Greek epigrapher,
and when I asked him whether he did not feel a gulf between
his teaching activities and the learned notes he contributed to
archaeological periodicals on the shapes of fifth-century
Athenian letters he said to me: "No. Why do you think I
spend my life on Athenian inscriptions? It is because they are
precious contemporary documents which can tell us how
Athenian democracy worked—and I am very interested in
democracy. And in its enemies." For him the two fronts were
interlocked. As in fact they are, or should be, for all of us.

America's Rome

Rome was not built in a day, nor was this book.[1] The metaphor is not inappropriate, for *America's Rome* is, in every sense of the word, a monumental work: a fully representative selection and profound analysis of American reactions to Rome, ranging from fascination to disgust (not to mention combinations of the two) over the lifespan of the American republic and the papacies of the fourteen Popes from Pius VII to John Paul II. The source material of William L. Vance's lavishly illustrated volumes is vast and varied—fiction, poetry, journalism, criticism, private correspondence, painting, architecture, and sculpture. And the book has much of interest and importance to say not only about Rome and the Romans but also, as Gore Vidal, himself a notable resi-

This essay originally appeared in the *Times Literary Supplement*, November 17–23, 1989.

[1]William L. Vance, *America's Rome*, 2 vols. (New Haven, Conn.: Yale University Press, 1989).

dent of the city, says in a tribute to the book, about America and the Americans. "It is," he says, "easily the best—and certainly the most unexpected—revelation of our national character since Tocqueville."

Volume 1, *Classical Rome*, tours the city's significant locations: chapters are devoted to the Forum, the Colosseum, the Campagna, the Pantheon, and, the last and by far the longest and richest, the Capitoline and Vatican sculpture galleries. The Forum, before the archaeologists got to work on it after 1870, was, as W. D. Howells described it, "a dirty cow-pasture" (Campo Vaccino, the Romans called it), and according to Howells it was also "obscenely defiled by wild beasts of men." Nevertheless, it served some Americans as a focus for their vision of the newborn republic as the heir of republican Rome, the Rome of Cincinnatus, who, like Washington, resigned his commission after victory was won and returned to his estates. The American image of the Colosseum, on the other hand, "in its complexity expresses an ambivalent attitude towards imperial power, its rise, its glories and terrors and its fall." It was also, for novelists, an "apt setting for madwomen and geniuses," a site for Gothic Romantic feelings and visions, as, for example, in Hawthorne's *Marble Faun*. The Campagna, stretching along the Via Appia Antica past the ruins of the great aqueducts all the way to Monte Albano, was, until modern development made it an endless, chaotic suburb, a "wilderness of sunny decay and vacancy," as Henry James described it in 1867. It was for American visitors, above all for painters, an ambiguous scene; they responded to it as "both Arcadia and Wasteland," evoking "two contradictory visions. One is melancholy and moralistic, the other pastoral and transcendent." The ruins made it a place of "desolate and tragic beauty," but the shepherds and their flocks recalled memories of Virgil's pastoral idylls.

Emphasizing the etymology of the word "Pantheon," a temple dedicated to "all the gods," Vance discusses American attitudes to Greek mythology (a subject of study by "the Transcendentalist circles of Concord–Cambridge–Boston in the 1840s"), and this leads him to the marble shapes of the ancient gods on display in the Capitoline and Vatican sculpture galleries. The young republic had no Ecole des Beaux-Arts, no British Academy, though one of its founders, Benjamin West, was "the first American artist in Rome to study directly the images in the Capitoline and Vatican museums." To study the nude, American artists had to go to Rome, where they could see the unveiled figures of Apollo and Venus, "the human form divine" in the shapes of *Apollo Belvedere* and the *Capitoline Venus*, just back in 1816 from their captivity in Napoleon's Paris. For those who could not afford a European journey, plaster casts were imported. In 1803 "the most enlightened citizens of New York" sent for "casts from the antique" including *Apollo* and *Venus*, still at that date in Paris; when they arrived, the "recipients promptly spent $12.50 to affix fig leaves to Apollo and the other males."

Fig leaves or no, these two Roman copies of (presumably) Greek originals became the American ideal of human beauty. As late as 1897, Stillman, one of the founders of America's first art journal, *The Crayon*, and a long-term resident in Rome, published a folio of photographic reproductions entitled simply *Venus and Apollo*. In his preface he championed, against "Darwinism, Realism and Impressionism," the "two types . . . Apollo and Venus" as "the purest form of male and female human beauty." Vance devotes the last two hundred pages of Volume 1 to "the ideals that these statues preeminently embodied in Rome and to the American effort to repossess them in art and thought." His rich interpretation of the varying re-creations not only of Apollo and Venus but also of Diana, Hercules, Orpheus, and others is an absorbing history of American artistic taste and higher culture, handsomely illustrated with the work of American painters and sculptors, famous and obscure, living and dead, from Benjamin West to a 1979 canvas of Peter Blume. Perhaps the most remarkable of these images is Raphaelle Peale's *Venus Arising from the Sea: A Deception*. Painted in 1823, it comments wittily on the prudishness of the American public (even as late as 1880 Mark Twain stigmatized Titian's *Venus of Urbino* as "the foulest, the vilest, the obscenest picture the world possesses") by showing a brilliantly executed *trompe-l'oeil* representation of a napkin that covers every part of the goddess except her feet and an arm raised to lift her wet hair. The napkin is, as Vance puts it, "a leap into the aesthetics of pure abstraction."

Volume 2, *Catholic and Contemporary Rome*, deals first with American reactions to the curiosities, splendors, and miseries of Rome under the rule of the Popes: incredulous astonishment at Roman adoration of the Santissimo Bambino, the "miracle-working doll" of the Ara Coeli; distaste for the glories of the Baroque ("freaks in marble . . . the lowest stage of degeneracy"); and political opinions ranging from enthusiastic approval of Pio Nono's initial liberal policies to outrage when he called in French troops to suppress the republican revolution his reforms had triggered. In 1870 Rome was occupied by the Piedmontese army of Vittorio Emmanuele II and became the capital of a united Italy, an event denounced by the Catholic Bishop of Baltimore but celebrated by Julia Ward Howe with new lyrics for her famous "Battle Hymn of the Republic": "Let them sound a victor strophe from the mountains to the sea. . . . Let Italy be one."

The years from 1870 to 1940 are, of course, the most fully documented, and they are covered in great and fascinating detail. The American presence in Rome was given stable centers with the consecration of "St. Paul's within-the-walls" in 1876, the first non-Catholic church in Rome, and, more influential, the establishment of the American Academy in 1874 and its move to its present site on the Janiculan in 1914. The Academy has left its mark on several generations of American artists, scholars, critics, architects, musicians, novelists, and above all poets: Anthony Hecht and Richard Wilbur, to name only two, have given us exquisite and moving images of the city's blend of beauty and *terribilità*. The American obsession with Rome even exhibited a remarkable fondness, especially in official circles, for Mussolini's strident regime. And it reached a grotesque high point in Mark Clark's stubborn insistence, in defiance of the obvious requirements of Alexander's overall plan for the destruction of Kesselring's army, on being first in Rome, to make what would now be called a photo opportunity and pose stagily as the latest conqueror of Rome in a long sequence that began with Brennus the Gaul and Alaric the Visigoth.

Geistosgeschichte
and *Quatsch*

Twenty-three of the articles in Sir Hugh Lloyd-Jones's academic papers[1] deal with what must always be the prime concern of a Regius Professor of Greek: the constitution, criticism, and elucidation of literary, and especially, since they are the most difficult, poetic, texts. Such work calls for a combination of training and talent that few can lay justified claim to: a firm grasp of the tangled intricacies of Greek grammar and syntax, a mastery of the nuances of dialect and changing idiom over more than a thousand years of the language's history, a sensitive ear for the daunting complexity of Greek lyric meter, a memory loaded with Greek poetry that can provide parallels to confirm or confute emendation or interpretation, familiarity with the errors of

This essay originally appeared in the *Times Literary Supplement*, March 8, 1991.

[1]Hugh Lloyd-Jones, *Greek Epic, Lyric and Tragedy* and *Greek Comedy, Hellenistic Literature, Greek Religion and Miscellanea* (New York: Clarendon, 1991).

scribes, both those of the medieval manuscripts and the older papyri, critical control of the vast and ongoing literature of the subject, not only in English but in all the principal languages of Europe, and, above all, discretion and judgment in the deployment of these skills.

The criticism and commentary provided for the texts in these articles is exemplary. Not the least admirable feature of Sir Hugh's method is its comparative conservatism; he avoids both heroic emendation and speculative supplement. This is all the more remarkable because his skill in Greek verse composition, especially in lyric meters, is legendary; he could in every case have improved spectacularly on the supplements he dismisses, but forbears to do so. Outstanding among these articles are the defense of the passage in the recognition scene of the *Choephoroe* that features Orestes' footprints, and its near-parody in the Euripidean *Electra* (they had both been branded as interpolations by no less an authority than Eduard Fraenkel); the lengthy, detailed demonstration that the poem on the "seal of Poseidippos" is in fact the work of the contemporary of Callimachus; and the three articles that deal with the text and interpretation of passages in the *Agamemnon* of Aeschylus.

But professionally exacting work of this kind is only one side of the duties of the Regius Professor, at least as Sir Hugh sees them. In his inaugural lecture of 1961 he praised the inaugural lecture of his predecessor Eric Dodds, which he characterized as "a warning against allowing the humane element in Greek studies to be submerged by the preoccupation of scholars with the technique of their profession." He echoed this emphasis in his own statement that "professional scholars have three different duties: one to their subject, one to their pupils, and one to the general public." He was aware that the scholar writing for the general public can hardly avoid reading into ancient texts the thought of his own time, and that to a later generation his work will seem, at least in some aspects, dated. But he thought that danger might be avoided and said so in a characteristically polemical statement:

> I believe in the possibility of understanding ancient thought, at least in some degree, without importing modern prejudices. If we carefully control every statement we make about an ancient theory or belief by reference to the evidence, if we are constantly on the watch against importing Christian or other modern preoccupations into antiquity, it seems to me that we have a slender chance of getting at the truth. Most likely we shall fail; at best we may get at that fraction of the truth which it is possible for our generation to comprehend.

As it turned out, importation of Christian preoccupations was not the main problem he had to face during the twenty-nine years of his tenure of the professorship. Quite different modern preoccupations were, even as he spoke, making their entry on the scene, as classical scholars, notably at first in France and the United States, began to apply to the study of Greek literature, thought, religion, and society methods developed by followers of Freud, Jung, and Lévi-Strauss, not to mention Dumézil and Marx.

The winds of change, however, had no effect on the course steered by the Regius Professor. In 1985 he published an acerbic survey of psychiatric and structuralist approaches to Greek myth and literature, in which among the very few brands saved from the burning are "a mildly interesting comment" by Georges Devereux, a "valuable contribution to comparative mythology" in the work of Otto Rank, valuable, that is, only if we remove its "framework of psychoanalytic theory," and an interpretation of the Oedipus myth by Jean-Pierre Vernant, who is complimented for his "learning, ingenuity, and courage" but taken to task for the "Gallic neatness and tidiness of some of the structures" which "contrasts disquietingly with the precariousness of the method by which they are obtained." The article ends, however, with a generous tribute to one scholar whose work owed much to modern psychological and anthropological theory—his predecessor Dodds, whose "famous book," *The Greeks and the Irrational,* he describes as "beyond comparison the most influential application of post-Freudian psychology to the study of the ancient world." The analysis that follows, however, is critical of many of Dodds's basic theses, and he concludes that though Dodds's "splendid book, fully documented, elegantly written, and giving a detailed account of many concrete phenomena, will still be useful many years from now," yet "the parts of it that are already showing signs of wear are just those parts in which the influence of psychoanalysis and of the social anthropology that sprang from it is most perceptible."

One thing Lloyd-Jones did inherit from Dodds (and from Dodds's predecessor Gilbert Murray) was a sympathetic interest in ancient Greek religion with an emphasis on local cult and sacrifice—a real attempt to take a polytheistic religion seriously rather than regarding it as "essentially a crude superstition." Dodds was especially urgent on this matter. I met him once in Athens when he had just returned from a hike on Mount Hymettus with Kevin Andrews, to visit the cave of the nymphs at Vari. "You can learn more about ancient Greek religious feeling sitting in that cave for half an hour," he told me, "than you can from reading both volumes of Nilsson's *Geschichte der griechischen Religion.*" In one of the longest articles of the third section of Volume 2 ("Religion and Intellectual History"), Sir Hugh sets out to buttress his claim (made twenty years previously) that the Artemis who demands the sacrifice of Iphigenia in the *Agamemnon* acts not as "the protectress of the weak and helpless" but as the goddess to whom sacrifice was made by generals before joining battle, a goddess, in the words of Walter Burkert, whom he quotes, "who is and remains a mistress of bloody sacrifices." He does this by assembling a wealth of evidence on human sacrifice in Greek myth, on the cults of Artemis (especially the Attic cult at Brauron), on the roles of Orestes and Iphigenia in those cults, and on Artemis as a goddess presiding over initiation rites and sacrifice. He then uses all this to fit the demand of Artemis for a maiden's blood into the pattern of the trilogy that is first and last the fulfilment of the will, which is also the justice, of Zeus.

The Justice of Zeus is, of course, the title of Lloyd-Jones's Sather lectures, published in 1971 and reprinted in 1983 with a preface that gave him a chance "to do for the book's many hostile critics what the army of Israel has just done for the Palestine Liberation Organization." The military metaphor is a typical Lloyd-Jonesism, but it has a certain appropriateness, for the hostile critics were reacting strongly to a hard-hitting offensive against the prevalent belief that Greek literature from Homer to Plato and Aristotle was a record of intellectual progress, from an inchoate conception of the human personality to a full realization of its powers and possibilities, an evolution of religious sensibility from the worship of primitive, capricious deities to the identification of divinity with the highest standards of justice and morality. Dodds had charted an evolutionary course for the development of the Greek mentality in his great book, and Sir Hugh respectfully takes issue with him on the matter. In his preface he quotes Dodds's urbane comment on his own book. "I stressed the element of change in Greek beliefs, you stress the element of continuity; we are both of us right, though both of us at times exaggerate the partial truth we are stressing."

In the collection of Lloyd-Jones's academic papers this preoccupation with continuity is evident throughout, especially in his frequent dismissal of *Geistesgeschichte*. He counts himself among the "English empiricists who in their youth were often told by a famous scholar who began his career in Germany but finished it with us, that *Geistesgeschichte* was only a politer name for *Quatsch.*" Its most brilliant, if flawed, exhibit was of course Bruno Snell's *Entdeckung des Geistes*, with its claim, based on a careful analysis of the Homeric vocabulary, that the Homeric poems are the product of an age in which "man's understanding of himself" was "primitive," of a mentality that did not recognize its body *"qua* body, but merely as the sum total" of the limbs, and had no clear conception of either the intellect or the soul. Though Sir Hugh frequently expresses his affection and admiration for Snell as a man and scholar, he has no use for theories that depend on lexicographical evidence for their attempt to trace the development or evolution of the Greek mind.

Evolution is another favorite target. In an early article,

"Zeus in Aeschylus," printed in 1956 but first delivered as a lecture in 1953, he expressed vehement disagreement with the idea, first proposed by Dissen and later adopted by Wilamowitz, Nilsson, Festugière, and Dodds, that in the Prometheus trilogy the character of Zeus evolved; the youthful tyrant of the first play was transformed into "the beneficent ruler who of his own free will releases his noble enemy." He did not content himself with citing "such eminent authorities on Greek religion" as Farnell and Karl Reinhardt to the effect that the notion of a god changing his character was one that Aeschylus could not possibly have entertained, but went on to reexamine the evidence for the general conviction that the Zeus of the *Prometheus Bound* was incompatible with the "purity, nobility and refinement of the theology of the other plays of Aeschylus."

The result was a radical reassessment of what had become an *idée reçue:* that Aeschylus had developed, in the figure of Zeus, an individual theology that bore remarkable resemblances to the monotheism of the Hebrews, and endowed his supreme being with a benevolent attitude to, and purpose for, mankind. The Lloyd-Jones Zeus is a very different figure. From a sober analysis of the passages, especially the choral lyrics, of the *Supplices* and the *Oresteia* that describe or address Zeus, supplemented by a full discussion of the *Dike* fragment (now Radt 281a) and a comparison of all these passages with lines from Hesiod that deal with Zeus and *Dike*, he draws what he himself calls the "startling conclusion" that Aeschylus' conception of Zeus contains "nothing that is new, nothing that is sophisticated, nothing that is profound." In a footnote to this reprint of the original article (which, in accordance with the principles announced in his preface, he has not revised) he says that though he still agrees with a great deal of it, he "has grown to dislike its tone" and reprints it "with reluctance." ("Unlike Zeus," he remarks in a different context, "I have evolved.") He reprints the article for the very good reason that it "played its part in the discussions of the time." He now refers readers to his "later writings on related topics" with the comment: "If Aeschylus' theology is comparatively simple, that does not mean that it is not profound."

The original statement was indeed too sweeping, but for those of us who had been taught to see Aeschylus as some kind of Greek counterpart to the Hebrew prophets and psalmists it was a salutary shock. And his conclusion about the final scenes of the *Oresteia*—"The Eumenides do not change character, but they do a deal with Athena and in consequence, their attitude changes"—also struck a grating note at the time, but is now in tune with the darker and more troubled views of the ending of the trilogy that have been put forward in recent years.

These papers consist of seventy-seven items, ranging in length from less than one page (a note on Aristophanes' *Acharnians* 393–94) to forty-four pages ("Modern Interpretations of Pindar"). Each volume is equipped with an excellent set of indexes—Authors and Texts, Greek words, Modern Authors, General—and a bibliography listing the 232 articles and reviews from which the author has made his selection. (Fifty-three of them have appeared in previous collections under the titles *Blood for the Ghosts* and *Classical Survivals*, both published in 1982.) The bibliography, though impressively large, is not complete; it omits, for example, contributions to the *London Review of Books* and the *New York Review of Books*—

perhaps they were thought insufficiently academic. And though connoisseurs of Sir Hugh's caustic wit may regret the absence of such classic dismissals as his review of *Der verlorene Aischylos* by H. J. Mette, they will still find plenty of Attic salt sprinkled on the sometimes formidable fare offered here.

That this review has so far singled out what might be viewed as the negative aspects of Sir Hugh's writing is due simply to the fact that he has played a leading role in exposing the flaws not only in the older, sentimental vision of Greek religious feeling and morality, but also in the newer, radical methodologies that have been enthusiastically but often rashly brought to bear on the ancient evidence. But these two volumes contain also much that is positive: not only the masterly reconstitution and elucidation of fragmentary and corrupted texts but also sensitive interpretation of poetry, in particular of the work of a poet whose importance has been generally underestimated, the Theban poet Pindar, to whom 130 pages of the first volume are devoted. Besides a rewarding analysis of two fragmentary texts, one of the famous *nomos basileus* passage and the other a *katabasis* that may well be one of the sources of Book 6 of the *Aeneid*, the volume contains three long articles which constitute what is perhaps the best introduction available to the work of this great but difficult poet.

These academic papers have been published, the Clarendon Press tells us, "to commemorate" Sir Hugh's "retirement from his distinguished position." The somewhat valedictory tone of this announcement seems, however, a little premature. For one thing, they make their appearance in the same year as the splendid new text of Sophocles—*Recognoverunt brevique adnotatione critica instruxerunt H. Lloyd-Jones et N. G. Wilson*—accompanied by *Sophoclea*, a commentary on the text that is full of sound judgment and great learning. For another, item 90 in the bibliography at the end of the two volumes is announced as "Forthcoming." Readers will hope that it is to be the first of many.

Achilles in the Caribbean

After playing a decisive role in the defeat and surrender of Cornwallis at Yorktown in 1781, the French fleet, under its Admiral De Grasse, sailed south to carry on the war against England in the Caribbean. In April of the following year, in a naval engagement known to the English as the Battle of the Saints, De Grasse in his turn was defeated, by Admiral Rodney of the British navy, surrendering his person and his flagship, the 120-gun *Ville de Paris*. "Her name," says Mahan in his classic work on the influence of sea power,[1] "commemorating the great city whose gift she had been to the King, and the fact that no French naval commander-in-chief had before been taken prisoner in battle, conspired to bestow a peculiar brilliancy upon Rodney's victory," which was

This essay originally appeared in *The New York Review of Books*, March 7, 1991. Reprinted with permission from *The New York Review of Books*. Copyright © 1991 Nyrev, Inc.

[1]A. T. Mahan, *The Influence of Sea Power upon History 1660–1783* (Boston: Little, Brown, 1890).

also "particularly . . . marked by a maneuver that was then looked upon as exceptionally daring and decisive—'breaking the line.' "

The battle acquired its name from three small islands, Les Saintes, that lie in the waters between Dominica and Guadaloupe. The French base was Port Royal on Martinique; Rodney's, some thirty miles away, was the more southerly island of St. Lucia.

St. Lucia is the birthplace of the poet Derek Walcott and the scene of most of the action in his magnificent narrative poem *Omeros*,[2] in which the memory of the battle is one of the multiple threads that weave the lives and deaths of his characters into a dazzling pattern, as varied and swift in motion as the waves and clouds of the Caribbean, a pattern that connects visions of Lisbon, London, and Dublin with the original African home of the island's inhabitants and the Ghost Dance of the Sioux at Wounded Knee, a pattern that merges the island chain of the Antilles with that other archipelago, the isles of Greece, where Homer, who gives the poem its name, composed his *Iliad* and *Odyssey*.

Omeros is the modern Greek form of the name. The poem's narrator heard it first from a "voice / that hummed in the vase of a girl's throat: 'Omeros.' / 'O-meros,' she laughed. 'That's what we call him in Greek.' " He appears in the poem in various guises: as the blind man known as Seven Seas, who lives in the fishing village of Gros Ilet on St. Lucia, as the "white-eyed storyteller" who in Africa sings the tribal tale,

[2]Derek Walcott, *Omeros* (New York: Farrar, Straus & Giroux, 1991).

reminding "who perished in what battle, who was swift with the arrow," and as a vagrant bargeman, "clutching in one scrofulous / claw his brown paper manuscript," who is driven off the steps of St. Martin-in-the-Fields in London by an irate churchwarden. Modern scholarly recreations of Homer (about whose life we have no solid evidence whatsoever) usually build on the picture of Demodocus, the court minstrel of the Phaeacians in the *Odyssey*, who is honored and served at royal banquets. But Walcott's poor fisherman, African griot, and London tramp are closer to an ancient tradition. In the life of Homer attributed (falsely) to Herodotus, Homer appears as an illegitimate child who became a schoolteacher (a despised profession in ancient Greece) and, after losing his sight, wandered from city to city reciting his poems to earn his bread.

Seven Seas is blind, and Philoctete, another inhabitant of the village, has a stinking ulcer in his leg that refuses to heal. Hector and Achille are two fishermen, who quarrel over the affections of Helen, a young woman who works as a housemaid and a waitress and whose proud beauty turns the head of every man that sees her. All these people are black, as is Ma Kilman, who runs the No Pain Café, but Major Plunkett, who fought with Montgomery's Eighth Army in North Africa, and his Irish wife, Maud, are white. The complicated interaction of these people is the narrative base of the poem. Helen loves Achille, but quarrels with him and goes to live with Hector, who deserts the sea to become a taxi driver with a huge "chariot" called The Comet; he dies at its wheel in an accident. Helen had been dismissed by Maud Plunkett for appropriating a pale lemon frock; Major Plunkett is half in love with Helen and because of her ("the island," Walcott tells us, "was once named Helen") decided "that what the place needed / was its true place in history, that he'd spend hours / for Helen's sake on research. . . ." He makes himself an expert on the Battle of the Saints. Maud dies of cancer; Helen, pregnant, returns to Achille; and Philoctete's ulcer is cured by Ma Kilman, who recaptures an ancestral African memory of a healing plant.

The narrator too—"Phantom narrator, resume," Walcott says to himself at one point in the poem—is a native of the island, but one who lives abroad, in Boston, who has traveled widely in Europe and who returns to the island to visit his mother, a widow living in a home for the aged. He too is involved in the crosscurrents of emotion that bind and divide the figures of the poem; he too is fascinated by Helen, of whom he says: "Sometimes the gods will hallow / all of a race's beauty in a single face." His first sight of her is that of

> a woman with a madras head-tie,
> but the head proud, although it was looking for work.
> I felt like standing in homage to a beauty
>
> that left, like a ship, widening eyes in its wake.
> "Who the hell is that?" a tourist near my table
> asked a waitress. The waitress said, "She? She too proud!"
>
> As the carved lids of the unimaginable
> ebony mask unwrapped from its cotton-wool cloud,
> the waitress sneered, "Helen." And all the rest followed.

All these characters come fully and movingly to life in Walcott's hands; black and white are treated with equal understanding and sympathy as they go their complicated ways. This does not, however, look at first glance like material that calls for Walcott's evocation of his great predecessor, or the epic scale of the poem—between eight and nine thousand lines. Yet in his fluent tercets, linked by a dazzling play of rhyme, half rhyme, and assonance, the scene expands, as in the *Odyssey*, to the farthest reaches of the known world and also, when Achille speaks to his African ancestor, the narrator to his dead father, and Plunkett to his dead wife, beyond our world to that of the dead. And time dissolves, as black slaves, one of Achille's forefathers among them, hoist Rodney's cannon up to the cliff tops on St. Lucia, young Plunkett and his sweetheart, Maud, take leave of each other in Ireland before he boards the troopship, and Achille, swept eastward in a dream to the African shore, talks to his ancestor Alfolabe in a village on a branch of the Congo, just before it is attacked by another tribe in search of captives to sell "to the slavers waiting up the coast."

The poem's apparently narrow focus expands to infinity as images of Plunkett's desert war—Montgomery's triumphal entry into Tobruk—mesh with reverberations of the end of empire—the flag "sliding down from the hill-stations / of the upper Punjab, like a collapsing sail"—and, farther west, the "Southern towns and plantations . . . maintained by convicts and emigrants who had fled / persecution and gave themselves *fasces* and laws / to persecute slaves" are paired with the colonists of Concord who displaced the Indians— "all colonies inherit their empire's sin / and these, who broke free of the net, enmeshed a race." And Homer's *Odyssey* is omnipresent, in the figure of Joyce by the Liffey—"eye-patch and tilted hat / rakish cane on one shoulder"—in the old name of Lisbon, Ulissibona, a "mud-caked settlement founded by Ulysses," and most memorably in the narrator's final interview with Omeros, in which he confesses that he has never read the *Odyssey*, "Not all the way through."

> Then there was the silence any injured author
> knows, broken by the outcry of a frigate-bird,
> as we both stared at the blue dividing water,
>
> and in that gulf, I muttered, "I have always heard
> your voice in that sea, master, it was the same song
> of the desert shaman, and when I was a boy
>
> your name was as wide as a bay, as I walked along
> the curled brow of the surf; the word "Homer" meant joy,
> joy in battle, in work, in death, then the numbered peace
>
> of the surf's benedictions, it rose in the cedars,
> in the lauriers-cannelles, pages of rustling trees.
> Master, I was the freshest of your readers."

Seven Seas—Homer takes him to the island's volcanic crater at Soufrière but the name Walcott gives it—Malebolge—announces that this is not Homer's dead world but Dante's. There, in the Pool of Speculation, he sees

> the traitors
>
> who, in elected office, saw the land as views
> for hotels and elevated into waiters
> the sons of others, while their own learnt something else.

This is a salute to Dante, whose *terza rima* he has adapted for the English ear, but the passage also sounds one of the

poem's obsessive themes: exploitation. The returning emi-
grant finds the island he left changed by the advent of tourism
and "progress":

> the sandy alleys would go and their simple stores,
> the smell of fresh bread drawn from its Creole oven,
> its flour turned into cocaine, its daughters to whores,

> while the DJs screamed,
> "WE MOVIN', MAN! WE MOVIN!"
> but towards what?

The history of the island ever since its "discovery" by Co-
lumbus—

> A Genoan wanderer
> saying the beads of the Antilles named the place
> for a blinded saint

—had been one of exploitation, once colonial, now native.
The opening lines of the poem show us the felling of the trees
that were the gods of the displaced Aruac Indians to make
canoes for the fishermen. Displacement, too, is a major
theme. The place of the Aruacs is taken by enslaved Africans:

> So there went the Ashanti one way, the Mandingo another,
> the Ibo another, the Guinea. Now each man was a nation
> in himself, without mother, father, brother.

The narrator himself is a displaced person, living in Boston, where he warms to the sight of the black sailor in Wins-
low Homer's painting *The Gulf Stream*, but is chilled by the

atmosphere once he leaves the museum. He remembers some words of Melville:

"Having for the imperial colour the same imperial hue . . .

giving the white man ideal mastership over every dusky tribe."
Lawd, Lawd, Massa Melville, what could a nigger do
but go down dem steps in de dusk you done describe?

So I stood in the dusk between the Greek columns
of the museum touched by the declining sun
on the gilt of the State House dome, on Saint Gaudens's

frieze of black soldiers darkening on the Common,
and felt myself melting in their dusk. My collar
turned up in a real freeze. I looked for a cab,

but cabs, like the fall, were a matter of colour,
and several passed, empty. In the back of one, Ahab
sat, trying to catch his whaler. I looped a shout

like a harpoon, like Queequeg, but the only spout
was a sculptured fountain's. Sic transit taxi, sport.
Streetlights came on. The museum windows went out.

I have quoted this passage in full not just for its content but also for its sample of the wit and verbal play that enliven every page of this extraordinary poem. Above all, for its mastery of rhyme, a constant source of surprise and delight from stanza to stanza, a music so subtle, so varied, so exquisitely right that it never once, in more than eight thousand lines, strikes a false note. Early in the poem the narrator's dead father shows him a vision of the women of his race carrying coal in hundredweight baskets on their heads up a steep wooden ramp on the hull of a ship; they are "Helens from an earlier time." "Kneel to your load," he says to his son,

"then balance your staggering feet
and walk up that coal ladder as they do in time,
one bare foot after the next in ancestral rhyme.

Because Rhyme remains the parentheses of palms
shielding a candle's tongue, it is the language's
desire to enclose the loved world in its arms. . . ."

And he sets his son a task:

"Look, they climb, and no one knows them;
they take their copper pittances, and your duty

from the time you watched them from your grandmother's
    house
as a child wounded by their power and beauty
is the chance you now have, to give those feet a voice."

And he has.

Index

Index

Index

Electra (Sophocles), 198–99, 200
Eliot, T. S., 66, 67, 304
Elizabeth I, Queen of England, 258
Empedocles, 173
Engels, Friedrich, 14
Ennius, Quintus, 91, 108
Entdeckung des Geistes (The Discovery of the Mind)
    (Snell), 50–51, 224, 328
Entretiens XXIV Sophocle, 191*n*
Ephialtes, 144
Epicrates, 164
Epistulae ex Ponto (Letters from the Black Sea) (Ovid),
    109, 110–11, 117
Erasmus, 251
Erechtheum, 128, 134
Eros, 80, 81, 174–80
Eumenides (Aeschylus), 200, 203
Eupolis, 57
Euripides, 70–85, 144, 165, 324
    divine intervention in, 82–84
    English translation of, 294
    lost works of, 79
    polis in, 200
    posthumous success of, 75, 84–85
    prophetic vision in, 70–78, 84–85
    reactions to extreme adversity contrasted in,
        186–88
    sense of instability conveyed by, 71, 76,
        80–81, 240
    on two kinds of shame, 227

Fagles, Robert, 19*n*, 247*n*
Faulkner, William, 80
Fifteen Decisive Battles of the World, The (Creasy), 138
Fitts, Dudley, 294
Fitzgerald, Robert, 49*n*, 296
"Flawed Crystals" (Nussbaum), 166
Flint, F. S., 92
Fondation Hardt, 191*n*
Fontenrose, Joseph, 154–57, 159–62
Ford, Henry, 13
Fordyce, C. J., 89
Forum, 319
Foucault, Michel, 164–65
Fraenkel, Eduard, 324
Fragility of Goodness, The (Nussbaum), 164*n*–90
French Revolution, 13–14
Freud, Sigmund, 309, 314, 325
Frogs (Aristophanes), 80
funeral games, 37
Fustel de Coulanges, 191

Gaisford, Thomas, 307
Gaius Silius, 262
games, athletic, 37, 57–58
García Márquez, Gabriel, 119

Geistesgeschichte, 328
Geischichte der römischen Literatur (Teuffel-Schwabe),
    110
Gemellus, 256
Germanicus Caesar, 255, 256, 259
Gibbon, Edward, 106, 107, 110
Gildersleeve, Basil Lanneau, 313
Glasgow University Magazine, 89
Goethe, Johann Wolfgang von, 13, 192*n*
Golden, Leon, 186
Goold, George, 97–98
Gorgias, 128
Gottschalk of Orbais, 272, 273
Grand Street, 19*n*
Grasse, François-Joseph-Paul de, 333
Graves, Robert, 138–39, 253, 285
Greek city-states:
    colonial expansion of, 128–29, 154
    Macedonian conquest of, 151, 152
    see also Athens
*Greek Comedy, Hellenistic Literature, Greek Religion and
    Miscellanea* (Lloyd-Jones), 323*n*
Greek cultural ethics:
    concepts of responsibility in, 224–32
    divine necessity and, 225–27, 232–33,
        239–42
    progressivist views of, 221–26, 328
    slavery and, 233–38
Greek Epic, Lyric and Tragedy (Lloyd-Jones), 323*n*
Greek literature:
    modern context for, 325–26
    religion in, 326–30
Greeks, The (Dover), 237
Greeks and the Irrational, The (Dodds), 155, 220–21,
    326
Green, Peter, 114, 268*n*, 278*n*
Grote, George, 28–29
Grundgedanke, 61, 62
guilt cultures, 221, 231–32

Hall, E. F., 284*n*
Harmodius, 137
Hawthorne, Nathaniel, 319
Hebrew monotheism, 329, 330
Hecht, Anthony, 322
Hecuba (Euripides), 166, 186–88
Hegel, G.W.F., 241, 242
Heine, Heinrich, 106
Helen:
    characters' reactions to, 48, 55
    human responsibility vs. godlike aspect of,
        19–21
Helots, 146
Henry II, King of England, 258
Heracles (Euripides), 82–83, 84–85
Heraclitus, 22, 163

Index

Index

Index

Index

LaVergne, TN USA
17 August 2010
193620LV00001B/38/A